Milos Forman

MILOS FORMAN

A Bio-Bibliography

Thomas J. Slater

Bio-Bibliographies in the Performing Arts, Number 1

GREENWOOD PRESS
New York • Westport, Connecticut • London

Library of Congress Cataloging-in-Publication Data

Slater, Thomas J.
  Milos Forman : a bio-bibliography.

  (Bio-bibliographies in the performing arts,
ISSN 0892-5550 ; no. 1
  Bibliography: p.
  Filmography: p.
  Includes index.
  1. Forman, Milŏs—Bibliography. 2. Forman, Milŏs.
3. Moving-picture producers and directors—
Czechoslovakia—Biography. 4. Moving-picture producers
and directors—United States—Biography. I. Title.
II. Series.
Z8309.24.S57 1987 016.79143'0233'0924 [B]   87-7494
ISBN 0-313-25392-7 (lib. bdg. : alk. paper)

Library of Congress Catalog Card Number: 87-7494
ISBN: 0-313-25392-7
ISSN: 0892-5550

First published in 1987

Greenwood Press, Inc.
88 Post Road West, Westport, Connecticut 06881

Printed in the United States of America

The paper used in this book complies with the
Permanent Paper Standard issued by the National
Information Standards Organization (Z39.48-1984).

10 9 8 7 6 5 4 3 2 1

Contents

Preface

Few film directors have ever achieved the degree of critical and commercial success that Milos Forman has. His films appeal both to the average spectator and to the intellectual, dealing with such diverse topics as mental illness and classical music. He was the leading light of the Czech New Wave of the sixties and since then, during his career in America, has won two Academy Awards for Best Director. Yet, no comprehensive publication on this important artist currently exists. This volume brings together most of the widely-scattered materials written about Milos Forman, offering an annotation for each piece as well as a plot summary, brief analysis, and survey of criticism for each of his films. Therefore, it will help other researchers efficiently pursue their studies of Forman and contribute further useful analysis about his work.

Several topics are obvious whenever a filmmaker and his films are examined. The director's relationships to producers and methods of working with actors, cinematographers, editors, and other professional people are all important areas of interest. However, a study of Milos Forman opens up a broad range of other possible topics as well. Forman's status as an immigrant from an East European communist country introduces questions of the structure and potential of a nationalized cinema versus that of a commercialized industry and of the differences between the methods and messages of his filmmaking in Czechoslovakia and in America. Forman's frequent focus of intergenerational struggles and the importance of music in his films provide other potentially rich areas for investigation. His theory of and relative success at adapting novels and plays, his philosophies about political and social institutions, and the degree of consistency or change in his films also are significant topics of study. A topic related to Forman's career is the changing critical response to his films and the factors that influenced the criticism over the years.

The biography and filmography chapters in this volume provide some answers to many of these questions. However, the guide to the annotated bibliography will assist scholars in finding support for their own ideas about Forman. Eventually, though, scholars will need to return to Forman's films and view them again and again. Encouraging others to do so is a major goal of this book. Ultimately, it is the images that provide all of the questions and answers, and understanding those of a major filmmaker in this visually-oriented age is no small matter.

My own study of Milos Forman began in the fall of 1981 when I was beginning my doctoral studies. For providing me with guidance and encouragement, I must thank my advisor, Dr. Peter C. Rollins, and film instructor Dr. Leonard J. Leff. Both provided invaluable advice and consideration beyond what was required of them as teachers. This work could also not have been completed without the dedicated assistance of my typist, Ronda Dakan, of Northwest Missouri State University. She proved herself remarkably conscientious in performing this demanding task. But my deepest gratitude must go to my wife, Mary Ann, for providing me with a purpose, giving me support, and working unselfishly as an irreplaceable proofreader and editor. Our daughter Gretchen also supplied priceless inspiration through her endless curiousity.

Milos Forman

1. Overview of Forman's Life and Career

Over a twenty-one year period, Milos Forman has built an enviable directorial career. Of his nine features, four have been nominated for major Academy Awards: Lasky jedne plavovlasky (Loves of a Blonde, 1965), Hori, ma panenko (The Firemen's Ball, 1967), One Flew Over the Cuckoo's Nest (1975), and Amadeus (1984). Each of the last two films captured the Best Director award for him and also won as Best Picture.

Forman's success is especially admirable because of the honesty in his work. His heroes are neither very successful nor totally appealing; he presents social leaders who are either corrupt or incompetent; and his conclusions contain no clear resolution or promise for a better future. Yet, Forman is basically an optimist. The endings of his films provide a reason for hope, even though they do not suggest that much will ever change.[1]

These seemingly contradictory attitudes both find their basis in Forman's focus on individual rights and responsibilities.[2] Most of his films examine a clash between a solitary person and a restrictive society. In all of his Czech films (Forman was born in Czechoslovakia and lived there until 1967) except for The Firemen's Ball, the main character is a young person seeking to find his or her identity while also attempting to stay within society's limitations. However, the vague and confusing nature of society's rules, geared more towards preserving order than allowing individual development, is a major problem for each youngster. No matter how much the main characters in Konkurs (Competition, 1963), Cerny Petr (Black Peter, 1963), and Loves of a Blonde attempt to do what they think is being demanded of them, they are continually frustrated. The rules simply do not make sense.

In The Firemen's Ball, Forman shifted his focus to show how the self-centered manipulation of power by those in control affects the elderly as well as the young. Forman's concern for the young and the old in his films demonstrates his compassion for those who lack power in society, whose lives are run by forces beyond their control.[3] Forman even demonstrates sympathy for those who are responsible. Though always foolish, they are also understandably human.

Forman's American heroes also attempt to express themselves within a highly structured and restrictive society. They too fight a social system more concerned with maintaining order than providing personal freedom. They become examples of Forman's belief that social institutions must serve people rather than the system. In this sense, the heroes are all admirable, but each of them fails because he lacks knowledge about his environment.

Forman always emphasizes that freedom and responsibility are inseparable and that those who do not understand their world, for whatever reason, must pay a price. Larry Tyne in Taking Off (1971), Randle Patrick McMurphy in Cuckoo's Nest, George Berger in Hair (1979), Coalhouse Walker, Jr., in Ragtime (1981), and Antonio Salieri and Wolfgang Amadeus Mozart in Amadeus all fail to act responsibly when given the chance. Each has the opportunity to accomplish more than he actually does if he can learn to work within his limitations rather than continually oppose them. The possibility for freedom within a given set of restrictions is the major theme in Milos Forman's films and represents his optimism. Obtaining that freedom depends upon the person. Individual responsibility is as much a part of Forman's message as the need for institutional humanitarianism. Of Forman's American film heroes, Larry Tyne is the only one to survive because he alone comes to recognize his limits.

Forman repeats these themes of freedom and responsibility in each one of his films, yet his work is also constantly changing to reflect both his own concerns and contemporary social themes. His Czech films show an increasingly negative attitude about the society's inflexibility, reflecting the growth of President Antonin Novotny's anti-intellectual measures prior to the "Prague Spring" of 1968.[4] The American films also all relate directly to their point in history. Taking Off demonstrates the confusion of a middle-age, middle-class parent in a youth-oriented culture. Cuckoo's Nest comments on the nature of power, an appropriate topic for the post-Watergate era. Hair relates to America's need to heal the wounds left from the Vietnam war. Ragtime presents a powerful statement about individual responsibility, the relationship of technology to power, the role of terrorism in twentieth-century life, and the struggles of minorities to share the resources of wealth and power. Amadeus focuses on the role of the artist in society and the need to recognize the difference between substance and form.

Besides these features, Forman also directed a short piece titled The Decathlon for the film about the summer Olympics of 1972, Visions of Eight. For this international event, Forman appropriately selected a universal theme. He focuses on a group of athletes enduring the most grueling Olympic event. But he also notices the judges, who self-importantly oversee the competition, and the spectators, whose attention fluctuates according to their own whims. In Forman's eyes, the whole spectacle becomes a parallel for modern life. Some people are the high achievers in society and constantly strive towards a goal. They must contend with both an authoritative superstructure that controls their actions and a passive audience that cares very little about their success. At the end, they are either rewarded or forgotten. In sum, The Decathlon contains the same blending of comedy and tragedy present in each of Forman's films. It encapsulates his vision of life.

Milos Forman's vision has, therefore, remained consistent through all his work. He always presents life as a mixture of comedy and tragedy. Forman's themes are also constant. He insists on the need for both individual responsibility and institutional humanitarianism. Yet, Forman's films relate significantly to their specific cultural and historical contexts as well. In addition, Forman has consistently altered his techniques to complement both his material and his role as an artist. Each of these factors, along with his virtuosity in adapting contemporary American drama and literature for the screen, have made Milos Forman one of the most important directors of the present era. Examining Forman's creative methods in regards to each of his films, including his screenwriting, camera work, editing, and use of other film elements, reveals the reasons for his work's continual relevance. But all of Forman's creative achievements have their origins in his childhood and development as a young artist. This period of his life covered the years 1932-1962.[5]

Even though they occurred in the midst of a great historical cataclysm, Milos Forman remembers the early years of his life, 1932-1945, as essentially happy ones. World War II was especially tragic for the

boy from Caslov because the Gestapo arrested both his parents when he
was eight years old. Forman remembers seeing his father at his school
one day, standing between two men wearing long raincoats. The young
Milos did not understand when his father said that the men were taking
him to a camp, because the only kind he knew about were of the summer
vacation variety. Forman's father asked him to tell his mother not to
worry, but she too was arrested a short time later. Both of them eventually died in the Nazi concentration camps.[6] The loss of his parents
did not have an immediately devastating effect on the young Forman.
Instead, his guardians felt such sympathy for him that they usually gave
him a great amount of freedom to do as he pleased. Forman thus
remembers his childhood as a relatively happy one.

Two important qualities in Forman's films stem from these early
experiences. First, he always shows compassion for all victims of the
drive of certain members of society to achieve prominence and power. In
his first three films, Forman makes these victims his main characters.
They are youngsters confused by the conflicting demands of society. In
his American films, these innocent victims become the silent bystanders:
for example, the little boy and the grandfather in Ragtime. Forman
focuses on them significantly a few times to remind the audience of the
lives being affected by the main characters' actions. His true sympathy
is with them because of the way their lives are being tossed about.

A second aspect of Forman's films that relates closely to his
childhood experiences is his blending of comedy and tragedy.[7] In the
Czech films, his young lead characters often act comically foolish, but
then evoke sympathy for the undue pain that their actions cause them.
Similarly, the firemen in The Firemen's Ball perform hilarious antics
throughout the film, but Forman concludes by focusing on three old men
who are the victims of the firemen's folly.

Forman's American films contain a similar intertwining of the comic
and tragic. Taking Off is a comedy that originated from a true story
about the murder of two runaway teenagers. The parents in the film
behave absurdly while seeking their missing children. McMurphy, Berger,
and Mozart are all comic figures who die in the end. Only Ragtime has a
completely serious main character, but Forman adds humor to the tragedy
of the film through the person of Evelyn Nesbit (Elizabeth McGovern) and
the use of silent comedy techniques during the tense climax.

But not until Forman was sixteen years old did he realize that pleasure and pain are not completely distinct feelings. His school class saw a documentary film about the concentration camps. Only then did he understand the horrors of his parents' deaths. The experience changed his perspective of his childhood and helped him form a vision of the world that has been the basis of his work. In Forman's films, heroes are also fools, villains are very practical, and people buy freedom and innocence at a price that ultimately must be paid. Individuals must understand this complex world or suffer for their ignorance.

As a teenager, Milos Forman became interested in drama. His older brother was a performer with the East Bohemian Repertory Theater, and the young Forman was allowed to wander around backstage at performances. One night in 1944, the company was performing its final presentation before the Germans closed all the nation's theaters. At one point during the third act, the cast was unable to continue. Everyone on stage suddenly began to cry. Forman was moved so strongly that he decided to make the theater his life (Liehm, Milos Forman, 4).

In high school, Forman began performing in plays and helped organize a drama club, the Musical Comedy Theater, during his senior year. The group was fairly successful. Established Czech stage director E. F. Burian allowed them to use his theater one night a week for rehearsals, and they were once invited to give a guest performance at a regional Communist Party conference in Kolin. Unbeknownst to the Party regulars who attended, Forman's company performed a banned play that was a huge success with the audience. Later in his career, Forman would similarly discover that his films had a relatively easy time with official review boards because the examiners did not consider comedies to have a serious message (Liehm, Milos Forman, 47).

In the fifties, having been rejected from the Prague Drama School, Forman gained admittance to the Film Faculty of the Academy of the Performing Arts (FAMU) in film dramaturgy. His decision to go there resulted from a desperate desire to do anything to avoid two years of military duty. At this time, Czech cinema was in horrible condition. Its problems resulted from cultural policies initiated in the socialist world during the 1930s by Soviet leader Josef Stalin and A. A. Zhdanov, the Soviet Central Committee's official expert on cultural affairs. These policies dictated that all art must adhere to Communist Party ideology.[8] Forman remembers that, in 1950, Czechoslovakia produced only three feature films, all tremendously boring (Slater, "An Interview, Part I," 12).

FAMU did not teach Forman anything about cameras or directing, but it did allow him to see hundreds of films from all over the world and spend five years of his life thinking and talking about film and art with his fellow students and teachers. The students included people such as Ivan Passer (Forman's life-long friend, co-screenwriter on all his Czech films, and accomplished director) and other future members of the Czech "film miracle" of the sixties. Some of the excellent professors were experienced directors Otakar Vavra and Elmar Klos and authors Milan Kundera and Milos Kratochvil.

FAMU provided Forman with a secure and independent position from which to examine Czech film, culture, and society. His experience there began an important decade of personal and artistic growth. Forman says that in the years at film school he had no strong objections to Stalinist-Zhdanovist philosophy. He struggled with ideas about how to conform to the demands of socialist realism. But the pathetic films resulting from the process convinced him that it was unworkable (Slater, "An Interview, Part II," 11).

While at film school, Forman wrote at least three screenplays: one on the Czech humanist Jan Amos Komensky, one based on the 1930 play The Bath House by Soviet writer Vladimir Mayakovsky, and the final one a simple story about a boy, a girl, and a horse. The nature of each of these projects makes them an outline of Forman's artistic development out of the stifling confines of socialist realism.

The first screenplay follows directly in the accepted path for Czech artists at that time.[9] A standard method for stretching the state's thematic limitations was to base a work on a historical figure or period. Otakar Vavra, Vaclav Krska, and Martin Fric were three of the prominent Czech directors choosing this response to cultural policy. Forman, therefore, took a politically safe path in his screenplay on Komensky. Such topics produced broad statements of unimpeachable national integrity.

With his next script, based on Mayakovsky's work, Forman believed himself to be continuing in that path. The play was a satire on socialist leaders who, in order to maintain their power, resist leaping

forward by means of a time machine into the perfect communist world of
the future. Officially, Mayakovsky was an accepted artist, but in
reality, the theory and practice of socialist realism were two different
things. With the rejection of this work, Forman began moving further
away from the state's cultural policy and towards his own artistic
philosophy because he realized that the authorities were not criticizing
him, but Mayakovsky, a supposedly acceptable artist. Therefore, the
system did not make sense (Slater, "An Interview, Part II," 12). The
final step in Forman's disillusionment with the operations of official
Czech culture occurred when he attended a meeting of one of the commit-
tees that was to decide whether or not a specific film would be made.
Forman remembers that although he respected each member of the committee, their final decision was very narrow-minded and stupid. It was
final proof that such groups should not control art (Slater, "An
Interview, Part II," 11-12). Thus, Forman's third film school screenplay
indicates his turning away from great themes and a broad perspective and
towards simplicity. The completion of this movement eventually resulted
in the creation of his first directorial efforts, Competition and Black
Peter, in 1963. Both films relate very simple stories about young
people attempting to cope with their society and find self-expression.

In the fifties, Forman also learned the persistence that a serious
artist needs. Experiencing the rejection of his early work, Forman
says, actually helped him when other projects later in his career were
also refused (Slater, "An Interview, Part I," 8). Another lesson came
when Forman worked as an assistant screenwriter with established
director Martin Fric on a film called Nechte to na mne (Leave It To Me,
1955). A light-hearted comedy about a man who keeps taking on new work
to help other people until he finally exhausts himself, this film was
Forman's first professional job following film school. One day, he
attended a screening of some of the unedited footage. A number of
official reviewers were present. This material was typically unexciting, and everyone was very bored, except for one man who kept laughing
and enjoying himself: Martin Fric. At first, even Forman felt annoyed
by Fric, but then he realized that the veteran director was the only one
present who really cared about artistic creation. Though political
circumstances limited the depth of his expression, Fric created a large
number of films in his career and worked on every project he could.

Forman felt that he had done the best work possible under the circumstances, and no one had a right to criticize him (Liehm, The Milos
Forman Stories, 15). At the end of the fifties, and again ten years
later, when for a variety of reasons Forman was unable to do projects he
had developed or make the ones that he was working on the way that he
wanted to, these lessons in perseverance aided him in maintaining the
level of quality that he desired in his work.

In 1956, Forman worked with director Alfred Radok on the film
Dedecek Automobil (Grandpa Automobile). Forman says that Radok "was
considered the very avante-garde, the very inventive man in the theater"
(Slater, "An Interview, Part II," 13). Grandpa Automobile was one of
the films that Radok occasionally made, and the experience was very
valuable to Forman. For the first time, he learned something about the
necessary requirements for directing a film, and he also got the chance
to employ his own inventiveness. Forman and Radok would spend time
creating ridiculous gadgets like a butterfly-catching machine to be used
in the film. Forman also worked with Radok on Laterna Magika, a combination of theater, slides, dance, and film that formed part of the
Czechoslovakian exposition at the 1958 Brussels World's Fair (Liehm,
Closely Watched Films, 48-51). Artistically, Forman did not like the
experience. After coping with that bewildering variety of art forms and
equipment, he was very happy to return to the simplicity of film's
direct expression.

In 1957, in between the two projects with Radok, Forman's own
artistic personality quietly began to emerge. His screenplay for Ivo
Novak's Stenata (The Puppies) represented an important break with the
typical Czech film because it focused on an ordinary situation in contemporary life.[10] In the story, two young people from Prague decide to
get married so that the girl can avoid a work assignment to a remote
rural district. Unfortunately, this decision represents only the beginning of their troubles. To avoid their disapproving parents, they have
to search for a place to stay, going through a number of comic situations in the process. Although the film has little substance, it
represents the beginnings of a fresh look at Czech society that characterizes the work of Forman and the other "New Wave" directors during the
sixties. The Puppies has the virtues of at least being based on an

actual situation present in Czech society and showing that all young people are not happy with government control of their lives.

In 1959, Forman was released from his duties with Laterna Magika for political reasons of which he was completely unaware. Feeling free to begin his own directorial career, Forman, with writer Josef Skvorecky, coauthored a screenplay of Skvorecky's short story, "Eine Kliene Jazzmusick."[11] He had wanted to develop Skvorecky's novel The Cowards, but it had been heavily criticized by the government at the January 1959 Banska Bystrica cultural conference and so was out of the question. So, they went ahead with the other project. Unfortunately, shortly before beginning production, the radio announced the scheduled filming of a Skvorecky work. President Antonin Novotny heard the item and, assuming The Cowards was the piece in question, quickly intervened to cancel the project.

Shortly thereafter, Forman found out that because of his firing from Laterna Magika he did not have the proper credentials that would allow him to direct anyway. So, in 1961, he was forced to work as assistant director on a film called Tam za lesem (Beyond the Forest) by Pavel Blumenfeld. He thoroughly detested the experience, but he went through it in order to re-establish himself. The incident exemplifies Forman's grim acceptance of the world as a cruel place in which random incidents control destiny and his insistence on personal responsibility in spite of that fact. Forman's personal and artistic struggles from the loss of his parents, through the restrictiveness of socialist realism, and beyond the injustice of his firing from Laterna Magika form the basis for his beliefs. In spite of severe social and intellectual environments, he has attained the pinnacle of his profession. His films relate his concerns about individual responsibility and insensitive institutions while still showing sympathy for human weaknesses and failure.

During his work on Beyond the Forest, Forman was already beginning to collect material for his own film. At the same time (the early 1960s), several factors coalesced to provide a fertile soil in which the Czech New Wave could take root.[12] First, the nation's economy was one of the poorest in Eastern Europe, and the already harsh conditions discouraged Party officials from being unduly severe in cultural matters. Second, the two men placed in control of the national film industry following Banska Bystrica, Alois Polednak and Jan Vesely, were surprisingly sympathetic to filmmakers' desires. At that time, Soviet Premier Nikita Kruschev decided that his national film industry needed a boost, which meant giving support to young filmmakers. The decree had its impact on Czechoslovakia. New directors like Forman, fresh out of FAMU, began receiving support, and old production groups were revived. In addition, the Union of Czechoslovak Film and Television Artists functioned as a shield from bureaucratic interference (Liehm, Closely Watched Films, 222-23).

At last, the stranglehold of Zhdanovist aesthetics over Czech filmmaking was broken, and the new directors could honestly examine their society and restore the national cinema to a healthy condition. The New Wave artists foresaw an era of creative freedom that could exist comfortably within the socialist system. Forman remembers filmmakers all tended to believe the ideological restrictions would eventually disappear (Slater, "An Interview, Part II," 9).

The early sixties also saw the availability of new lightweight movie cameras. In 1962, Milos Forman saved all his money earned by writing nightclub stage shows and bought a hand-held sixteen millimeter Pentaflex camera. At that time, documentary filmmakers in America and France were achieving great success with the new equipment by using a style known as cinema-verité. Their films were notable for providing a more direct presentation of reality than what was visible in stylized Hollywood productions.[13] Forman's use of cinema-verité methods and the new environment in Czechoslovakia allowed him to create an honest portrait of Czech youth and society in Konkurs (The Audition).

Once he had his new camera, Forman called his friend Miroslav Ondricek, cinematographer on all but three of his films, to show him how to use it.[14] Together with Ivan Passer, they began shooting on the streets around the Semafor Theater, which was in the forefront of the burgeoning Czech youth culture.[15] Semafor stars Jiri Suchy and Jiri Slitr agreed to hold mock auditions of girl singers for him to film. The scheme worked perfectly. Hundreds of girls came, and most of them were so serious about performing that they completely ignored the cameras. Forman took his material to Barrandov Studios, which asked him to develop it into a twenty-minute documentary. Instead, Forman pursued his own ideas and created a forty-five minute story about two girls who go to audition and fail. The result was a film that is both an authentic look at the rock and roll craze sweeping Czechoslovakia in the early sixties and a realistic depiction of teenage hopes and disappointments.

In his next two projects, Forman continued examining Czechoslovakia's youth culture. The Audition satisfied the Barrandov Studio chiefs enough to earn Forman his first opportunity to direct a feature. He chose to direct a story based on an autobiographical novel called Cerny Petr (Black Peter), by his friend and co-author Jaroslav Papousek. The story, which involves a youngster working as an apprentice grocery store clerk, also reflected Forman's own childhood experience (Slater, "An Interview, Part II," 10). It was originally set in World War II. But, when he began rehearsing his young actors in their roles, Forman discovered that they were most effective when he allowed them to be themselves and to relate to their own desires. So, with production already scheduled to begin, Forman and his co-writers almost completely rewrote the entire script. These changes caused the production committee to have second thoughts about approving the project. Only the intervention of Vojtech Jasny, a well-established director, saved the film (Liehm, Milos Forman, 41-43). Forman's struggle proved worthwhile. The result was an honest story about a shy, contemporary young person beginning his first job as a grocery store apprentice. Amidst the confusion of trying to please both his boss and father and win a girlfriend, he also quietly seeks his own identity.

Forman's next film, Kdyby ty musiky nebyly (Why Do We Need All Those Brass Bands?), was made on weekends during the shooting of Black Peter. Forman created it in order to fulfill the studio's demand for another short film to distribute along with The Audition. The title Konkurs (Competition) refers to both works as a whole.

In Brass Bands, Forman repeats his theme from Black Peter that young people should be allowed to develop their own identities and interests. Jan Vostrcil, who played Peter's father, provided Forman and co-author Ivan Passer with the idea for their film. As a brass band leader, Vostrcil worried about the lack of young people interested in the music. He agreed to appear in Black Peter only if Forman would also make a film about that subject.

Brass Bands reflects Vostrcil's concerns, but it also recognizes the fact that modern young people have other interests. In the film,

Vladimir Pucholt and Vaclav Blumenthal portray a pair of teenage motorcycle enthusiasts. Each of them plays in a brass band scheduled to
perform in an upcoming festival, but on the day of the competition they
both decide to attend a professional motorcycle race instead. The
conductors of the bands fire the boys, but the young men find an easy
solution for continuing their musical careers. They simply join each
other's former bands.

Forman ends Brass Bands on an upbeat note. One of the bands plays
at a private party where the guests range in age from the young to the
very old, and almost everybody, musicians included, is getting drunk.
The picture is one of both diversity and unity. As Forman pans across
the bandstand in the final shot, he adds the sound of a jazz saxophone
at the very end. A performer who is lifting his instrument away from
his lips appears to be playing the music. The jazz is energetic and
represents a lively new cultural influence. In Brass Bands, Forman is
indicating that Czech culture can only become strengthened by incorporating such influences.

The ending also expresses Forman's general optimism in 1963. His
outlook is understandable. The year had seen a liberalization in Czechoslovakia's cultural policy, enabling Forman to consolidate his knowledge and move forward in new artistic directions. He now had a firm
beginning to his career. However, Forman's optimism diminished in his
two remaining Czech films, both of which satirize government attempts to
regulate people without really understanding them. All of Forman's
Czech films share the common theme of society's need to remain open to
the people and to new ideas. But in Loves of a Blonde and The Firemen's
Ball, he sees such liberalism as increasingly unlikely.

Both Loves of a Blonde (1965) and The Firemen's Ball (1967) demonstrate a closeness to the Czech people, whom Milos Forman revealed with
great honesty. He attempted in these films to get the public to laugh
with him at their often comic responses to their nation's tragic situation. The final irony, of course, is that the situation is not comic
at all. Forman thus reveals his sympathy for society's victims. The
origins of both films were from actual events. Forman created Loves of
a Blonde, for example, from a conversation with a girl who was walking
along a Prague street late one night with a suitcase in her hand. She
had come looking for a boy with whom she had had a romantic encounter,

but he gave her a false address and now she was alone in the big city.[16]
Similarly, a visit with Ivan Passer and Jaroslav Papousek to an actual
firemen's ball produced the idea for Forman's last Czech film.

Milos Forman's success thus represents an interesting contrast to
Czechoslovakian President Antonin Novotny's failure. As Forman freely
responded to his environment, Novotny, entrapped by his own ideology and
an entrenched bureaucracy that resisted progressive reforms, became
increasingly isolated from the people (Weisskopf, 163-68). Their contrasting fates exemplify one of Forman's major themes: people who do
not understand reality will suffer. By the end of 1967, Antonin Novotny
had been forced out of power in humiliation while Milos Forman had
produced two more feature films that accurately portrayed the tragi-
comic nature of Czech society in both their content and style.

Milos Forman did not intend directly to address the political
situation of the times in either Loves of a Blonde or The Firemen's
Ball. But as examinations of Czech society, these films could not keep
from having important social and political implications. Such was the
nature of Czech film and popular culture in the mid-sixties that many
entertaining works were automatically raised to a level of serious
social comment (Liehm, "Some Observations," 140). In Loves of a Blonde,
for example, Forman's depiction of two state workers, the control of
personal lives through public policy, and personal relationships all
reflect a society based upon dishonesty and foolishness. In The
Firemen's Ball, the presentation of a group of likable but self-centered
firemen attempting to control the distribution of a few rewards creates
an apt analogy for a bumbling regime that is out of touch with its
people. In both cases, Forman heightens the absurdity by adopting
techniques increasingly removed from the documentary realism of Competition and Black Peter. His camera is not strictly tied to a human
point-of-view and is free to roam. However, Forman always establishes
the rationale for each shot at the very beginning of his film and never
allows his camera to stray outside the limitations that he establishes.
Yet the appropriateness of these techniques to the film's contents
actually increases the accuracy of Forman's depiction of society in
Loves of a Blonde and The Firemen's Ball.[17]

Milos Forman's first four films combined simple stories with entertaining comedy to reveal the complexity of Czech daily life. In 1967,

Paramount Pictures was hoping that Forman could repeat his success in
America. They gave him a contract, but decided, after seeing his
initial script for Taking Off, that they could not support his project
(Forman). Since then, however, Forman has become one of the most successful immigrant directors ever. Milos Forman's American films have
continued to be primarily entertaining works, often confounding critics
with their subtle complexity. Most importantly, Forman's films have
always addressed some of the most important issues of their times,
revealing the problems and urging the audience to search for solutions.
During the late sixties, Forman was greatly concerned with remaining
both contemporary and consistent, gradually evolving so that his work
maintained both a high quality and also constant social relevance.[18]
Each of Forman's films since then prove that he has achieved his goal.
Taking Off, for example, though somewhat disappointing in its conclusion, accurately portrays the journey of an American middle-class adult
male towards self-identity in a world dominated by youth culture.[19]
Forman had to struggle to make Taking Off the way he wanted to, but even
though it was a commercial failure, the film contains some character-
istically Formanesque techniques and themes. Perhaps too many, for
audiences did not feel that a Czech adolescent's responses to his
society were appropriate for an American adult.

    For possibly the last time in his career, Forman relied, in Taking
Off, on personal experience as the basis for his work. In America,
Forman found out that his proven skill provided him with very little
capital. He learned that his prior accomplishments did not automatically entitle him to Hollywood's bountiful resources. Forman worked
hard for what he got and learned to be satisfied within the limitations
of his lowly Hollywood status while maintaining his self-esteem. Possibly as a result, Taking Off focuses on a man of the same age learning
a similar lesson. In the film, Forman sympathizes with the desires and
frustrations of a man in his mid-thirties and skillfully juxtaposes the
illusory freedom of youth with the harsh limitations of adult responsibilities. As in The Audition, Forman once again effectively presents
young people within the context of a try-out session for female singers.
The setting allowed him to incorporate many aspects of the youth counterculture that was dominating national attention at the time. Yet,
Taking Off failed at the box-office because its ending is cautious and

conservative.[20]   Where Forman's Czech teenagers were moving out into the world, his American adult was retreating from it, and audiences were not excited by the outcome.

Forman has worked and suffered to achieve consistency in his career, one of his most important goals. The film industry does not make it easy for a commercially unproven director to do only the work that he wants. Taking Off's failure at the box office forced Forman to wait for two years until he was again offered a feature film that he considered worth making. Forman's persistence attests to his artistic integrity and his ability to maintain his values.

In the early seventies, Forman developed screenplays for three films, none of which even went into production. These were Bulletproof (a script very similar to The Firemen's Ball), Vital Parts (based on a novel by Thomas Berger, with whom he collaborated on the filmscript), and The Autograph Hunter (co-authored with film critic Paul Zimmerman, whose story later became the basis for Martin Scorsese's King of Comedy). As a result, Forman's only work for three years was directing a Broadway play (The Little Black Book, starring Richard Benjamin) and a fourteen-minute film, The Decathlon, for David Wolper's 1972 Olympic film Visions of Eight. In The Decathlon, Forman attempted to parallel the tragedy and comedy of the event with life in general. But most critics, perhaps unfairly, detested his effort, and the entire production is now mainly a forgotten film.

During this period, producer Michael Douglas sent Forman a copy of Ken Kesey's One Flew Over the Cuckoo's Nest. Douglas was nearing the end of a long struggle to bring the novel to the screen. Forman loved the novel and immediately agreed to direct. In doing so, he accepted a significant challenge. Cuckoo's Nest was extremely popular with college students in the late sixties and early seventies, and the work's established audience would naturally want to see the meanings they took from the novel displayed on the screen. But Forman also needed to make the story contemporary. He was mainly successful because he gave the story's unusual narrative perspective to his camera and transformed Kesey's mythic characters and surrealist setting into human beings in a unique but recognizable world.

Cuckoo's Nest tells the story of Randle Patrick McMurphy, who fakes insanity in order to get transferred from a prison work farm to a state mental institution. Once there, he leads the patients in a revolt against the ward's oppressive head nurse, Nurse Ratched. At the end of the novel, all of the men leave the hospital. But in the film, only Chief Bromden, a six-foot-eight Indian who narrates the novel, escapes, because he is the only one who has gained enough courage to act on his own. In Forman's hands, Cuckoo's Nest achieves a strong relationship to the dominant event of the seventies, Watergate, and American attitudes toward it. Forman tells the story as a struggle for power among McMurphy, Nurse Ratched, and homosexual patient Dale Harding. On its surface, Forman's film appears to have a conservative message because the hero is battling an oppressive social system dominated by a woman and a homosexual. But his film is neither sexist nor anti-gay. His depiction of all three characters as failing to achieve or maintain power because of their very lust for it presents his true theme. Forman shows that, like Richard Nixon, people who strive for power are suscep- tible to their own human weaknesses, and others cannot depend on them to provide freedom. In the end, each individual is responsible for either working towards his or her own freedom or remaining entrapped by the whims of those who have power.

Winning his first Oscar for Cuckoo's Nest enabled Milos Forman to maintain a gradual evolution in his career by giving him the time to develop each project in his own manner. Forman's evolution over the past ten years has been as much in terms of technique as in terms of theme, but with each story that he brings to the screen, he adds ele- ments that make it relevant to its own time period. This ability is remarkable, first because each film takes two to three years from con- ception to release, and second because each film that Forman has made since Cuckoo's Nest has been set increasingly further back in history. But, time and his own creative methods allow Forman to give contemporary meanings to by-gone eras because he is dedicated to a story first and to a theme second.

Sometimes Forman is able to choose his own story, and sometimes the story chooses him. His next film, Hair (1979), resulted from a combina- tion of both. Forman expressed an interest in filming the play when he saw the first off-Broadway public preview, and he remained interested throughout the seventies. But financial support never materialized. When it finally did, Forman nearly panicked because he was not sure if

he was still enthusiastic about the project. But he listened to the
music again and found that he still liked it (Slater, "An Interview,
Part I," 11-12).

Near the end of the seventies, three major films attempted to
remind Americans of the deep divisions caused by the Vietnam war that
still needed to be resolved. In 1978, Hal Ashby's Coming Home and
Michael Cimino's The Deer Hunter were released, followed in 1979 by
Francis Ford Coppola's Apocalypse Now. Amidst the large amount of
public attention that each of these films received, critics failed to
notice Milos Forman's Hair as another work addressing America's need to
resolve its differences over the war. The strong topicality of the
original stage production a decade earlier blinded reviewers to the
possibility of the work having a contemporary theme. Yet Forman and
co-screenwriter Michael Weller were able to look beyond Hair's original
purpose as a celebration of the "hippie" lifestyle to its inherent
capabilities as a musical for bringing opposites together.[21] In Hair,
Forman suggests that those who were divided by the war can find a common
basis for agreement in devoting themselves to people rather than to
institutions, though he reaffirms that society needs its formal structures. Forman's achievement in Hair is in adapting the optimism of
traditional musicals to the uncertainty of the modern age. The result
maintains his focus on the significance of individuals while addressing
an issue peculiarly relevant to its times.

Ever since Milos Forman began filming Hair, he has been constantly
involved with his filmmaking career. Forman was offered Ragtime (1981)
before filming Hair and became interested in Amadeus shortly afterwards.
In Ragtime, Forman was able to find themes from a story set at the
beginning of the twentieth century that apply directly to the 1980s.
The tale is about the changing nature of America due to the rising power
of immigrants and minorities, about the struggle to create a fair system
of justice in the face of a society dominated by racism and archaic
Puritan values, about a world in which terrorism now constantly
threatens established institutions, and mainly about the clash of the
human spirit with technology and the need to either understand the
modern world or be controlled by it.

Ragtime's author, E. L. Doctorow, strenuously objected when he
heard that Forman planned to make the rebellion of Coalhouse Walker,

Jr., the central part of the film (Higham). In the story, Walker is an eloquent young black man who turns to violence to obtain his rights when some racist volunteer firemen desecrate his car and the legal system offers him no possibility of reprisal. Yet, Walker's story makes the film relevant not only because Americans had to cope daily in 1980 with the spectre of terrorism in Iran, but mainly because the use of violence as a means of expressing grievances has been a fact of life throughout the twentieth century.[22]

Coalhouse Walker's story is central to Ragtime, but it is not the sole basis for Forman's theme. Forman is intent on showing that people's understanding of their history and their world must go deeper than simply acknowledging that minorities and underdeveloped countries lack adequate resources for advancement, because individuals who do not comprehend their environment, for whatever reason, are doomed to suffer. In Ragtime, two people die and a family collapses as a result of mis-interpreted images. Forman uses the film's structure, a few key shots, his actors, and colors to extend the significance of these events to the viewers, who are left with an important choice to make. They can either relate to the world superficially and suffer for their ignorance or learn how to define it properly and progress along with the twentieth century.[23]

By the time he finished Ragtime, Milos Forman was all set to begin work on his most recent film, Amadeus. Ragtime represents Forman's most thorough assessment of American culture, concerned with temporal issues in contrast to Hair's spiritual ones. In Amadeus, Forman turns to new issues that have been important to Americans in the eighties while continuing to examine the nature of man and his individual responsi-bility.

Milos Forman first saw the stage version of Peter Shaffer's Amadeus at one of its initial London public previews and immediately decided to try to make it his next film after Ragtime. The strength of the main characters attracted him to the story. Amadeus is about Antonio Salieri, court composer for Emperor Joseph II of Austria, and his jealous rivalry with the young and talented Wolfgang Amadeus Mozart. Salieri, after methodically working his way into a prestigious position by producing popular, but decidedly unspectacular, music, feels slighted by God for not being granted the talent to create great works. Because

the vulgar and unconventional Mozart does possess such skill, Salieri
seeks revenge against the Almighty by attacking His servant. Music is
Mozart's very being: his blessing and also his curse. He composes
great works as easily as breathing, but spends the rest of his time
pursuing the sinful pleasures of a world from which he feels alienated.
In the end, both composers achieve their goals, but only at the cost of
losing everything they had while gaining nothing in the process.

Forman makes his own presence in Amadeus obvious, but he uses it
ironically. The fates of the two composers reflect on the status of the
film director, who must reject both the flippant self-assurance of
Mozart and the lifeless pragmatism of Salieri, and yet learn also to
combine them somehow.

Ragtime spoke only to the responsibilities of the audience, but
Amadeus also addresses the position of the artist. Forman's standard
themes about individual responsibility, the need for self-knowledge, and
the human basis of spirituality still persist, but this time he uses
them to comment about his own role, and that of other artists, to a far
greater extent than in any of his other films. The conclusion, the most
negative of Forman's career, represents a warning to himself, to other
filmmakers, and to society. Like Larry Tyne in Taking Off, Salieri and
Mozart both attempt to completely transform themselves, and unfortunately they succeed, thereby wasting all of their talent. Salieri goes
insane because he cannot be satisfied with his own limitations, while
Mozart dies because of his constant physical indulgence.

The most sensible character in the whole film is actually Mozart's
wife, Constanze, who initially appears to be completely witless.
Constanze knows little about music or politics, but she does understand
that comfortable living depends upon money, and so she pushes Mozart to
get in touch with reality and earn what they need. More than anyone
else, she most adequately combines the emotional and the practical. At
the end, she returns to Mozart's bedside where their son (Milan
Demjanenko) wakes him up by playing with some coins spread out over the
sheets. As important as Mozart's music is, the boy also needs to learn
about the significance of money as his father never did. This simple
shot thus demonstrates the important implications of Forman's theme.
Though people might desire to build a future based on spiritual notions
and philosophical ideas, practical necessity will always play just as

important of a role. Governmental figures and the financially powerful
may be inept, but the artist must cope with them. For the sincere
artist to make truly meaningful contributions to society, he must relate
as much to reality as to his own artistic, moral, and spiritual
concepts.

Milos Forman's concern in the late sixties about his ability to
fashion a career based on a gradual evolution of his talent and themes
is now far behind him. Through a combination of vision, skill, persistence, and luck, Forman has developed in a manner enjoyed by few
other directors in world cinema. Each of his films, despite occasional
failures with the public and critics, is an intellectually challenging
and basically entertaining work that demands serious attention. The
recognition of Amadeus at the 1985 Academy Awards guarantees that Forman
will continue to be able to make exactly the kinds of films that he
desires for some time to come.

Notes

[1]Explaining his philosophy, Forman says, "you want to be part of this cleansing process of the human soul. We will never beat the stupidity of bureaucracy, and so on, but we must never stop fighting it" (Murphy).

[2]Joseph Skvorecky quotes Forman as saying,

> I think all that which is noble, and which has remained in art and literature since ancient times . . . and which is also significant for strong contemporary works of art, has always concerned itself with injuries and injustices perpetrated against the individual. That is because we always perceive the work of art as individuals. There, at the bottom of all those great works, are the injustices, which no social order will eliminate. Namely, that one is clever and the other is stupid, one is able and the other is incompetent, one is beautiful while the other is ugly, another might be honest, and yet another dishonest, and all of them are in some way ambitious. And it indeed does not matter that we are arriving at eternal themes. (All the Bright, 84)

[3]In Forman's Czech films, he focused his sympathy entirely on the young and those past middle-age because he considered them to be the most powerless. Forman told Peter Cowie that in the prime of life, "we pursue our professions, go after money, after women, after position, and we mercilessly spin the wheel of society which carries both young and old in its whirl, whether they like it or not, because they cannot protect themselves against it--they have neither the sense nor the strength necessary" (50 Major, 90). See also Kopanevova (2) and "Spotlight on Prague" (94).

[4]Forman commented about his apprehension for the future of Czech film following the making of The Firemen's Ball in both his own article "Chill Wind on the New Wave" and in an interview with Czech critic and historian Antonin J. Liehm. He told Liehm,

> I don't know why it is, but I am afraid that if we get our hands slapped, then in a few years, when an optimum situation starts to form again--and it will happen, that can't be stopped--we won't know how to start all over again either. A subconscious defensive reflex against this outlook urges us to learn quickly to do what they call pure entertainment, clean fun, which is theoretically (but for the most part also practically) independent of the political and social situation. (Closely Watched, 232)

The big slap against the Czech New Wave came, of course, with the Russian invasion. Despite that fact, Forman still hoped in the early seventies to work in his native country again, but various factors prevented it.

[5]Brief summaries of Forman's life are available in several sources. My own account derives from Forman's in Liehm's The Milos Forman Stories (3-34) and Lipton's in "A Critical Study" (127-130, 151-171).

[6]One of Forman's oldest friends, director Ivan Passer, comments, "it must have been a traumatic experience for him. You can see it. At the heart of his pictures is almost always a family or the lack of it, and the parents are inadequate in one way or another" (Buckley, "The Forman Formula," 51).

[7]Lipton discusses how Forman's method of drawing comedy out of real life tragedy is similar to Charlie Chaplin's, citing the origins of Taking Off as a specific example (127-151).

[8]Liehm and Liehm discuss the origins and early impact of Zhdanovist aesthetics (36-55). Stoil covers this issue also (68-82), and Skvorecky reveals its impact on Czech films in All the Bright (32-40).

[9]See Liehm and Liehm (105-07, 228-30) and Skvorecky (All the Bright, 35-45).

[10]See Liehm (Milos Forman, 157-58) and Skvorecky (All the Bright, 70-71).

[11]Skvorecky's story is printed in Mihailovich's White Stones and Fir Trees (351-64). It is very similar to his novel The Cowards.

[12]Several histories of Czech filmmaking and the birth of the New Wave, all annotated in this volume, are available. See Liehm, Closely Watched Films, "Some Observations," and "Success on the Screen," Liehm and Liehm, The Most Important Art, Skvorecky, All the Bright, and "The Birth and Death," Dewey, "The Czechoslovak Cinema," Lipton, "A Critical Study" (22-46), Broz, "Grass Roots," and The Path of Fame, Bocek, Modern Czechoslovak Film, Zvonicek, 25 Years, and Hames, The Czechoslovak New Wave.

[13]Cinema-verité actually originated in 1919 in the work of Russian filmmaker Dziga Vertov. New lightweight equipment gave the style a strong impetus in the early sixties. For a brief definition, see Issari and Paul (3-8).

[14]Forman's method, though inspired by cinema-verité, is actually much different because he very definitely shapes his raw footage according to his own vision of reality through editing. In his interview with Galina Kopanevova, Forman discloses that his originality results from his lack of knowledge about directing when he first began (1-2). He started with no preconceptions and so was forced to develop his own style.

[15]Forman's account of the origins of The Audition is in Liehm's The Milos Forman Stories (33-38). Forman needed help from his friends "because, despite my FAMU diploma, I didn't know how to use a movie camera" (33). Skvorecky details Competition's creation in All the Bright (75-79).

[16]Forman recounts the origins of Loves of a Blonde in Liehm's The Milos Forman Stories (59-62), Howard Thompson's "The Nude Boy," and Joseph Gelmis's The Film Director (733-34).

[17]Other writers such as Bruce Williamson ("The Loves") and Leonard Lipton comment about the actual complexity behind Forman's apparent simplicity. Lipton makes especially detailed analysis of a few shots from the dance hall sequence in Loves of a Blonde (215-37).

[18]Forman has always viewed consistency as an inherent quality of filmmaking. During the shooting of The Firemen's Ball, he remarked, "The critics expect . . . that a new work is totally new. That's impossible. Throughout his life a man retells the same story over and over again" (Skvorecky, All the Bright, 68). At the same time, he also seeks to grow with each film. As Forman describes it, consistency is only a means of maintaining artistic integrity while changing:

> Here is a question for somebody: Is a person capable of seeing to it that the unrepeatable, the unique, does not repeat itself? Can a person avoid allowing the unique to be transformed into constant repetition? Because, in the end, both the artist and—with a certain delay—the audience cease to be amused. It would be ideal if a person could evolve smoothly and progressively from one stage of his work to the next stage, as 'unrepeatable' as the last. But perhaps only Chaplin had conditions like that. In our own situation, the way things stand, it definitely isn't possible. (Liehm, Closely Watched Films, 228)

Forman's own gradual evolution marks one of his most important achievements.

[19]Not only was the sixties' youth counterculture bewildering to adults, by 1971 it was also falling apart as a result of commercial absorption, fragmentation into various causes and styles, and too many incidents of young people falling prey to dope dealers and other exploiters. Forman captures the ugly and unappealing aspects of youth in the film's audition sequence. The girls' desperateness and lack of touch with reality are just one of the film's accurate portraits of the time. For a full discussion of the counterculture's collapse, see David Pichaske (153-227) and William L. O'Neill (233-74).

[20]Forman admits to Todd McCarthy "the problem of the film was . . . the ending. The film built bigger expectations than the ending delivered" (18).

[21]Charles F. Altman's analysis of the film musicals reveals that

> Instead of focusing all its interest on a single character, following the trajectory of his progress, the American film musical has a dual focus, built around parallel stars of opposite sex and radically divergent values. This dual-focus structure requires the viewer to be sensitive not so much to

chronology and progression--for the outcome of the male/female
match is entirely conventional and thus quite predictable--but
to simultaneity and comparison. (11)

[22]William Borderer's report of the company's having to build a
facade of the J. Pierpont Morgan Library because Library trustees did
not want the idea of holding the building for ransom to spread
demonstrates the relevance of the terrorism issue.

[23]David Thomson, in the most thorough and intelligent analysis of
Ragtime, accurately describes it as a film about looking:

> Thank God Robert Altman wasn't allowed to make a carnival of
> the project. The film has to be as precise as the book. The
> faces are always examining an issue, just as the novel never
> forsakes the numb inability of the present to intervene in,
> or stop contemplating the past. (13)

Bruce Williamson ("Movies," February 1982) similarly claims that the
film is about cinema and rejects a simplistic liberal interpretation of
its conclusion.

Works Cited

Altman, Charles F. "The Film Musical." Wide-Angle Winter 1970:10-17.

Bocek, Jaroslav. Modern Czechoslovak Film 1945-1965. Prague: Artia, 1965.

Borderer, William. "Mailer, Dying for a Part in 'Ragtime.'" New York Times 17 December 1980:C25.

Broz, Jaroslav. "Grass Roots." Films and Filming June 1965:39-42.

------------. The Path of Fame of the Czechoslovak Film. Prague: Ceskoslovensky Filmexport, 1967.

Buckley, Tom. "The Forman Formula." New York Times Sunday Magazine 1 March 1981:28,31,42-43,50-53.

Cowie, Peter, ed. 50 Major Film-makers. New York: A. S. Barnes and Co., 1975.

Dewey, Langdon. "The Czechoslovak Cinema: Go! Stop! Go! Go?" Film Autumn 1968:20-32.

Forman, Milos. "How I Came to America to Make a Film and Wound Up Owing Paramount $140,000." Show February 1970:38-40,86-88.

Gelmis, Joseph. The Film Director as Superstar. Garden City, NJ: Doubleday and Co., Inc., 1970.

Hames, Peter. The Czechoslovak New Wave. Los Angeles: University of California Press, 1985.

Higham, Charles. "How 'Ragtime' Led to Discord." New York Times 26 September 1976:2:1,15.

Issari, M. Ali and Doris A. Paul. What is a Cinema Verite? Metuchen, NJ: Scarecrow Press, 1979.

Kopanevova, Galina. "Two Hours with Milos Forman." Ceskoslovensky Film: Foreign Film Bulletin 5 November 1968:1-12.

Liehm, Antonin J. Closely Watched Films: The Czechoslovak Experience. White Plains, NY: International Arts and Sciences Press, Inc., 1974.

------------. The Milos Forman Stories. White Plains, NY: International Arts and Sciences Press, Inc., 1975.

-----------. "Some Observations on Czech Culture and Politics in the
      1960s." Czech Literature Since 1956: A Symposium. Ed. William E.
      Harkins and Paul I. Trensky. New York: Bohemia, 1980:134-55.

-----------. "Success on the Screen." Survey: A Journal of Soviet and
      Eastern European Studies 5.1 (April 1966):12-20.

Liehm, Antonin J. and Mira Liehm. The Most Important Art: Eastern
      European Film After 1945. Los Angeles: University of California
      Press, 1977.

Lipton, Leonard Joel. "A Critical Study of the Filmmaking Style of
      Milos Forman With Special Emphasis on His Contributions to Film
      Comedy." Ph.D. Dissertation: University of Southern California,
      1974.

McCarthy, Todd. "Milos Forman Lets His Hair Down." Film Comment March
      1979:17-24.

Mihailovich, Vasa D., ed. White Stones and Fir Trees: An Anthology of
      Contemporary Slavic Literature. Cranbury NJ: Associated
      University Presses, 1977.

Murphy, Robert. "No Politics, Please. This is Comedy." Village Voice
      26 July 1976:109.

O'Neill, William L. Coming Apart: An Informal History of America in the
      1960s. New York: Quadrangle/The New York Times Book Co., 1971.

Pichaske, David. A Generation in Motion: Popular Music and Culture in
      the Sixties. New York: Schirmer Books, 1979.

Skvorecky, Josef. All the Bright Young Men and Women: A Personal
      History of the Czech Cinema. Toronto: Peter Martin Associates,
      Ltd., 1971.

-----------. "The Birth and Death of the Czech New Wave." Take One 2.8
      (November-December 1969):9-12.

Slater, Thomas J. "Milos Forman: An Interview, Part I." Post Script
      4.3 (Spring/Summer 1985):2-15.

----------. "Milos Forman: An Interview, Part II." Post Script 5.1
      (Fall 1985):2-16.

"Spotlight on Prague." Newsweek 18 July 1966:93-94.

Stoil, Michael Jon. Cinema Beyond the Danube: The Camera and Its
    Politics. Metuchen, NJ: Scarecrow Press, Inc., 1974.

Thompson, Howard. "The Nude Boy Needed Three Days to Think it Over."
    New York Times 23 October 1966:2:13.

Thomson, David. "Redtime." Film Comment January–February 1982:11–16.

Weisskopf, Kurt. The Agony of Czechoslovakia '38/'68. London: Elek
    Books, Ltd., 1968.

Williamson, Bruce. "The Loves of a Blonde." The National Society of
    Film Critics on Movie Comedy. Eds. Stuart Byron and Elizabeth
    Weis. New York: Grossman Publishers, 1977:255–56.

––––––––––. "Movies." Playboy February 1982:28.

Zvonicek, Stanislav. 25 Years of Czechoslovak Socialist Cinematography
    and Its Prospects. Prague: Czech Film Institute, 1970.

2. A Forman Chronology

1932   Born on February 18 to Rudolf Forman, schoolteacher, and Anna (Svabova) Forman in Caslov, Czechoslovakia.

1937   Forman sees his first film, a silent version of Smetana's opera, The Bartered Bride. He views very few other films until the war ends.

1940   Forman's father arrested by Gestapo while he is at school; Forman's mother is arrested a few months later while at home. Milos spends the rest of his childhood with relatives and friends in Nachod, Caslov, Kutna Hora, Podebrady, and Prague.

1943   Anna Forman dies at Auschwitz.

1944   Rudolf Forman dies at Buchenwald.
On the night the Germans close all of Czechoslavakia's theatres, Forman views an emotional performance by the East Bohemian Repertory Theater, for whom his brother works. Forman decides to make theatre his life.
Forman meets lifelong friend and co-author of all his Czech films, Ivan Passer, at a Podebrady Boarding School.

1948   Forman first realizes the horror of his parents' deaths when his high school class sees a documentary film about the concentration camps.

1949   Forman and a friend organize The Musical Comedy Theater. They perform Ballad of Rags by banned playwrights Jiri Voskovec and Jan Werich for a group of Party officials, who are delighted.

1950   Refused from drama school, Forman desperately applies to Prague's Film Faculty of the Academy of the Performing Arts (FAMU) in film dramaturgy and is accepted. Being a student was the only way to escape two years of military duty. Forman also considered law school as a final alternative.

1950-55 Forman studies scriptwriting and gets to view films from all over the world.

1955   Forman graduates from FAMU, works as a television announcer, and co-authors the script for Nechte to na mne (Leave It To Me) with director Martin Fric.

1956   Forman works as assistant director to Alfred Radok on Dedicek Automobil (Old Man Motorcar).

1957   Forman co-authors Stenata (The Puppies) with director Ivo Novak, based on his own scenario.

1958   Forman marries Czechoslovakia's only real movie star, Jana Brejchova, who played the lead in Stenata. He assists Alfred Radok on Laterna Magika (The Magic Lantern), a combination of

music, film, and theatre that becomes a major success at the
Brussels World Exposition. Shortly afterwards, the whole crew
loses their jobs due to the manipulations of some politically
powerful figures.

1960   Forman co-authors a script of Josef Skvorecky's "Eine Kliene
Jazzmusick" with the writer. He plans on directing the film,
but President Antonin Novotny cancels the production. Novotny
harbors a deep dislike for Skvorecky because of his novel The
Cowards, which had been condemned the previous year.
Forman co-authors floorshows under a pseudonym with Jan Rohac
for the Alhambra night club, considered a den of depravity.

1961   To re-establish his credentials, Forman works as assistant
director to Pavel Blumenfeld on Tam za lesem (Beyond the
Forest).
With his nightclub earnings, Forman purchases a 16 mm.
Pentaflex camera and begins shooting the raw material for his
first directorial effort Konkurs (The Audition) around Prague's
Semafor Theatre with friends Ivan Passer and Miroslav Ondricek.
Ondricek has to teach him how to use the camera.
Forman's brother Blahoslav dies in an accident. He is survived
by one other brother, Pavel, a painter.

1963   Prague's Barrandov Studios releases Forman's first two films,
Konkurs (Competition) and Cerny Petr (Black Peter).
Competition consists of two parts, Konkurs (The Audition) and
Kdyby ty muziky nebyly (If There Were No Music). Black Peter
wins the 1963 Czechoslovak Film Critics' Award, the grand prize
at the 1965 Locarno, Switzerland International Film Festival,
and earns Forman his first trip to America for the 1964 New
York Film Festival.

1964   Forman marries Vera Kresadlova, star of The Audition, who gives
birth to twin sons, Petr and Matej.

1965   Forman's Lasky jedne plavovlasky (Loves of a Blonde) wins the
CIDALC Award at the Venice Film Festival, the Etoil de Cristal
(French Academy Award), the Bambi (West German Academy Award),
and is nominated for Best Foreign Film at the American Academy
Awards (1966).

1966   Forman directs a film version of The Well-Paid Stroll, a play
by the Semafor Theater's Jiri Suchy and Jiri Slitr, for Czech
television. Forman agrees to make a film being co-produced by
Italy's Carlo Ponti.

1967   Loves of a Blonde opens the New York Film Festival and meets
with considerable success in America.
Forman sees the first off-Broadway production of Hair. After-
wards, he goes backstage to try to get the playwrights' permis-
sion to produce a film version of the work in Czechoslovakia.
After official delays and a removal of funding by Carlo Ponti,
Barrandov Studios releases Hori, ma panenko (The Firemen's
Ball). French filmmakers Claude Berri and Francois Truffaut

save Forman from a possible jail sentence for economic sabotage
when they replace Ponti's money with their own. Ball is
nominated for an American Academy Award as Best Foreign Film
(1968).

1968   Alexander Dubcek comes to power in Czechoslovakia, initiating a
period of liberalism which lasts until Russia invades the
country in August.
Forman and Jean-Claude Carriere work on the screenplay for
Taking Off in New York, Paris, and Prague.

1969   Forman and Ivan Passer occupy a house on Leroy Street in New
York's Greenwich Village, leaving an open door for runaways and
others while writing the script for Taking Off. Playwright
John Guare is also a resident sometimes.

1971   After many negotiations, budget cuts, and a change of production companies from Paramount to Universal, Taking Off debuts
to much critical acclaim but no box office success.
Forman plans production of a film titled Bulletproof but never
completes a script that he feels is strong enough to overcome
his weak position in the industry.
Barrandov Studios informs Forman that he has been fired after
he asks Czechoslovakia for an extension of his exit visa.
Stunned from Taking Off's commercial failure, Forman suffers
from depression and insomnia. Ivan Passer visits a psychol-
ogist, giving Forman's symptoms as his own, and brings back
instructions until the recovery is complete.
Forman works on a screenplay of Thomas Berger's novel Vital
Parts but never completes it. Forman moves into New York's
Chelsea Hotel, home for many artists, where he is able to live
for months without paying rent.

1972   Forman co-authors a screenplay The Autograph Hunter with film
critic Paul Zimmerman. Years later, Zimmerman uses his idea as
the basis for Martin Scorsese's King of Comedy.
Forman films The Decathlon at the Munich Olympics for producer
David L. Wolper's Visions of Eight. Critics generally detest
Forman's effort and the complete film is a box-office failure.
Forman directs Jean-Claude Carriere's The Little Black Book on
Broadway, starring Delphine Seyrig and Richard Benjamin. The
play has only a short run.

1973   Forman begins work on One Flew Over the Cuckoo's Nest for
co-producers Saul Zaentz and Michael Douglas.

1975   United Artists releases One Flew Over the Cuckoo's Nest to
great critical and popular success. At the 1976 Academy
Awards, it becomes only the second movie to ever capture the
Oscars for Best Picture, Best Director, Best Actor, and Best
Actress in one year. It also wins for Best Screenplay
Adaptation.

1976   Lester Persky completes arrangements for a production of Hair
with Forman directing.

Producer Dino DeLaurentiis fires director Robert Altman from the production of Ragtime and hires Forman to replace him.

1978   Forman and Frantisek Daniel, his former instructor at FAMU, become co-directors of the Film Division of Columbia University's School of the Arts.

1979   United Artists releases Hair to general critical success but weak commercial response.
        Forman attends the very first preview of Peter Shaffer's Amadeus at the National Theatre in London. Afterwards, he expresses his desire to make a film of the play to Shaffer.

1981   Paramount releases Ragtime, which achieves mixed critical and box-office success.

1982   Forman and Shaffer begin working on the screenplay for Amadeus.

1984   Orion Pictures releases Amadeus to great critical and box-office success. At the 1985 Academy Awards, the film wins eight Oscars including ones for Best Director and Best Picture.

1986   Forman makes his screenacting debut in Mike Nichols' Heartburn.

3. A Critical Filmography

This part of the book contains citations in the "Plot Summary" and "Analysis" sections that refer to a "Works Cited" list at the end of the chapter. In these instances, specific page references were necessary. However, numbers in parenthesis in the "Summary of Criticism" sections refer to the complete bibliography because this material merely summarizes the writers' opinions.

1955 <u>Nechte to na mne</u> (<u>Leave It to Me</u>)

Script: Milos Forman. Director: Martin Fric.

Plot Summary: Light comedy about a sacrificing worker who keeps volunteering for tasks until he finally breaks down under the strain.

1956 <u>Dedecek Automobil</u> (<u>Old Man Motorcar</u>)

Director: Alfred Radok. Assistant Director: Milos Forman.

Plot Summary: A documentary-styled look at the turn of the century, when inventors and individualism were prominent.

1957 <u>Stenata</u> (<u>The Puppies</u>)

Script: Milos Forman and Ivo Novak. Director: Ivo Novak. Assistant Director: Milos Forman. Director of Photography: Jan Novak. Music: Jan F. Fischer. Art Director: Karel Skvor. Editor: Jan Kohout. Executive Producer: J. Jilovec. Players: Jana Brejchova, Rudolf Jelinck, Jaroslava Panyrkova, Jan Pivec, Blanka Waleska, and others. Produced by F. S. Barrandov, Czechoslovakia.

Plot Summary: A young couple decides to get married against their parents' wishes so the girl can avoid a work assignment to a remote district. Due to a housing shortage in Prague, they encounter several mishaps while trying to find a place to stay. This film was an important precursor to the Czech New Wave because it focuses on a contemporary social problem and reveals that not all Czech youths are happy with the social system.

1963 <u>Konkurs</u> (<u>Competition</u>)
Part I. <u>Kdyby ty musiky nebyly</u> (<u>If There Were No Music</u>)
Part II. <u>Konkurs</u> (<u>The Audition</u>)

Script: Ivan Passer and Milos Forman. Director: Milos Forman. Director of Photography: Miroslav Ondricek. Music, Part II: Jiri Suchy and Jiri Slitr. Executive Producers: Rudolf Hajek

and Milos Bergl. Editor: Miroslav Hajek. Players: Part I--
Vaclav Blumenthal, Vladimer Pucholt, Jan Vostrcil, and Frantisek
Zeman; Part II--Ladislav Jakim, Marketa Kratka, Vera Kresadlova,
Jiri Slitr, Jiri Suchy, and others. All actors portray them-
selves. Produced by F. S. Barrandov. Distributed by Films Inc.,
440 Park Avenue South, New York, NY   10016, (202) 889-7910.

Plot Summaries: In Part I, two young motorcycle enthusiasts who
also play in brass bands attend a professional race on the same
day that they are expected to perform in a band contest. As a
result, each boy's band leader fires him. But they simply trade
places and keep on playing.

In Part II, two girls attend a talent competition for a
female singer. One works in a beauty parlor and the other sings
in an amateur rock band. Both fail their audition, but manage to
maintain their dignity. The worker tells her boss that she was
selected but will not start until next year. The singer lies to
the other band members about where she was.

Analysis: Milos Forman's directorial debut came in this little
film entitled Competition. Although it seems insignificant in
scope, few other films have ever been such a clear product of
social, political, technological, and artistic trends as well as
a signal for the direction of a nation's film industry. After
his graduation from film school in 1955, Forman had a couple
scripts produced by other directors. Martin Fric made Leave it
to Me (1955) and Ivo Novak directed The Puppies (1958). Both
films, in their own ways, gently satirized the idealism of
socialist realism. But Forman was not entirely happy with the
final version of either one (Liehm, Milos Forman, 13-16). During
the late fifties, he worked on two projects with director Alfred
Radok and on a screenplay with novelist Josef Skvorecky. When
President Antonin Novotny personally halted the latter project,
Forman turned to a more direct, but also more risky, means of
getting his career started (Skvorecky, All the Bright, 73-74).

While working as an assistant director on a film called Tam
za lesem (Beyond the Forest, 1961), Forman began filming on
Prague streets with his own hand-held sixteen millimeter camera
(Liehm, Milos Forman, 33). Through this simple act, Forman was
actually building on a major trend in international filmmaking at
the time known as cinema-verité. Lightweight equipment had made
this new form of "direct cinema" possible (Issari and Paul, 3-8).
By choosing to film at the musical-comedy theater of his friends
Jiri Suchy and Jiri Slitr, Forman was also incorporating an
important national phenomenon. Suchy, Slitr, and their Semafor
Theater were very popular at the time (Liehm, "Some Observations," 140).

None of these developments were actually conscious artistic
decisions. Forman was working mainly for fun and, perhaps, with
a bit of desperation, because his future as a director did not
seem too promising. But having the time to experiment turned out
to be fortunate. It allowed Forman to begin heading down his own
path, away from the status quo. Then, more good fortune struck.
Soviet Premier Nikita Kruschev declared that young filmmakers
should be given more encouragement and the pronouncement had an

impact throughout Eastern Europe. So, when Forman took his raw
footage to Barrandov Studios, they were receptive. They asked
him to make a fifteen-minute documentary, but Forman took another
chance. He made a forty-five minute fictional film instead
called The Audition, which became the second half of Competition
(Liehm, Milos Forman, 34-36).

The Audition tells the story of two young girls who come for
an audition at the Semafor. One of them is a manicurist and the
other a singer in a rock-and-roll band. Both fail but manage to
keep their pride. Forman thus presents a cultural message,
indicating that young people must be free to pursue their own
interests. He also explores the differences between fantasy and
reality, revealing the importance of being able to distinguish
between the two.

While using his rough footage as a basis, Forman ultimately
rejected the cinema-verite approach of working strictly from
"captured" events. Instead, he and Ivan Passer constructed a
script involving the two girls and incorporating sections in
which the camera would be free to observe the crowds of hopeful
auditioners. The result was a film that has an important place
in the history of the Czech New Wave because it marks the beginning of a period in which the nation's cinema began taking honest
looks at contemporary life. Several reviewers were upset with
Forman because many of the auditioners are neither talented nor
pretty. They thought of his film as cruel exploitation (Liehm,
Milos Forman, 36-37). But Forman considered the performers
important precisely because of these reasons. He perhaps in-
stinctively knew that the virtue of rock-and-roll is not its
professionalism but its honesty. Whether it strikes the listener
as pleasant or not is secondary.

When Forman brought his completed film to Barrandov, the
studio chiefs did not know what to do with it either. Were young
people really like that? Should they allow these movies to be
released? Finally, they decided to accept it if Forman would
produce another forty-five minute film to accompany it (Liehm,
Milos Forman, 36-37). Forman eventually made one called If There
Were No Music (also called Why Do We Need All Those Brass Bands?)
on the weekends while making his first feature, Black Peter.

In Music, Forman mainly relies on editing to compare and
contrast the new and the old cultures represented by the bands
and the motocycle racers. His basic message is that Czech
culture has room for both groups, but, in order to grow, the old
must make room for the new. Quite by accident, Music formed an
appropriate companion piece to The Audition as it focuses on two
boys while the earlier film centered on two girls. An additional
contrast is that the young men here are successful while the
older generation appears blundering. This perspective balances
nicely with The Audition's display of young people's negative
qualities. What both films contain is an implicit recognition of
historical trends as a major factor in the characters' lives.
Like its young subjects, Competition is also technically un-
polished. But, as film art, it too marks the path of important
historical changes.

Survey of Criticism: Because Competition was not seen in the
United States until 1968, very little has been written about it.
Leonard Lipton discusses it in terms of its realism, editing, and
use of non-actors (208). In the winter of 1966-67, a Sight and
Sound writer excitedly summarized the plots for his readers
(034). Upon its American release, Variety (091) praised it as
representing "the essence of Forman's cinematic art," noting in
particular how Brass Bands subtly reveals the flow of history and
life as the cause of its characters' problems. Gideon Bachmann
comments in "Is There a New Wave?" (015) that Competition proves
Forman's primary concern is with the individual and not society.
Only in Black Peter does Forman show interest about his characters' entrance into society.

1963 Black Peter (Cerny Petr)

Script: Milos Forman and Jaroslav Papousek. Director: Milos
Forman. Assistant Director: Ivan Passer. Director of Photo-
graphy: Jan Nemecek. Music: Jiri Slitr. Artistic Director:
Karel Cerny. Editor: Miroslav Hajek. Executive Producer:
Rudolf Hajek. Players: Vladimir Pucholt (Cenda), Ladislav Jakim
(Peter), Pavla Martinkova (Pavla), Jan Vostrcil (Peter's Father),
Bozena Mastuskova (Peter's Mother), Pavel Sedlacek (Lada), and
others. Produced by F. S. Barandov. Honors: 1964, Grand Prix
and the Young Critics Award at the International Film Festival at
Locarno, Switzerland; The Award of the Federation of Italian Film
Clubs and of the journal Cinema at the Venice Film Festival; the
Czechoslovak Film Critics' Award; 1965, Best Foreign Film, Great
Britain. Distributed by Films, Inc.

Plot Summary: Peter is a shy adolescent beginning his first job
as a grocery store apprentice. The boss tells him to spy on the
customers to catch them stealing. Peter is totally incompetent.
At one point, he follows a suspect all the way across town only
to give up and go home. He later discovers the man was a friend
of his boss. In the end, Peter revolts against being an informer
by not reporting a woman he catches stealing.
    At home, Peter must face countless lectures from his father
about being a good worker. However, the comments are almost
totally irrelevant, and the film ends with the father being
unable to explain what he is talking about.
    With his girlfriend, Pavla, Peter is also very shy, though
she gives him many opportunities to impress her. He takes her to
a dance, but spends most of the evening buying lemonade or practicing by himself. When Pavla gives him a final chance to say
how much he likes her, Peter only complains about his parents.

Analysis: Milos Forman's Black Peter, through its successes at
the Locarno and Venice Film Festivals, revealed to the world that
rumors of a revitalized Czech film industry were indeed true.
Many elements of Forman's style were plainly evident for the
first time. Once again, the focus was on contemporary youth, but
it did not start out that way. The source for Black Peter is a
novel by Forman's co-screenwriter Jaroslav Papousek, which is set
in World War II. However, while Forman was rehearsing his young

actors, he discovered that their performances improved when they were allowed to use their contemporary attitudes and styles. Therefore, with production already scheduled to begin, Forman decided to update the script, a move that jeopardized the entire film. Luckily, established director Vojtech Jasny used his influence to help preserve the project (Liehm, Milos Forman, 41-43).

Forman developed his screenwriting method while working on Black Peter, not as a calculated design, but completely spontaneously. While working with Papousek and Ivan Passer, Forman discovered that the best ideas came through a process of open argumentation. Each man felt totally free to criticize the other's ideas, and nothing went down on the page until all of them had agreed to it (Liehm, Milos Forman, 39-40). As an artist, Milos Forman sincerely believes in the value of his artistic vision; any successful artist must. But he does not have a big enough ego to believe that he can always produce a flawless script. One way that he guards against his own weaknesses is by working with writers who feel free to criticize him.

Forman's use of nonprofessional actors, also plainly evident in Black Peter, serves something of the same function. One of the reasons Forman liked using them was that a nonactor will question a line that sounds awkward. A professional, by contrast, will do the best possible work regardless of the script's quality. Working with amateurs thus helps Forman guarantee that the quality of his film is in its substance and not merely superficial (Skvorecky, "The Birth," 10). Still, Forman's penchant for working with nonactors did not begin with this artistic consideration. This technique actually began because professional actors were generally not available for films. The use of nonactors is in fact a common characteristic of Czech films in the 1960s (Dewey, 27-28).

One final reason for Forman's use of nonactors is that he believes they help preserve a film's realism. With an unknown playing a role, the audience can believe in the reality of the character instead of being conscious about watching someone who is merely pretending to be someone else. In his American films, Forman has, for the most part, quit using nonactors, and he even uses well-known stars on occasion. But he still constructs his casts mostly out of unknowns (Forman, "Closer," 57).

Milos Forman's films thus find their basis in exploring what is corrupt, weak, foolish, and false about the strong and exceptional characters of the world and also what is wonderful, admirable, pitiable, and true about average people. He has been accurately termed one of the major minimalists currently working. Most critics admired Black Peter precisely because of the mundane nature of the characters, which Forman nevertheless finds fascinating and encourages his audience to view in the same way. A film about a young person who is not radical, rebellious, or totally disillusioned, and who does not become involved in any adventure, is very unusual. Although Peter does not represent all Czech youth, he is very ordinary. Audiences and critics found this view of everyday life insightful and refreshing.

In Black Peter, Forman is once again arguing that young people need to have the freedom to learn from their own mistakes.

He received inspiration for the film from the style of Italian neo-realism, particularly Emberto Olmi's Il Posto (1961), which tells practically the same story. In his film, Olmi used the camera as a type of "engaged observer" and Forman also uses the camera this way in Black Peter (Lipton, 179-81). Forman attaches the camera's viewpoint to that of an actual observer who looks around before deciding what to focus on and sometimes even gets bored and looks away. This technique establishes the film's credibility as simply a picture of everyday life. The viewer gets an accurate sense of contemporary reality and comes to understand the important relationship of Peter to his environment by interpreting the camera's view.

Italian neo-realism was the product of Italian directors successfully adjusting to the devastated conditions of their country and film industry following World War II. Rather than trying to create fantasies for their audiences, they incorporated the reality around them. Similarly, Forman's camera observes a Czech society that is decidedly unglamourous. Peter's home and the store where he works are both very mundane. Yet, his father and his boss insist that everything is fine and that he must work to get into their world. They use art to support their own material and commercial philosophies, but beauty seems to have vanished. Forman thus shows that socialism has not come close to producing an ideal society. The town looks appropriately like a war-torn area.

The irony is that Peter does attempt to fit into this world. He tries to help customers while doing his work. But when his boss insists that he be inconspicuous, he realizes that the purpose is not to encourage honesty but to trap people into being dishonest. Peter suddenly becomes isolated and uncertain within the small store. Forman incorporates a variation on the classic silent comedy chase scene when Peter follows a suspected thief across town. However, both Peter and the man are too embarrassed to confront each other. Instead of becoming increasingly frantic, the "chase" simply dwindles to a halt. The camera pulls further and further away until it just quits looking altogether. The man later turns out to be a friend of Peter's boss.

Another important shot occurs during a scene when Peter's father is lecturing him, trying to tell him how he should have acted with the possible shoplifter. The camera simply stares at Peter for a very long time as he sits stirring his soup. Eventually, the viewer should realize that Peter is silently rebelling. Though he shows respect for his father by not arguing, he also does not agree. Instead, he quietly maintains his dignity. Peter is thus an admirable figure, while his father becomes increasingly trapped within the contradiction he is trying to support. Forman finishes the film by capturing Peter's father in a freeze frame as he tries to explain once more what life is all about. But he is ultimately unable to impose his views on Peter. He does not have all the answers, and Forman suggests that despite Peter's uncertainty, the boy must have the freedom to search for his own.

Survey of Criticism: Critics were almost universal in their
praise of Black Peter. Liehm felt that it proved what Czech
filmmakers could do when given the chance (213). The London
Times (009) gives an excellent brief analysis of the film,
recognizing Forman's observation of his characters as affectionate, but avoiding sentiment. The reviewer also notices that
Peter's family relationships are based on love and gives the film
high praise as a unique work. Other reviewers also considered
Black Peter unique. Gordon Gow (036), who includes Loves of a
Blonde in his comments, describes Forman's method of achieving a
natural look through a combination of tight control and improvisation. Gow also praises Forman for successfully meeting the
challenge of focusing on quiet and ordinary youngsters in normal
settings, which is far more difficult than presenting openly
rebellious teenagers in unusual circumstances because the drama
is less apparent. Forman comments that he thought his films
would be too slow for Western audiences to appreciate.

   Andre Techine (072) analyzes Forman's undercutting of narration, progression, and standard resolutions, creating instead a
comedy of observation. By depicting the present, Techine argues,
Forman refuses to distort the past. Richard Roud (012) praises
Forman's style as "controlled improvisation" and admits finding
difficulty in describing a film that he likes which has neither a
strong plot nor a flashy style. Roud feels that Forman is honest
and not at all condescending. Lindsay Anderson (007) praises
Black Peter as a fresh, personal film of graphic elegance, and
Variety (004) commends Forman's basic understanding and his handling of the actors and the pacing. Joseph Morganstern (099), in
a retrospective article about the New Wave, cites Black Peter as
the first indication to the West of the great work to come out of
Czechoslovakia in the sixties. He states, however, that the film
was not particularly revolutionary except in comparison to the
Czech films of the fifties.

1965   Lasky jedne plavovlasky   (Loves of a Blonde)

Script: Jaroslav Papousek, Ivan Passer, and Milos Forman.
Director: Milos Forman. Assistant Director: Ivan Passer.
Director of Photography: Miroslav Ondricek. Music: Evzen
Illin. Art Director: Karel Carny. Editor: Miroslav Hajek.
Executive Producer: Rudolf Hajek. Players: Hana Brejchova
(Andula), Vladimir Pucholt (Mila), Antonin Blazelovsky (Tonda),
Josef Sebanek (Mila's Father), Milada Jezkova (Mila's Mother),
Jana Novakova (Jaruska), Jan Vostrcil (The Major), Josef Kolb
(Factory Supervisor), Vladimir Mensik (A Soldier), Ivan Kheil (A
Soldier), Jiri Hruby (A Soldier), and others. Produced by F. S.
Barrandov. Honors: The CIDALC Award at the Venice Film Festi-
val, 1965; Etoile de Cristal (French Academy Award); Bambi (West
German Academy Award). Distributed by Films, Inc.

Plot Summary: Andula is a teenage worker at a shoe factory in a
remote town where the girls outnumber the men sixteen to one. At
night, Andula dreams of love. She tells another girl about her
boyfriend and a brief encounter that she has with a forest
ranger. When the factory supervisor gets the army to station a

troop of reservists near the town, Andula spends a night with the piano player of the band that comes to play at the welcoming dance.

After a speech on virtue by the girls' housemother, Andula goes to Prague to visit her new boyfriend. When she gets to his apartment, only his parents are home, watching television. They spend the entire evening questioning Andula's morality while their son is out attempting to seduce yet another girl. When he finally arrives home late at night, his mother takes him into bed with her and his father. Andula breaks down in tears when she listens outside their door and learns that none of them care anything about her.

Back in her dormitory, Andula tells a friend that she had a wonderful time in Prague and will probably be going there often. The next day, she is back at work as usual.

Analysis: Loves of a Blonde, through its successes at the New York Film Festival and elsewhere, brought Milos Forman international fame. Some critics may still consider it his greatest work. Once again, Forman drew directly on contemporary Czech life for his story. While driving home during the early morning hours, he spotted a girl with a suitcase. Finding a girl by herself on a Prague street at that hour was a very unusual occurrence. Forman picked her up and learned that she was looking for a boy's house. She was from the country and had met this boy once. He had given her an address and suggested she visit him sometime. Of course, the address he had given her was false (Liehm, Milos Forman, 60-61). This story is the same one that Forman tells in Loves.

Forman varies his visual perspective somewhat in Loves. Although he does use a human observer's viewpoint a few times, he does not maintain it throughout the film as he did in Black Peter. Instead, Forman's camera takes an omniscient perspective. For example, at one point, a middle-aged soldier who is anticipating an encounter with a young girl removes his wedding ring. He drops it and it rolls across the dance floor. Wherever it is kicked, the camera is right on top of it, following it to a halt under the table of three girls. The scene is hilarious, but had the camera been limited to the viewpoint Forman used in Black Peter, this action would not have fit into the film.

Forman justifies this freedom of camera movement right from the beginning because the whole film takes the form of a dream by its main character, Andula. Right from the start, action takes place that seems incongruous. Loves opens with a girl staring straight into the camera, playing the guitar, and singing a rock-and-roll song about a lousy boyfriend. As she finishes, the camera pans down from her to a table where the guitar is lying even though the music is still playing. The action then begins with Andula and a friend talking in bed together. The two of them live in a dormitory as part of an all-girl workforce at a shoe factory in a remote town. The fact that the action begins with the girls going to bed further supports the film's dreamlike nature. Forman focuses on hands and feet sticking out of

blankets in the dark. The camera is thus taking a perspective
similar to Andula's, settling down into her dream. Andula tells
about her boyfriend who gave her a ring that he said is a
diamond. Her friend suggests that Andula should give him
something in return.

Forman then cuts to a strange scene of Andula walking
through a snow-filled woods toward a tree with a tie hanging
around it. A forest ranger strikes up a conversation with her
and asks her to come back to his cabin with him. Forman then
cuts back to Andula and her friend in bed together again. They
talk about the ranger. Andula thinks he may be her new boyfriend, but the fact that he is married makes her uncertain.
Coming between the two scenes in bed with abrupt cuts to and from
it, the scene with the ranger appears like a dream. Forman
completes this pattern at the end of the film when Andula is
again in bed talking with her friend, but now light is coming in
through the window. Thus, her dream is ending.

Andula often behaves foolishly during the film, as in her
response to the forest ranger, but she deserves sympathy because
she is looking for love and has no basis for knowing how to find
it. Her motives are pure, but her resources are few. The
government stations a company of aging reservists in the factory
town, and the young piano player for the welcoming dance (Mila)
manages to seduce Andula. She tells him that her parents do not
love her and that she has attempted suicide, but he merely uses
these confessions to get her up to his room. Later, while he is
making love to her, Andula finally decides that she trusts him.
The scene is comical, but Andula's pathetic nature checks the
laughter.

Later, when Andula goes to visit Mila in Prague, her trip
seems foolish because he never seriously intended her to come.
But Andula is responding to a speech by the girls' housemother
that they not cheapen themselves through flirting but stick to
one man. By this point, Andula has had three boyfriends and gone
to bed with one. Her trip therefore represents her attempt to
stabilize her values and her life, and the housemother's speech
represents an example of unintentionally misapplied social
values.

Andula's troubles come from the fact that she believes what
each one of her "boyfriends" tells her. She accepts the world as
an honest place and feels guilt when the housemother tells the
girls that morality is their responsibility. Her resulting
search for romance produces some truly comical misadventures.
But viewers cannot be condescending toward Adula, for her
ignorance and vulnerability are a direct result of her isolation.
Instead, Forman makes the viewers feel like intruders on Andula's
dream, and their laughter stops when they see her being used by
Mila or crying later at his apartment because of her loneliness.
Thus, Forman catches the audience in laughing at Andula and
builds sympathy for his heroine. He therefore forces the
audience to face the important question of how a society can
justify Andula's isolation.

Forman also reveals that isolation and ignorance are not
solely the fault of public policy. Many people simply create
their own isolation. Therefore, Andula's attempts to end her

loneliness actually make her an admirable figure. When Andula
arrives in Prague, she has to spend the evening with Mila's
parents. Since they sit night after night watching television,
they have isolated themselves from the world. When a strange
girl unexpectedly shows up at their door, they immediately fear
the worst. In a matter of minutes, the mother has imagined that
Andula and her son will have to get married, will probably get
divorced, and then will leave their children in some kind of
desperate situation.

In the end, Andula returns from her disastrous trip to
Prague and tells her friend that she had a wonderful time.
Several writers have concluded that since she also told stories
at the beginning of the film, she has learned nothing. But that
interpretation conflicts with the idea that Andula is emerging
from a dream at the end of the film. If she is waking up, she
must be waking up to something. An accurate interpretation could
be that she has realized the deceitful nature of the world, and
her final lie shows that she now knows what she has to do to get
by. This view also agrees with Forman's consistent blending of
comedy and pathos. Andula's enlightenment is positive, but the
world she now understands is not a hopeful one.

The music for the final scenes is "Ave Maria." Thus, the
music changes from humorous and upbeat at the beginning to serious and sorrowful at the end, contrasting with the plot movement.
The basis of Andula's maturity is her loss of virgin innocence.
She is now another capable member of a deceitful society. She
will endure, but the society simply continues in the same path.
Forman's view of his country was not particularly positive, but
he made his audience laugh while telling them about it.

Survey of Criticism: Jean Collet (063) uses the opening and
closing scenes to explain Loves as taking place within Andula's
dream since the film begins with her going to sleep and returns
to the dorm at the end with the light just coming in through the
windows. The viewer looks on with mounting embarrassment and
curiosity, which creates the humor. Collet thus finds that Loves
fulfills the essence of cinema: to reveal secrets and dreams.
The multiple examples in the film of individuals discovering
other people's secrets supports this analysis.

Phillip J. Hartung (037), who did not admire the film as
much as Ivan Passer's Intimate Lighting, and Newsweek (032),
which rates it with the work of Griffith, Vigo, and Renoir, both
felt that Andula learned nothing from her experiences. Most
other reviewers, such as Arthur Knight (040), Brendan Gill (035),
Moira Walsh (049), John Peter Dyer (018), Robert Kotlowitz (041),
and Bosley Crowther (022) also praised the film. The dissenters
are Kirk Bond (089), who argues that Loves of a Blonde is just an
ordinary film that gives no indication of what the Czechs are
really doing, and Robert Hatch (038). Hatch finds the film
endearing but artless and ill-constructed. He sees no relationship between the ballroom scene and the one at Mila's house and
does not believe the ending.

1967   <u>Hori, ma panenko</u>   (The Firemen's Ball)

Script: Milos Forman, Jaroslav Papousek, and Ivan Passer.
Director: Milos Forman. Assistant Director: Jaroslav Papousek.
Director of Photography: Miroslav Ondricek. Music: Karel
Mares. Art Director: Karel Cerny. Editor: Miroslav Hajek.
Executive Producer: Rudolf Hajek. Players: Vaclav Steckel
(Fire Brigade Commander), Josef Svet (Old Man), Jan Vostrcil
(Chairman of the Committee), Josef Kolb (Josef), Frantisek
Debelka (1st Committee Member), Josef Sebanek (2nd Committee
Member), Karel Valnoka (3rd Committee Member), Josef Rehorek (4th
Committee Member), Milada Jezkova (Josef's Wife), and others.
Produced by F. S. Barrandov. Honors: Nominated for the Academy
Award for Best Foreign Film in 1968; shown at film festivals in
Cannes, New York, and San Francisco. Distributed by Cinema 5,
1585 Broadway, New York, NY 10036.

Plot Summary: A group of small town firemen decide to have a
ball during which they will award a special hatchet to their
honorary fire chief of fifty-one years. But then, everything
goes wrong. They decide to have a beauty contest, but the girls
they select are not very attractive and basically shy. When the
contest starts, they escape to an upstairs bathroom. The firemen
chase after them while the guests go beserk, dragging women to
the front of the auditorium. They select a fat middle-age lady
as the winner.

  In the midst of this chaos, a fire starts, but the fire
truck gets stuck in the snow and an old man's house burns down.
The firemen attempt to hold a tombola, but the guests gradually
steal all the prizes. One fireman's wife even steals a head-
cheese, and her husband is later caught trying to return it.
While the firemen meet in private to decide how to handle this
disgrace, all the guests leave. The firemen finally decide to
present the hatchet to their honorary chief, only to discover
that it too has been stolen. In the end, the old man who lost
his house goes to bed in the middle of a field of snow with
another old fireman who was left outside to guard his
possessions.

Analysis: <u>The Firemen's Ball</u> represented a number of firsts for
Milos Forman as well as a continuation of some of his standard
themes and techniques. It is a unique film for him because there
is no main character. Forman is basically interested in the
functioning of two groups: the firemen and the rest of the
townspeople. Forman also changed focus in directing his sympathy
toward the elderly instead of youth. His concentration on either
end of the age spectrum in his Czech films reflects Forman's
beliefs at that time that middle-aged people are basically strong
and secure individuals who create havoc in the lives of those who
have less power (Cowie, 90). Although his views have since
changed slightly, even Forman's most recent films, <u>Ragtime</u> and
<u>Amadeus</u>, demonstrate these feelings. Finally, <u>The Firemen's Ball</u>
is Milos Forman's first color film. At this point, Forman did
not seem to look at color in terms of symbolism. He was mainly
interested in it in terms of enhancing realism and probably would

have made his earlier films in color as well had he been given
the opportunity.

Forman also had more advanced technical capabilities on the
set during The Firemen's Ball, and he exploited them fully. His
camera is more free than in any of his other films, and Forman
once again established its role in the opening scenes. The film
begins with the firemen passing a commemorative hatchet around a
table. The entire film basically hinges on their attempt to
present it to their honorary chief for fifty years of service,
but they fail at even this simple task. Merely giving it to him
would not be enough. The plans for the bestowal have to be so
elaborate that they will honor the brigade as well. In fact,
that is really their main purpose. They want to exalt themselves
as protectors and distributors of rewards. They even want to act
as judges by holding a beauty contest. Unfortunately, they are
unable to live up to their self-image. But they stick to it,
even as their ball turns into a shambles. Part of Forman's theme
is that people often try to determine reality rather than simply
recognize it and react logically. Usually, their stubborn
refusal to admit an error produces disaster. As a result, The
Firemen's Ball appears to be a clear analogy for the communist
system. But, in reality, the model applies anywhere.

The townspeople who come to the ball are no more admirable
than the firemen. Logically, they ignore the firemen's attempts
to control them and, instead, do exactly as they please. But,
throughout the evening, tombola prizes keep disappearing.
Instead of waiting for the firemen to say who has won what,
people just take what they want, and that includes more than what
the firemen are offering. At one point, a girl looking to
recover beads from her broken necklace crawls under the prize
table. Her boyfriend sees a wonderful opportunity and follows in
after her for a brief erotic encounter. The fireman guarding the
table simply watches helplessly as the prizes tip over one by
one.

The primary conflict between the firemen and their guests
occurs with the handling of the beauty contest. The firemen use
a picture from a magazine of a professional contest as their
model. But they cannot decide on how many candidates to select.
And what should be the basis for deciding: faces, busts, or
legs? Eventually, the selection committee has most of its decisions made for them. The girls they really want refuse to participate. Wives tell them whom to include or not; friends bribe
them. When the contest finally does take place, most of the
girls are too shy to go to the front of the ballroom. While the
band takes a beer break during the processional, the contestants
take the chance to bolt for the upstairs women's room. The
firemen head after them while the crowd goes beserk. Women are
dragged or carried to the front. Finally, the crowd selects its
own queen: a fat middle-aged woman who stands on stage laughing.
On paper, the firemen's plans all seem very workable. But they
never consult any of the people about what they might want to do,
and they never take human unpredictability into account. Meanwhile, the townspeople have no great standards either. They are
merely greedy individuals who want to grab all they can.

The camera reacts to all of their activity by trying to remain somewhat above it even though it is also a part of it. For example, when the beauty contestants break for the bathroom, the camera watches them head for the stairs, but then it is in the upstairs hallway as they arrive at the top. Forman then uses several shots overlooking the crowd as they drag other women up to the stage. After the contest, a fire breaks out and the crowd rushes to the door to go see it. The bartender stands in their way to try and make them pay before leaving. Forman first shoots from inside behind the crowd, but then he cuts immediately to a shot looking at the door from the outside as the people throw the bartender into a snowbank.

Forman creates the basis for this freedom of camera movement during a second opening scene in which a few men are decorating the ballroom. One of them is standing on a ladder, burning the edges of a poster. The two men holding the ladder start arguing over the disappearance of a tombola prize and the ladder falls. While the man who was on it holds onto a wire, the picture catches fire and the men down below try unsuccessfully to use an extinguisher. During the scene, the camera shifts back and forth between looking up at the man hanging and looking down on those with the extinguisher. Forman maintains this freedom throughout the film and employs it effectively in the very last shot.

During the film, an old man's house burns down. The firemen are unable to stop it because their truck gets stuck in the snow. The people take the old man in but leave an elderly fireman out in the cold all night to guard his possessions. They promise to send someone to relieve him, but he is evidently forgotten. In the meantime, the firemen finally get around to awarding their honorary chief his hatchet after everyone has gone home. But when they go to do so, they discover that it too has been stolen. The sad look on the old chief's face is the final commentary on their bungling.

The film ends with the fire victim looking through his possessions scattered throughout the snow. He goes over to the bed, takes off his slippers as he normally would, and crawls in with the old fireman who was left on guard. With this scene, the camera rises up into the sky as new snow begins to fall on the two men. By distancing his camera from the action, Forman preserves the comic elements of the scene. But, again, he provides no easy laughter. The film's conclusion is a pessimistic vision of the way the society has left its most helpless members out in the cold. The new snow indicates that their troubles are not over. In The Firemen's Ball, Milos Forman once again uses the large ballroom setting to explore the hopes and follies of his society. His conclusion is pessimistic, and he finishes by distancing himself from involvement with the action. Perhaps it is appropriate that he now took his career to the United States.

Survey of Criticism: Marion Armstrong (109) does no more in her review than recount the film's events, not always accurately. Harriet R. Polt (101) feels that Forman should have shortened some of the sequences, but basically admires the film for revealing most of mankind's weaknesses and the disasters they produce at a ball where everyone still manages to have a good time anyway. Bruce Williamson (119) praises some of the film's hilarious sequences, but laments its lack of focus on a specific character. Williamson feels that Forman's theme is the effects of a faulty bureaucracy and finds the humor less subtle than in Loves of a Blonde. Nevertheless, the review closes by stating that Forman may single-handedly revive the golden age of screen comedy. Renata Adler (079) agrees with that opinion, mentions several incidents from the film, and notes Forman's ability to escalate both comedy and sadness at the same time. Antonin Liehm comments on the film by comparing Forman to Gogol as a master satirist with intimations that he will probably be equally misunderstood and attacked by his countrymen for showing the average citizen to be just as callous and capable of doing harm as social and political leaders (213).

Time's reviewer (103) saw The Firemen's Ball as having a different meaning in relation to each of the three regimes before, during, and after Dubcek, and thought that the film worked well in each context. By contrast, David Wilson (104) describes the film as a very human story with its political overtones only an afterthought. Wilson finds the ending saved from despair by Forman's compassion. Roger Ebert (309) is not sure whether the film is an allegory or not, but finds the humor unforced and Forman's presentation of how the best intentions often go awry to be very realistic.

1971 Taking Off

Script: Milos Forman, John Guare, Jean-Claude Carriere, and John Klein. Director: Milos Forman. Director of Photography: Miroslav Ondricek. Photographer: Louis San Andres. Editor: John Carter. Players: Lynn Carlin (Lynn Tyne), Buck Henry (Larry Tyne), Linnea Heacock (Jeannie Tyne), Georgia Engle (Margot), Tony Harvey (Tony), Audra Lindley (Ann Lockston), Paul Benedict (Ben Lockston), Vincent Schiavelli (Mr. Schiavelli), David Gittler (Jamie), the Ike and Tina Turner Revue (Themselves), and others. A Forman-Crown-Hausman, Inc., Production, in association with Claude Berri. Produced by Alfred W. Crown. Associate Producer: Michael Hausman. Copyright by Universal Pictures and Forman-Crown-Hausman, Inc. Honors: Special Jury Prize, Cannes Film Festival, 1972; Best Picture Award, Belgrade Film Festival, 1973 (Buck Henry named Best Actor at Belgrade Festival). Distributed by Swank, 350 Vanderbilt Motor Parkway, Hauppauge, NY 11787.

Plot Summary: Larry and Lynn Tyne are afraid that their daughter Jeannie has run away. Actually, she is merely at a talent audition for girl singers. But Lynn sends Larry out to look for her. The trouble is that Larry would like some excitement in his own life as middle-class existence is getting to be a bore. Therefore, instead of looking for Jeannie, Larry and his neighbor go out and get drunk. In the meantime, Jeannie returns. But when Larry comes home and angrily slaps her, she actually does run away.

Larry continues searching for Jeannie, but is still unsuccessful. During the first search, he gets chased by a group of

Hell's Angels and begins an attempt at seducing the mother of
another runaway girl, Ann Lockston. But when he calls Lynn, she
tells him they must immediately go to upstate New York to pick up
Jeannie. The trip is fruitless, but in a resort hotel that
night, two men try to pick up Lynn, who then attempts to seduce
the bewildered Larry.

Later during their search, the Tynes attend a meeting for
the Society of Parents for Fugitive Children where a young
hippie, as a means of helping them understand their children,
shows a number of the parents how to smoke marijuana. Larry and
Lynn return home with Ben and Ann Lockston for a game of strip
poker, unaware that Jeannie has come back in the meantime. As
Larry stands naked on the dining table, singing an aria from La
Traviata, Jeannie appears on the upstairs landing. Larry
recovers enough from his shock to talk with Jeannie and tells her
to ask the man she has been staying with over for dinner.

Jeannie's boyfriend, Jamie, is a silent long-haired musician. At dinner, he gives Larry another shock by revealing that
he earned $290,000 the previous year. Larry reacts by finally
starting to relax. He gives signs that he is ready to stop
worrying and be happy with his natural self. At the end of the
film, he sings "Stranger in Paradise" while Lynn accompanies him
on the piano.

Analysis: When Milos Forman came to America, he could not and
did not leave his Czech sensibility behind. Working within a new
production system, in a new culture, and with a new language,
Forman clung to many of his standard techniques and motifs as a
basis for his work. Like most of his Czech films, Taking Off
also focuses on generational conflict, but this time more from
the adult side. Like The Audition, it includes a try out for a
singing job. Forman even repeats one montage of several girls
all singing a line from the same song. He also employs his by
now standard ballroom scene twice. This degree of continuity is
understandable and responsible for Taking Off's critical success.
Forman did not approach his American project by trying to do
something totally new. He believes that people everywhere are
basically alike, and, through his understanding of human nature,
he was able to produce one of the most thoughtful studies of
American generational conflicts ever. But his reliance on the
past also led to the film's commercial failure. What seemed
optimistic when applied to Czech youth was not uplifting in terms
of American adults.

Forman began his first American project with the attitude
that he would enjoy this new challenge. Unfortunately, he was
unprepared for the complex negotiations and deceptions of studio
executives, lawyers, and agents. Czech filmmaking had provided
him with no comparable experiences. Similarly, Forman lacked the
connections with the American culture and people that he had
enjoyed in Czechoslovakia. Nevertheless, he went about writing
his script in the same manner that he had used for writing The
Firemen's Ball. He and Ivan Passer rented a house in New York's
East Village and Forman immersed himself in the lives of young
hippies, runaways, and their parents (Conaway, 10). These
experiences provided the basis for Taking Off. But Forman has

since admitted that it is very difficult to tell when enough of
the culture has been absorbed to interpret it correctly (Liehm,
Closely Watched, 235). Since Taking Off, Forman has never again
worked from the basis of his own experience. He has consciously
chosen to do adaptations of others' visions (Slater, "An Interview, Part I," 15).

Taking Off involves the story of Jeannie Tyne, who runs away
from home, and her parents Larry and Lynn, who become involved in
various mishaps while searching for her. Jeannie initially goes
to an audition for a show, and Forman injects scenes from the
audition into the story of the Tynes' search for their daughter
throughout the film. The songs provide a commentary on the
action and also contrast the seemingly timeless and creative
world of young people with the highly structured world of adults.
The major irony in the film is that the members of each generation are attempting to enter the other's society. For young
people, the process is natural and they have a right to make
fools of themselves while going through it. The adults simply
look foolish. Forman thus shows a number of hopelessly
incompetent girls at the audition trying to prove they have
talent, and a group of adults repeatedly acting ridiculous. Some
critics have accused him of exploiting his characters. But for
those who find fault with the girls, the problem lies with them
and not with the young people, while those who criticize the
adults may not understand them fully.

Some of the auditioners, Carly Simon for example, are very
talented, and from them adults form their impressions of the
youthful world. They make the young world seem like the fresh,
alive, and exciting one for which adults yearn. Simon sings,
"Long term physical effects are not yet known/So I think I'll
have another drag and just get stoned." In the film's climactic
scene, Larry and Lynn Tyne get high on pot for the first time in
their lives and play strip poker with a pair of friends. The
short term effects do seem "groovy" to them. However, they have
not yet experienced the long term physical effects of hysterical
paranoia, the feeling that the world is falling apart. Earlier,
Forman showed a girl at the audition who believed that acid
enabled her to sing beautifully. But she then has to be dragged
away screaming. The Tynes are about to experience the same
emotional shift themselves.

Unknown to the Tynes, Jeannie is up in her bedroom, and she
discovers her parents while Larry is standing on the table, nude,
and singing opera. Just when he had finally shaken his inhibitions and was about to "take off" himself, Larry comes literally
crashing down. The long term effects hit him, and he evidently
decides that he is very happy and comfortable in his father role
after all. With the strip poker game over, Larry goes to
Jeannie's bedroom to talk to her. Forman shoots the scene from
behind an open closet door to show how Larry feels comfortable
within a restrictive environment. Shortly afterwards, Forman
again shows him in a confined area with a specific role to play.
When Jeannie's boyfriend arrives for dinner, Lynn stands in the
pantry closet crying, still unable to face her daughter. Larry
goes to her and comforts her. These two scenes show him the most
confident that he has been in the entire film. When Jeannie's

hippie boyfriend reveals he earned $290,000 the previous year
from his music, Larry also gives up his futile attempt to quit
smoking. Lynn looks surprised, but it is his most natural act in
Taking Off. Larry finishes the film by singing "Stranger in
Paradise" as Lynn plays the piano.

Larry is thus the only leading male character in one of
Forman's American films to discover that he can be happy within a
set of limitations and therefore survive. He is the primary
example of Forman's point that freedom within a restrictive
environment is possible. But through most of Taking Off, Larry
does not realize this fact. A psychiatrist tells him that in
order to quit smoking and enjoy life, he must restrict his
natural inclinations. Blocked off in one area, however, they
emerge in others. When Jeannie runs away, Larry sees everything
that he has worked for falling apart. Worse, he does not seem to
be having any fun anymore, and when Lynn sends him out to look
for Jeannie with a large framed portrait, he feels like a fool.
So he finishes his first search for Jeannie by getting drunk at a
bar. Another search appears to be leading to a sexual encounter
with the woman who later plays strip poker with the Tynes. But
when Larry calls home, Lynn tells him Jeannie has been found and
they have to drive to upstate New York to get her. Thus, parental responsibilities once again interfere with his pleasure. But
each time they do so, Larry responds. These situations reveal
his natural inclinations and show that he has his priorities
straight. They also establish that Larry feels most comfortable
within a restrictive environment.

By contrast, the world at large is very confusing. Forman
evokes New York City as a place that offers endless possibilities
but that can also be overwhelming. This idea is evident during a
scene in which Larry Tyne enters Manhattan early one morning
looking for Jeannie. Forman shoots him from a low angle with the
sun coming up behind him and skyscrapers towering overhead while
Antonin Dvorak's "Stabat Mater" plays on the soundtrack. It is a
beautiful new day, full of possibilities. But Larry is dwarfed
in this environment. His confusion builds until a short time
later he is caught in a silent-comedy inspired chase involving
some Hell's Angels, a runaway girl, her mother, and an irate taxi
driver. Forman thus shows Larry futilely attempting to cope with
conflicting ideas of happiness until he literally does not know
which way to turn. Larry's confusion, however, only reveals his
similarity to the other adults in the film, all of whom act like
foolish children while the young people attempt to take on the
mature responsibility of finding jobs and taking care of themselves.

In the end, Larry becomes contented with his family role.
But the conclusion is uninspiring because it contains some un-
foreseen negative aspects. Larry appears to be retreating from
the world, perhaps deciding that he does not want to take any
more chances. In Forman's Czech films, Peter and Andula could
reach new states of awareness and be ready to expand their lives.
Showing an adult who is ready to accept some type of "security"
is not as exciting.

Survey of Criticism: <u>Taking Off</u>'s detractors generally attack
Forman for belittling his characters. Benjamin DeMott, for
example (144), criticizes the parents in the film as people who
have no sustained concern for their children. He believes
Forman's vision of suburban domesticity is unrelentingly cruel.

George N. Boyd (156) basically echoes DeMott's criticism
that <u>Taking Off</u> lacks continuity. He finds no explanation for
Jeannie Tyne's running away and no evidence of self-revelation at
the end. Colin L. Westerbeck, Jr. (171) sees Forman as exploiting youth, tacking on an arbitrary ending, and trying to explain
all of America's problems. Robert Hatch (164) believes that
Forman is paternalistic and treats everything too much as a joke,
but admires him for reducing the generation gap problem down to
its actual size. Jay Cocks (158) also sees Forman as exploiting
young people and stating only that parents are self-centered
hypocrites. Stanley Kauffmann (166) congratulates Forman on not
trying to "say" anything about the generation gap, but is mainly
critical. He finds all of Forman's films heavy on atmosphere,
but light on theatricality, and his vision of America as
reflecting the social structure of Eastern Europe.

John Simon (169) was the most caustic critic, expressing
only pure disgust for Forman and his film, which he perceives as
a mere example of the director showing his superiority to the
rest of mankind. A more balanced notice comes from David Brudnoy
(157), who admires the film, but registers some complaints about
Forman over-caricaturing, such as when the adults smoke dope and
play strip poker. Paul D. Zimmerman (174) generally likes the
film, focusing his comments on Forman's effective use of the
auditions and his examination of the parents. But he also finds
Lynn and Larry Tyne's reunion as lacking motiviation.

Richard Schickel (168) and David Wilson (173) give the film
its highest praise. Schickel places the film directly within its
time period as an explanation of national problems that cites
mere human frailty instead of a corrupt system as the basic
cause. Schickel admires Forman's depiction of both youth and
adults as foolish but deserving compassion and the American
tendency to respond to a problem by forming an organization. The
film may not be as flawless as Schickel states, but he presents
an excellent, concise sociological analysis. Wilson begins by
attacking the film's critics and then illustrates Forman's skillful timing, beauty, realism, and comic style. He notes Forman's
optimistic view of human frailty and depiction of the inadequacy
of communication, chronicling the differences between "what is
said, what is meant, and what is understood." Penelope Gilliatt
(161), Vincent Canby (140), Charles Champlin (142), Sandra
Hochman (147), Hollis Alpert (153), Molly Haskell (163), and
Susan Rice (134) also give <u>Taking Off</u> positive reviews.

I. C. Jarvie (322) cites <u>Taking Off</u>'s similarity with a
number of other films of its time in depicting the lost sexual
basis of marriage, accompanied by a guilty search for pleasure
outside of it. Adults are restless and bored, which inspires
their children to run away. He also comments that Larry Tyne is
still a decent and harmless man.

1972 The Decathlon (in Visions of Eight)

Directors: Milos Forman (Czechoslovakia), Kon Ichikawa (Japan),
Claude Lelouche (France), Yuri Ozerov (USSR), Arthur Penn (USA),
Michael Pfleghar (West Germany), John Schlessinger (Great
Britain), and Mai Zetterling (Sweden). Producer: Stan
Margulies. Executive Producer: David L. Wolper. Original
Music: Henry Mancini. Production Manager: Pia Arnold. Chief
Photographic Consultant: Michael Samuelson. Main title sequence
by Mel Stuart. Supervising Film Editor: Robert K. Lambert.
Assistant Editors: Bea Dennis and Geoffrey Rowland.

The Decathlon. Director: Milos Forman. Cameraman: Jorgen
Persson. Editor: Lars Hagstrom. Unit Manager: Dietmar
Siegert. "Rota-Sommerhanon" by Carl Orff. Beethoven's Ninth
Symphony performed by the Chorus and Orchestra of the Bavarian
State Opera, directed by Professor Wolfgang Sawallisch; Bavarian
folk music by Vita Bavarica and Platzl.

Plot Summary: Documentary about the ten-event competition at the
Munich Olympics of 1972. Forman injects performances of Bavarian
folk music and Beethoven's Ninth Symphony that both comment on
and parallel the action.

Analysis: The Decathlon presents Milos Forman's vision of the
world in a nutshell, just fourteen minutes. The subject of
sports must have reminded him of If There Were No Music because,
once again, Forman fuses an athletic competition with a folk
music contest. This time, the culture, year, and setting are
different, so there is no competition between the two forms of
expression. Instead, the folk music complements the sporting
event. It provides the starting music and simulates crowd reactions during different points of the competition. When the
athletic drama is at its highest, such as during the first event
or the completion of the last one, Forman often uses natural
sound, because that is when the spectators pay most attention.
However, during the middle events, such as the high hurdles, the
music may continue on merrily as an injured runner gets helped
from the track. As long as the events continue, no one seems to
care.
    Forman is basically using the music to show how he sees
competition existing in all aspects of life. And, though the
performers in both areas sometimes appear comic, Forman genuinely
admires their efforts. The shots of the runners pounding down
the track during the first race is a silent ode to their grace
and beauty. During the final event, the fifteen hundred meters,
Forman intercuts a performance of Beethoven's Ninth Symphony with
the race. The pairing of similar expressions and gestures of the
conductor and the runners reveals that both are practicing an art
form. The music evokes the glory and fulfillment of their
achievements, win or lose, which can only be reached through
pain.
    Most sports films might conclude by showing the winners in
triumph, but Forman instead focuses on the athletes suffering at
the end of the race, some of them unable to stand. The world

tends to forget their sacrifices just as it often forgets the
victors. Forman concludes by using a high-speed sequence to show
the awards ceremony, and then the athletes leave the field. Some
are given medals, others forgotten, and life goes on. In the
great spectrum of things, the entire event perhaps has little
significance. But, at the same time, the efforts are important.

Forman emphasizes his focus on the nature of the event
itself through his voice-over narration. He interrupts only a
few times to state what event is about to take place or who the
leaders are. This use of narration contrasts sharply with most
of the other directors of Visions of Eight. Many of them would
directly explain the focus of their film as exemplifying some
important aspect of man's basic nature. They would then show the
action as evidence to support their statements.

As in most of his films, Forman again attacks figures of
authority in The Decathlon. At various times, he uses slow
motion or high-speed action to mock the contest officials and
their sense of self-importance. Other shots reveal their lack of
connection with the competition. At the most dramatic moments of
the final event, one official sits asleep in the stands. This
aspect of the film serves to heighten, by contrast, Forman's
admiration for those who compete. Forman's films as a whole show
that he admires those who will take a chance, risk embarassment,
and become involved with life rather than just go through the
motions.

Survey of Criticism: Antonin J. Liehm was the only critic to
give The Decathlon a complete analysis and one of the few who
praised it. Liehm synopsizes the film in a manner that matches
Forman's editing and expresses the depiction of the event as a
mad rush toward a temporary goal under the watchful eye of men
committed to organizing events and lives. Liehm also shows how
Forman demonstrates the similarities among men more than the
Olympics themselves do (213). Other reviewers devoted only a few
sentences to each segment of Visions of Eight and therefore
reveal no careful analysis. Roger Greenspan (197) thinks that
Forman simply speeds everything up, demonstrating nothing but
witless humor and the worst sequence in the film. Stanley
Kauffmann (203) calls The Decathlon "so devoid of sympathy or
insight that it quickly becomes a detestable bore." Variety
(205) merely refers to Forman's juxtapositions as sometimes
gratuitous. John Coleman (201) manages to pay Forman a back-
handed compliment by pronouncing his segment mere self-parody
that helped relieve the dismalness of the film as a whole. In a
later review of Forman's career, Peter Cowie disagreed with the
dominant opinion, stating, "his episode in Visions of Eight makes
the other seven look hopelessly pompous and severe" (210).

1975   One Flew Over the Cuckoo's Nest

Script: Lawrence Hauben and Bo Goldman. Director: Milos
Forman. Producers: Saul Zaentz and Michael Douglas. Based on
the novel of the same title by Ken Kesey. Photography: Haskell
Wexler, William Fraker, and Bill Butler. Music: Jack Nitzsche.
Editors: Richard Chew, Lynzee Klingman, and Sheldon Kahn.

Associate Producer: Martin Fink. Designer: Paul Sylbert. Art
Director: Edwin O'Donovan. Assistant Directors: Irby Smith and
William St. John. Players: Jack Nicholson (Randal Patrick
McMurphy), Louise Fletcher (Nurse Ratched), William Redfield
(Dale Harding), Michael Berryman (Ellis), Brad Dourif (Billy
Bibbit), Peter Brocco (Col. Matterson), Dean R. Brooks (Dr.
Spivey), Alonzo Brown (Miller), Scatman Crothers (Turkle), Muako
Cumbaka (Warren), Danny DeVito (Martini), William Duell (Sefelt),
Josip Elic (Bancini), Lan Fendors (Nurse Itsu), Nathan George
(Washington), Ken Kenney (Beans Garfield), Mel Lambert (Harbor
Manager), Sydney Lassick (Cheswick), Kay Lee (Night Supervisor),
Christopher Lloyd (Taber), Dwight Marfield (Ellsworth), Ted
Markland (Hap Arlich), Louisa Mortiz (Rose), Phil Roth (Woolsey),
Will Sampson (Chief Bromden), Mimi Sackisian (Nurse Pilbow),
Vincent Schiavelli (Fredrickson), Marya Small (Candy), Delos V.
Smith, Jr. (Scanlon), Tim Welch (Ruckley). Academy Awards: Best
Director (Milos Forman), Best Picture, Best Actor (Jack Nichol-
son), Best Actress (Louise Fletcher), Best Screenplay Adaptation
(Lawrence Hauben and Bo Goldman). Distributed by MGM-United
Artists Home Video, 1350 Avenue of the Americas, New York, NY
10019.

Plot Summary: In order to escape duties at a prison work farm,
Randle Patrick McMurphy feigns insanity so that he can serve out
his term at a state mental institution. Upon arrival at the
hopsital, McMurphy discovers that the men in his ward are all
controlled by the strict Nurse Ratched. She subtly breaks down
their self-confidence and manipulates them into fighting against
each other. McMurphy bets that he will be able to drive her
crazy.
    Quickly becoming the men's leader, McMurphy fights Nurse
Ratched on whether or not the men will get to watch the World
Series, organizes a patients' basketball team, and steals a bus
to take the men on a fishing trip. He then discovers that Nurse
Ratched has the power to keep him at the mental ward for as long
as she wants.
    McMurphy tries to back out of his revolt, but the other men
now have some of their confidence back. When they start an
argument with Nurse Ratched over confiscated cigarettes, McMurphy
takes an active role in the dispute. This action earns some
punitive electro-shock therapy for himself and two other patients, one of them a huge American Indian named Chief Bromden.
    McMurphy decides to escape. But before he goes, he brings a
pair of prostitutes to the hospital for a farewell party on the
ward. McMurphy is about to leave when one of the patients, Billy
Bibbit, asks if he can spend some time alone with one of the
girls. McMurphy consents and falls asleep.
    In the morning, Nurse Ratched returns to find the ward in
chaos and Billy with the girl. She quickly reassumes control by
threatening to tell Billy's mother. McMurphy is about to escape
through a window again when he hears Nurse Ratched scream. Billy
has killed himself, and McMurphy responds by attacking Nurse
Ratched. In the final scene, a lobotomized McMurphy returns to
the ward. Chief Bromden mercifully smothers him with a pillow
and then escapes by lifting a four-hundred pound shower control

panel and throwing it through a window. McMurphy had attempted
the same feat much earlier.

Analysis: Winning an Oscar as Best Director for One Flew Over
the Cuckoo's Nest finally placed Milos Forman's directorial
career on a secure basis. In Czechoslovakia, ideological
restrictions always threatened a director's work. In America,
Forman's lack of commercial success forced him to struggle unsuccessfully for years, trying to get projects started. But since
producers see an Oscar as promise of future commerical success as
well, Forman has been able to be selective since Cuckoo's Nest.

For this film, Forman had a ready-made audience of thousands
who had loved Ken Kesey's novel, but pleasing them in the theatre
was not as easy a task as it might seem. The novel came out in
1962 and represented Kesey's view of American society at that
time. Many high school and college students were inspired by the
work throughout the 60s and early 70s. Forman had to maintain
the novel's spirit to please that audience, but merely illustra-
ting the book on the screen would only prove to be an excercise
in nostalgia. The story had to be relevant to the mid-70s as
well. A further problem in the adaptation was that the novel is
narrated by a schizophrenic patient and therefore contains many
surrealistic scenes. Forman's solutions to these problems of
relevance and narration reveal much about why he has become a
successful adaptor of others' work.

Milos Forman's philosophy about adaptation is that the
filmmaker must have the freedom to work with the raw materials of
the original source to create his own filmic vision. If not, he
will simply be attempting to illustrate the story and will inevi-
tably fail to recapture the experience of the novel (Slater, "An
Interview, Part II," 2-3). Thus, in Cuckoo's Nest, Forman simply
does away with the schizophrenic narrator. Instead, his camera
appropriately takes the role in the guise of an unseen patient on
the mental ward where the story is set. Forman establishes this
narrator's identity and role in the first two shots of the film.
Cuckoo's Nest opens with the shot of a mountain reflected in a
lake at dawn. A car bringing the main character, Randal Patrick
McMurphy, from a prison work farm to the mental institution,
emerges from the shadows and goes across screen from left to
right. Forman then cuts to inside the sleeping quarters of the
mental ward. The camera pans from right to left across the ward.
The combination of shots reveals the narrator to be a patient who
was standing at the window and then turns to look around inside.

This narrator does have many characteristics in common with
the novel's Chief Bromden, a large Native American who tells the
story in the book. He has been playing deaf and dumb for years
and is therefore not considered a threat by the hospital staff.
They tell all their secrets around him without worrying that he
will act on the information. Similarly, Forman's narrator also
demonstrates more freedom than the other patients. He is obviously out of bed while all the rest are asleep, and he is privy
to hospital staff meetings the same as the Chief is in the novel.
Also, despite the film's realism, Forman's narrator is not
limited to a realistic point of view. For example, at one point
in the novel, McMurphy takes the other patients on a fishing

trip. At the end of it, the Chief imagines himself high over the
boat, looking down on the scene. In the film, Forman copies this
perspective exactly.

The principal impact of this changed narrator is that the
main characters are on a human scale in his sight, though they
can still support mythic interpretations. In the novel, Chief
Bromden blatantly presents McMurphy as a Christ figure while
describing his nemesis, ward supervisor Nurse Ratched, as a
mechanical monster in service of a huge organization called the
Combine that intimidates people into playing a passive social
role. In the film, the narrator simply stares at McMurphy, who
can be interpreted as a Christ figure. But if he is one, he is
very unconscious of his role. For example, the first time the
narrator watches the men exercise, he views McMurphy stretched
out in the crucifix position. But the shot is from far behind
McMurphy, who is thus obviously unaware that he is being seen
this way. Forman also alters the plot structure to emphasize the
unconscious nature of McMurphy's sacrifices. In the novel,
McMurphy openly challenges Nurse Ratched after learning that she
has the power to keep him institutionalized indefinitely. In the
film, McMurphy instigates the fishing trip, organizes a patients'
basketball team, and ignores his work to announce an invisible
baseball game on TV, all defiant acts, before he finds out about
the Nurse's power.

Nurse Ratched also becomes a much more human figure in the
film. Her statements seem logical and reasonable, not openly
vindictive as in the novel. However, because she is more human,
she is ironically a greater source of evil in the film than in
the novel. In the novel, evil is everywhere because the Combine
controls everything. By contrast, the opening shot of the film
indicates a clear division between the inside and outside. On
the outside, the possibility of freedom exists for those who have
the courage to take a chance. Nurse Ratched thus becomes the
main barrier between the men and freedom. Forman demonstrates
this clearly late in the film after McMurphy has thrown a party
on the ward, turning it into a shambles. Nurse Ratched arrives
the next morning and lines up with her aides, directly across
from the patients, with the exit behind them.

Ultimately, Ratched and McMurphy both covet the same thing,
power. Both have their own vision of the world that they want to
enforce. Forman reveals Ratched's ideal in his first shot of her
entering the ward. She wears a long black cape and black hat,
perfectly contrasting her with the black aides, who wear all
white uniforms. Nurse Ratched likes a perfectly balanced world
in which all the dirtiness of reality is washed away or hidden.
Thus, the aides are mopping the floor as she enters. By contrast, the film's opening shot associates McMurphy with all the
wild forces of nature. His entrance to the hospital, during
which he jumps up and down and laughs like a monkey, further
emphasizes this association. Forman presents McMurphy's ideal
vision of the world at the end of the party scene. McMurphy sits
down and looks around contentedly. Forman keeps the camera on
him a long time so that the viewer can judge him. McMurphy has
finally created his ideal world, which is one of complete chaos.

Both Ratched and McMurphy eventually fail because they are interested in power solely for its own sake. One other character, patient Dale Harding, shares the same desires. Harding is a homosexual who runs the patients' card games and acts as their leader before McMurphy arrives. He tries to maintain power by counseling subservience to Nurse Ratched's wishes. He wants to keep the others' respect without taking any risks. Every time McMurphy supports doing something unorthodox, Harding objects to it or goes along very reluctantly. Harding once again tries to take control of the card games and is more than happy to help Nurse Ratched destroy the men's image of McMurphy when she has him taken away at the end of the film. Forman's Harding also contrasts with Kesey's character, who is intelligent and has McMurphy's respect. The importance of the difference is that Forman wants to show that those who quest for power are doomed to failure. In the novel, Harding leaves the hospital at the end. In the film, he remains on the ward. Forman's final shot of Harding shows him standing behind an iron grating, an image of how he is still trapped by his own desires. Forman's presentation of Harding, McMurphy, and Ratched as characters who all fail to maintain or achieve power because of their very lust for it is what makes his version of Cuckoo's Nest an important document of the immediate post-Watergate era.

Despite these differences between novel and film, Forman still maintains the spirit of Kesey's work by showing how America pressures people into conformity. But while Kesey does so very blatantly in the novel, describing suburban housing as all identical with children often returning to the wrong houses at night, Forman forces the viewers to do a bit more interpreting. Once again, his narrator's superior vision provides the insights. On the bus drive to the fishing trip, the other patients look at the outside world in wonder. But the narrator sees a couple pulling their chairs up to a TV set in a store window, an old man staring blankly into the camera, and crowds of people lining the docks as the men return from their trip. These are people who go places to observe life rather than participate in it. Or else, they just sit and stare. Their presence supports Forman's theme that individuals must take responsibility for their own lives and not rely on others to supply them with fulfillment. His different ending, in which the Chief alone leaves the ward instead of all the men, also reinforces his emphasis on individual responsibility. Like the men who are left in the ward, viewers must take that first step toward life by themselves. This theme is not essentially different from the novel, where the Chief, and not McMurphy, is the real hero. But it is the result of Forman's own cinematic vision.

Survey of Criticism: Unfortunately for Forman, some critics insisted on judging the film by comparing it with the novel, though their generally negative comments did nothing to hurt its commercial success. Marsha McCreadie (319) and Elaine B. Safer (320) present distinctly opposite views in the Spring 1977 issue of Literature Film Quarterly. McCreadie details how Forman kept the novel's spirit by retaining important characters, settings, and dialogue, even though he altered the point of view

and structure and completely discarded the surrealism. Safer
faults Forman for merely simplifying the novel, noting his use of
slapstick comedy techniques and realism. Donald Palumbo (498)
provides a detailed analysis of the novel, but concludes that the
film captures only its surface and therefore lacks a message.

John Simon's review (240) is the most offensive. Simon
blames the film for missing the essence of Kesey's novel even
though he admits to having never read the book. He finds Forman
more humane than in Taking Off, but cites what most other critics
see as the film's strengths as its weaknesses. The ambiguity of
the main characters displeases Simon. He would rather see the
mythic struggle of Kesey's broadly defined figures even though he
finds the author's position reprehensible. Simon asks for more
plainness and subtlety at the same time. Richard Schickel (239)
spends half of his review praising Kesey's novel while viewing
the film as shallow and too concerned with pleasing its audience
to provide any dramatic tension. Nevertheless, he denounces
Forman for only showing the ugly surface of asylum life in documentary fashion.

By contrast, Stephen Farber (285) praises Forman for realizing the story's irony and softening its tone, but disagrees with
almost every other critic as he finds Nurse Ratched completely
dehumanized and the film as misogynist as the novel. Jack Kroll
(236) refers to it as a well-made film that lacks the novel's
insight, complexity, passion, and terror. Similarly, Frank
Kermode (257) praises the ambiguity in Fletcher's and Nicholson's
faces, admiring Forman's focus on them, but sees the film as both
simpler and more mythological than the novel. Kermode builds his
analysis from Leslie Fiedler's explanation of the novel as an
updating of Huckleberry Finn, fitting an American literary
tradition depicting male flight from female sexuality. Pauline
Kael (234) produces an intelligent comparison of novel and film,
revealing why the story had to be changed and updated. She likes
the film solely for its story and acting.

Michael Wood (305) cites Forman's theme as one of individual
responsibility. But Wood does not carry his analyses through to
the film's conclusion. He accepts what seems like the only
obvious interpretation: that it is a racist and sexist film.

Among the film's other commentators, David Thomson (313)
likes Cuckoo's Nest and accurately notes its depiction of insanity in a manner that questions all standard concepts of reality.
The audience leaves the theater wondering whether or not its own
spirit will be crushed. Thomson also wonders about the contradiction in Jack Nicholson accepting an Oscar for playing a loser.
I. G. Edmunds and Reiko Mimuera (388) offer a terrible piece,
giving a brief, partially inaccurate, Forman biography and a
story synopsis based as much on the novel as on the film.

Vincent Canby (215) dislikes the film, but bases his analysis on false interpretations of McMurphy and the story. Canby
praises the excellent performances, but sees the film only in a
1960s context. He thinks that Forman has attempted to make
McMurphy into a hero fighting an oppressive system. McMurphy
does that, but the film does not work for Canby because he fails
to understand Forman's conscious creation of a hero who fails.
In a second review (216), Canby tries to be kinder, changing his

mind about Forman using the mental ward as a symbol for America,
but merely repeating most of his other remarks. Canby simply
does not understand the film and his review rambles pointlessly.
In a third article, Canby states his opinion that neither of
Forman's American films have the resonance of his Czech ones
(252).

Vernon Young (306) uses as many criticisms as he can to
condemn the film for being exploitative and incorporating every
liberal cliché. Judith Crist (282) praises Cuckoo's Nest, but
sees the thesis as simply a "free-spirit" fighting the system.
To her, the ending only proves once again that bureaucracy cannot
be beaten. Variety (237) interprets the film in heavily nostalgic terms, noting fine efforts on behalf of everyone involved,
but attributing little meaning to the whole. The reviewer makes
copious references to the 1963 play as the "legit" version.
Finally, Seth Cagin and Philip Dray interpret the film as equat-
ing manliness with sanity and showing Harding being won over to
McMurphy's side. (501)

1979 Hair

Script: Michael Weller. Director: Milos Forman. Based on the
musical play Hair. Choreographer: Twyla Tharp. Music: Galt
McDermot. Lyrics: Gerome Ragni and James Rado. Director of
Photography: Miroslav Ondricek. Editors: Stanley Warnow and
Alan Heln. Producers: Lester Persky and Michael Butler. Re-
leased by United Artists. Players: John Savage (Claude), Treat
Williams (Berger), Beverly D'Angelo (Sheila), Annie Golden
(Jeannie), Dorsey Wright (Hud), Dan Dacus (Woof), Cheryl Barnes
(Hud's Fianceé), Richard Bright (Fenton), Nicholas Ray (General),
Charlotte Rae (Party Guest), Miles Chapin (Steve), Fern Taller
(Sheila's Mother), Charles Deney (Sheila's Father), Herman Mack-
ler (Sheila's Uncle), Antonia Rey (Berger's Mother), George Manos
(Berger's Father), Linda Surk (Vietnamese Girl). Distributed by
MGM-United Artists Home Video.

Plot Summary: Sometime during the Vietnam war, Claude Bukowsky
leaves his Oklahoma home to report for duty in New York City.
Arriving at Central Park, Claude meets a small group of hippies
led by a guy named Berger and sees a wealthy debutante named
Sheila, to whom he is immediately attracted. The hippies initi-
ate Claude into the joys of illicit drugs and later crash
Sheila's coming out party with him. But when they play a practical joke that causes an argument between he and Sheila, Claude
decides to go through with enlisting.

During basic training in Nevada, Claude gets depressed and
writes to Sheila, who shows the letter to Berger and his friends.
They help her steal a car so that they can all go visit Claude.
Berger helps Claude sneak off the base to visit Sheila during a
full alert. While Claude is gone, the Army sends Berger to Vietnam in his place. The film ends with Berger's friends looking
down at his grave.

Analysis: With Hair, Milos Forman finally completed a film that
had taken him twelve years to produce. Forman saw the first

off-Broadway performance of Hair in 1967 and immediately went
backstage to see about gaining the rights for a film version.
Over the next decade, he remained interested in the project until
Lester Persky was finally able to put it together. At the time
of its release, the film had almost no audience. The late 60s
seemed too recent for nostalgia and too distant for relevance.
Those who had been optimistic at the time were so no longer, and
those who had painful memories of the era did not wish to re-
experience them (Morden, 227-28). Forman had made a 60s' vision
relevant in Cuckoo's Nest, but Hair seemed bound by its age.

Forman obviously faced a difficult task of adaptation once
again. On stage, Hair had broken through the barriers of
performer-audience separation, rigid plot structure, and taboos
against nudity and foul language. Forman had to maintain that
exhuberance while limiting the action to a formal plot played out
on the limited space of a screen. To make the problem even more
difficult, he had to provide this energy while also dealing with
the issues of war, drugs, sexuality, spirituality, freedom, and
responsibility without wallowing in any of them.

Milos Forman's version of Hair resolves these problems by
using the traditional structure of Hollywood musicals, a dual-
focus on two distinctly different characters who eventually come
together through music and dance (Altman, 11). Forman updated
the structure by focusing on two concepts of spirituality rather
than characters. Focusing on the need to resolve the conflict
between these concepts gives Hair its relevance for the seventies. A very traditional form of spirituality is evident in the
opening section of the film. The action starts in rural Oklahoma
where Claude Bukowski is leaving to report for military duty.
Forman's camera, which takes on a truly omnipresent perspective
in this film, adopting a different pace and viewpoint suitable to
each new environment, reveals a hidden structure within the wide
open landscape. This structure includes a farmhouse with animals
grazing outside and long stretches of road lined by a series of
fence posts and telephone poles. A tractor passing by contri-
butes to the slow-paced mood. A small white church on which
Forman focuses provides a physical and spiritual center to the
area. All of these details, captured with appropriately few
camera movements, reveals the imposition of order and conformity
upon the land and human spirit. When Claude's father tells his
son good-bye, he gives him a stiff, one-armed hug and remarks,
"It's only these smart people that got to worry. The good Lord
will take care of us ignorant ones." His comments reveal his
belief in the philosophy that God has provided an order in the
world, and the landscape tends to support that idea. As a
result, human relationships are also orderly and confined.

These notions hold little relevance for Claude when he
arrives in New York City to report for duty. There, he encounters an entirely different environment and people practicing an
alternative form of spirituality. Skyscrapers tower overhead.
Not God, but impersonal beings within these concrete structures
set the order by mailing out draft notices and other restrictive
edicts. Yet, the people Claude sees in Central Park are free-
spirited, wear wild clothing, and seek a new spirituality which
would unite them with earth and sky. The opening song,

"Aquarius," provides this theme. The black woman who sings it
stands up straight with white flower petals in her hair, making
it look like the nighttime sky. The camera dives through the
trees and swirls around her from both above and below, producing
unity between the two realms.

The song seems to provide the new harmony it is seeking.
Blacks and whites dance together. Even black and white police
horses do so. Other dancers also perform movements that emphasize a oneness with nature. The deceptive element here is that
the camera has actually provided all the unity. The characters
are never as free as they believe themselves to be because the
camera always has more knowledge than they do and actually confines them. They are incapable of achieving the spiritual unity
they seek. But Forman's camera can suggest a resolution of the
two competing concepts of spirituality, one that will humanize
the unfeeling institutions that dominate both city and country.
The camera can affect the nature of an environment as well as
reveal it. Meanwhile, the characters must continue on in
ignorance, unable to influence their surroundings.

Forman demonstrates his camera's capability in two scenes.
When Claude finally reports to the draft board after experiencing
the joys of hippie life, he walks down a New York street singing
"Where Do I Go?" Having rejected the counterculture as an answer
to his question, he now looks to conformity to provide a direction for his life. But as he walks, the actions of the other
pedestrians, all properly dressed for business or shopping,
foreshadow what Claude will find. Society has dehumanized these
people to the point where all their movements are robot-like.
They all walk, turn, stop, or kneel in unison. Meanwhile, Claude
heads onward, guided by a flag above the enlistment office. With
this new center to his life, he will soon be taking orders in the
same way. This dehumanization begins to bother Claude during
basic training, and he writes to Sheila, the girl he had met in
New York. Being from high society but also a friend of the
hippies, Sheila provides the combination of traditional values
and countercultural freedom that he desires.

A short time later, Sheila is driving out west to meet
Claude with the small group of hippies the two of them had met in
Central Park. She wakes up and begins singing "Good Morning,
Starshine." The entire group joins in, and they all appear to
gain a sense of unity, freedom, and purpose that they have thus
far lacked. But Forman ends the scene by using a high, rear
angle shot to show them heading down a long straight highway.
From the opening scene, Forman associates straight lines with
confinement and curved lines with freedom. Thus, though the
characters are travelling toward the wide open west and away from
the cold confines of New York, they are unwittingly headed for a
further restriction to their freedom. The camera is once again
showing how their lives are more limited than they realize.

Eventually, Berger, the leader of the hippie group, dies in
Vietnam when he substitutes for Claude, who is then able to sneak
off the base for a quick visit with Sheila. Forman thus completes two patterns that he started with the opening scene.
Forman introduces Berger and his friends during Claude's bus ride
to New York. As the bus enters a tunnel, the four hippies' faces

come into view individually, surrounded by darkness. They are in a Central Park tunnel, burning Berger's draft card. The dark tunnel resembles both a cave and a womb. As they warm their hands over the fire, a pair of mounted policemen arrive to chase them away, thus forcing them out into the world. Throughout the film, Berger and his friends attempt to maintain both their childlike innocence and a oneness with nature. But, as they become increasingly in contact with social institutions, they also become less self-reliant and direct in their actions. Berger must borrow money from his parents to get them all out of jail. He later disguises himself to help sneak Claude off the military base. Unconsciously, against his will, Berger conforms to society's demands, losing his "natural" identity.

The hippies also discover that they cannot cope with nature. In the beginning, they lose control over a rented horse. Throughout the film, they are increasingly exposed to the elements and must seek shelter somewhere. Thus, their journey from beginning to end represents both man's collective journey from a state of nature to civilization, and, in Berger's case, the individual's movement from birth to death. Along the way, the individual becomes increasingly dependent on institutions which, in turn, take away some of his or her identity. Hair is thus the primary example that Milos Forman is not anti-institutional. Instead, he believes that people need to force institutions to provide service and not allow them to become oppressive controllers of life.

In this sense, Hair's conclusion is optimistic despite Berger's death. As the camera rises from his gravestone, three couples representing three new families, with Claude and Sheila in the center, provide hope that this basic institution might now be directed toward self-fulfillment rather than social functioning. Individuals must give meaning to the social structures ordering their lives. Similarly, Milos Forman's Hair gave new vitality to the structure of the Hollywood musical, suggesting answers for America's spiritual dilemma following the Vietnam war. In Hair, Forman gave new relevance to the film's final song, "Let the Sun Shine In."

Survey of Criticism: The critical reaction to Hair was generally positive. Frank Rich (377) praises Forman and co-screenwriter Michael Weller for creating a musical based on believable characters that expresses exuberance while also showing movement from utopia to reality, with the songs and dances used for narrative purposes. Rich states that in the conclusion Forman at once resolves the plot, presents a reminder about the debate over our role in Vietnam, and brings the whole movie into a historical perspective. Ethan Morden (411) credits Hair's success to its combination of "intoxicating imaginative flights" and an accurate presentation of the era. The necessary realism, Morden suggests, was also the film's downfall. Sixties youth had moved on to other concerns, and older people did not care to review events they hated the first time. Leonard Quart and Albert Auster describe Forman's theme as the gains and losses of liberation. They find his meshing of design, dance, and music perfect, and also comment on his transformation of Central Park into Oz (376).

Auster repeats this statement of the theme in his individual
review (353), praising the film as Forman's best American effort.
Jack Kroll (372) praises just about every aspect of the film,
regretting only that some of the original numbers are cut. Kroll
says that Forman treats the material as a myth of our popular
consciousness, harking back to America's search for innocence in
the late sixties.

Other reviewers have very few positive comments. Stanley
Kauffmann (371) feels that the film offers some pleasantly imaginative escapes from reality, but fails to overcome its dated
topicality. Kauffmann sees the main character, Berger, as a
silly failure. Richard A. Blake (354) finds Hair upbeat even
though the times were not and offers the remark that selective
memory can be bad. He labels Forman's theme as anti-
institutionalism. Robert Asahina (352) simply cannot understand
the film and admits it. Forman's frank portrait of the hippies'
positive and negative values confuses him. Consequently, he
interprets all of Berger's bad qualities as only confirming what
he had thought about hippies all along. Vernon Young (386) also
uses the film as an excuse for venting his pent-up hatred of
hippies. He dislikes Hair for having no unifying style and
celebrating the "ugly" sixties.

John Coleman (359) apparently liked the music, dancing, and
photography, but hated the characters. He finds Berger arrogant
and concludes, "shutting the mind to the prevailing moral weather
permits incidental pleasures." Rob Edelman (363) also sees the
characters as superficial and the theme of freedom versus conformity poorly stated. Variety (366) likes the cast and praises
parts of the film for rising above other contemporary musicals,
even though, the writer contends, Forman fails to evoke the
potent nostalgia. Vincent Canby (340) takes a completely opposite view, praising the film as a combination of fable and Broadway polish that makes no pretensions to being contemporary.

Penelope Gilliat (364), in the midst of some generally
confusing comments about Hair, does remark that its lack of
exuberance rests on its shifty notion of where true exuberance
lies. Janet Maslin (347) and David Denby (360) also desire a
more exhilarating film, though Denby does praise Forman's objective view of the hippies and sixties' issues.

Several writers criticized Forman's filming and editing of
the dance sequences. John Simon, in a typically caustic review,
faulted these scenes and Forman's casting most heavily (380).
Colin L. Westerbeck, Jr. criticizes the dance sequences and
claims that Forman has a dangerously superficial view of American
culture. The film, according to Westerbeck, lacks the tension of
the original show (383). Twyla Tharp partially agreed with the
critics, suggesting that working with Forman was difficult and
that too much dancing was cut. Nevertheless, she still seems
happy with the outcome and has worked on both of Forman's films
since Hair as well (365). Forman describes Tharp as naturally
antagonistic. She often feins disgust with a project in order to
test her collaborator's commitment (543).

Eric Bradford (363) was the only reviewer to emphasize how
Forman met the challenge of making "let the sunshine in" a
meaningful phrase once again.

1981 <u>Ragtime</u>

Script: Michael Weller. Director: Milos Forman. Producer:
Dino DeLaurentiis. Based on the novel by E. L. Doctorow. Cin-
ematographer: Miroslav Ondricek. Editors: Anne V. Coates,
Antony Biggs, and Stanley Warnow. Art Directors: Patrizia von
Brandenstein and Anthony Reading. Music: Randy Newman. Execu-
tive Producers: Michael Hausman and Bernard Williams. Players:
James Cagney (Rheinlander Waldo), Brad Dourif (Younger Brother),
Moses Gunn (Booker T. Washington), Elizabeth McGovern (Evelyn
Nesbit), Kenneth McMillan (Willie Conklin), Pat O'Brien (Demas),
Donald O'Connor (Dance Instructor), James Olson (Father), Mandy
Patinkin (Tateh), Howard E. Rollins (Coalhouse Walker, Jr.), Mary
Steenburgen (Mother), Debbie Allen (Sarah), Robert Joy (Harry K.
Thaw), Norman Mailer (Stanford White), Eloise O'Brien (Mrs.
Thaw), Bessie Love (Old Lady), and others. Distributed by Films,
Inc.

Plot Summary: <u>Ragtime</u> mixes historical and fictional characters
in turn-of-the-century New York and its suburbs. The story
begins with the murder of architect Stanford White by Harry K.
Thaw, a Pittsburg steel magnate, enraged over White's former
daliances with his wife, chorus girl Evelyn Nesbit. In a rigged
trial, Thaw is found innocent by reason of insanity and sentenced
to treatments in a mental institution. He is eventually released. Meanwhile, Evelyn uses the trial's publicity to launch a
career as an actress.
    Shortly after the White murder, a New Rochelle family is
sitting down to dinner when the maid discovers a black baby in
the garden. Mother persuades Father to take the baby and his
mother into the house. The father, a piano player named Coalhouse Walker, Jr., eventually shows up and promises to marry the
woman. But, while Walker is driving to work, a group of racist
firemen stop him and desecrate his beautiful Model T Ford.
Walker tries every possible avenue for filing a protest, but
finds the system closed to him. A prominent black lawyer refuses
his case because it seems too trivial. But Walker will not
accept second-class status. After policemen club his fiancée to
death while she is attempting to appeal to the Vice-President,
Walker decides to take the law into his own hands.
    He forms a gang that goes around bombing and machine-gunning
firehouses. He demands that the racist fire chief Willie Conklin
be handed over to his justice. Finally, Walker's gang takes
occupation of New York's J. Pierpont Morgan Library, beginning a
long stand-off with the police. The suburban family's Younger
Brother, following a frustrated love affair with Evelyn Nesbit,
joins Walker's gang as an explosives expert. Thus, the family's
involvement continues. Father returns from a vacation to try to
negotiate with Walker and discover the whereabouts of Younger
Brother. Meanwhile, Mother becomes infatuated with Baron
Ashkenazy, the Jewish immigrant Tateh, who is now Evelyn's film
director.
    At the end of the film, Walker makes a deal to allow his men
to go free. They escape, but the police gun him down on the

Library's front steps. Mother leaves Father for a new life with
Tateh, and World War I begins in Europe.

Analysis: Milos Forman's Ragtime includes many issues relevant
to the 1980s: terrorism, the struggles of minorities to share
the resources of wealth and power, and the relationship of technology to power are just a few. Intertwining each of these
themes with three story lines presented Forman with another
challenging adaptation. To resolve these difficulties, Forman
decided to employ one of his constant themes since the beginning
of his career, the importance of understanding the visual image.
This theme is one that films can naturally present very effectively, and, like the movies themselves, it cuts across all
class, racial, and ideological barriers.

To frame the film, Forman goes all the way back to a device
that he first used in The Audition. He presents the same image
at both the beginning and ending of the film. Both times the
image is a facade. In The Audition, Forman shows some performers. In Ragtime, he shows Evelyn Nesbit dressed in a gown and
dancing with a man in a formal suit. With each final image, the
viewer should understand the factors that support it. The
actors' happy expressions result from hard work. A world of
corruption, poverty, and bigotry lies behind the image of Evelyn
and her partner. To truly understand our world, we cannot just
look at the images. We have to understand what produces them.

Forman gives his audience a clue to his theme with the
opening credits. The title Ragtime appears first and grows on
the screen until the camera moves through the hole in the "G."
Forman's name then appears and grows until the camera moves
through the "O" in Forman. The shot of the two dancers then
appears. When the rest of the credits finish, the camera pans
down to Coalhouse Walker, Jr. playing the piano for a series of
silent newsreels in a turn-of-the-century movie house. When he
concludes, Forman cuts to a lavish party being given by architect
Stanford White.

Forman thus unwraps his film as if he were unpeeling the
layers of an onion. The viewer should understand after the
opening credits that there is always something behind an image.
The newsreels are just superficial images of an era that the film
as a whole will explore in depth. Forman continues with this
structure throughout the entire first section of the film.
Following the introduction of Stanford White and his friends,
Forman shows an upper-middle-class family whose business and
manufacturing skills provide the economic stability for White's
extravagance. He then moves on to introducing the minority and
immigrant characters whose classes provide the large, cheap labor
force needed to support American wealth. Thus, the film gradually digs down to the very basis of society, and, when that basis
begins to change, the whole structure is shaken. It is therefore
appropriate that Coalhouse Walker and his gang eventually take
over the J. Pierpont Morgan Library, a bastion of knowledge for
the entire Western civilization. The revolt goes directly to the
philosophical roots of the corrupt structure that has oppressed
them.

As in Loves of a Blonde, those who suffer most in Ragtime are the ones who are unable to understand their world, regardless of their degree of innocence. At Stanford White's party, Harry K. Thaw, a Pittsburgh steel magnate and jealous husband of White's ex-mistress Evelyn Nesbit, bursts into the house and demands that the architect remove a nude statue of his wife from the roof of Madison Square Garden. White ignores him and does so again at the Garden's rooftop restaurant shortly before Thaw murders him. White's concern with his own image and refusal to recognize Thaw as a serious threat results in his demise.

A short time later, the suburban family's maid finds a black baby in the family garden. Right from the beginning, Father reacts to the discovery in terms of his narrow self-interests. He wants to send the infant away to a state institution, but Mother insists on taking the baby and its mother into the house. Father bases his idea of justice and morality on socially determined codes while Mother bases hers on human compassion. Coalhouse Walker, Jr., who turns out to be the baby's father, later becomes a rebel and occupies the Morgan Library. When the police come to Father and Mother and ask for Walker's son, Mother refuses to allow them to use the child as a pawn. Father, however, disagrees with her and decides to go with the police. Mother makes one final plea for Father to stand by her, but when he refuses, she decides to leave him for a film director. Father's ability to recognize ultimately the legitimacy of Walker's complaints is admirable. But he suffers the loss of Mother because he fails to recognize anything other than his most narrow interests. He accepts social authority completely.

Coalhouse Walker takes up his rebellion because a group of racist firemen desecrate his fancy Model T Ford. He turns to violence after exhausting all legal possibilities of redress. At one point, his fiancee, Sarah, leaves the suburban home to appeal to the Vice-President for help at a whistle-stop political rally. But Sarah has unrealistic expectations and very little knowledge. She does not even realize that she is not seeing the President or that, since William McKinley's assassination, the Secret Service are being especially wary. Therefore, when she starts moving toward the platform and yelling, the police converge on her and she later dies from the injuries she receives. Thus, like White and Father, her fate also results from ignorance about her environment.

Forman confronts his audience with this question of interpretation as well. When the family rushes out to see what the maid has found, Forman holds the shot of the baby lying among the vegetables for a long time. The image brings to mind the myth about babies coming from cabbage patches, which the viewer must naturally reject. But it is also similar to the story of Moses in the bullrushes. The mother is a member of a formerly captive people who has her child taken in by a well-to-do member of the oppressive race. The debate over whether or not to bring the child in should remind viewers of Christ's statement about treating the least of people well. It therefore challenges the viewer's concept of Christian charity. A true Christian must agree with Mother.

The similarities of the baby with both Moses and Christ indicate that the child might be a future leader of his people. Late in the film, Booker T. Washington's confrontation with Coalhouse Walker demonstrates the black person's dilemma over whether to take the Old Testament or New Testament path. While Walker is practicing the law of Moses, Washington speaks with the authority of Christ. He gains entrance to the Library simply by commanding the doors to open. He speaks of violence begetting violence, with the end only coming when one man has the courage to stand up and say "No." The film thus forces viewers to re-evaluate the traditional historical image of Washington as a subservient Uncle Tom. The flaws in Washington's argument are that it is hard for blacks to turn the other cheek when they seem to have no voice on earth to support them and that Coalhouse Walker does achieve some positive results through his actions. His goals are not merely selfish. Thus, Forman questions the efficacy of New Testament morality in every situation.

Forman also challenges the viewer through his use of the veteran Hollywood actors Donald O'Connor, Pat O'Brien, and James Cagney. In each case, he undercuts the actor's established image, Cagney being the most prominent. When Cagney, as Police Commissioner Rhinelander Waldo, first arrives at the showdown between Walker's gang and policemen, he appears to be the same type of figure that audiences remember from his classic gangster films of the thirties. He immediately assesses the situation correctly, gives orders, and sits back to relax and wait. However, when Coalhouse Walker leaves the Library, Cagney orders an officer to gun him down. The scene is exactly the opposite of the conclusion of The Roaring Twenties (1939) in which Cagney is gunned down on the steps of a cathedral. Here, Forman shocks the audience by showing him as the killer policeman. Viewers cannot simply assume that they understand his image and know how he will act. They must look deeper.

The scene also challenges all those who would agree with Cagney's actions. Many viewers might feel that since Walker is obviously guilty, he does not deserve a trial and therefore Cagney is simply carrying out direct justice. But Walker's actions have proven that when a fair system of justice breaks down, only chaos can result. The film thus faces racists and vigilantes with a choice between order and chaos.

After Walker's death, Forman wraps the film back up with a quick series of short scenes leading up to the image of the two waltzers that symbolizes the era. In the final brief scene, Harry Houdini is hanging upside down from a crane high above the street. Someone down in the crowd takes a picture of him. The visual image has now become the major form of communication in our world, easily available to almost everyone. To make sense of the world, people have to be able to interpret those images.

Survey of Criticism: Several critics, naturally, discuss the novel and make comparisons with the film. Andrew Sarris (451) discusses Doctorow's creation of Coalhouse Walker from an 1808 German novella, Michael Kollhaus, by Heinrich von Kleist. Sarris believed that people's opinions of the film would either stand or fall with their judgment of Elizabeth McGovern as Evelyn Nesbit.

His own feelings about McGovern are ambiguous, but he admires the
film as a liberal tract flying in the face of rising Reaganism.
Morris Dickstein (465) is unusual in finding Forman too heavily
swayed by Doctorow's fondness for sixties' historical revision-
ism. He praises Forman's handling of human problems, but believes that placing black insurrections of the sixties in the
century's first decade creates a historical travesty. Judith
Crist (434) reviews the film as doing honor to its sources.
Crist recounts the plot and applauds the performances and Forman's blending of stars and unknowns.

     Others sympathized with Doctorow. Stanley Kauffmann (442)
finds no evidence of recreating the novel in cinematic terms,
dismissing both Weller's script and Forman's direction as merely
conventional. He also feels that Doctorow's novel was unfairly
hounded by overly-patriotic right-wing critics. Margo Jefferson
(469) chastizes Forman and co-screenwriter Michael Weller for
doing nothing more than stripping the work of its psychological
and historical texture and replacing it with simplistic, stereo-
typed characters. Richard Corliss (433) calls the film impressive, but complains that Forman included only half of Doctorow's
novel. For Corliss, the film thus lacks historical sweep.
Michael Sragow (479) criticizes Forman for reducing the novel's
complexity to the theme of "the underprivileged and lower class
get screwed."

     John Coleman (464) admires the casting and performances but
regrets what is missing from the novel. Vincent Canby (418)
thinks that the film fails simply becuase the novel is unfilmable. He finds Forman's version too confusing. Pauline Kael
(441) primarily praises the novel and admits to simply not understanding the film.

     Other reviewers wish that Robert Altman had been kept as the
director. Altman would have been less predictable, William Wolf
argues (453), but more capable of creating a work of genius.
Altman reveals to Wolf how he had planned to make a film with
Doctorow much like the book. The first scene would have shown
Sigmund Freud arriving in America. Wolf feels that the only
artistic justification for adapting a highly successful or
classic work can be to express its spirit and essence. Leonard
and Barbara Quart (473) also state a preference for Altman. They
find Ragtime a safely accessible film that avoids intellectual
risks. Their entire review is a comparison of the film with the
novel.

     Kenneth R. Hey (468), another reviewer who wanted Altman,
argues that the film concentrates on characters' shortcomings
more than social change. Forman's film, Hey declares, must be
measured against "what this country has stood for." Bea
Rothenbuecker (450), who also wishes Altman had directed, praises
the casting, but finds the film disorienting.

     In terms of contemporary themes, Tom Pulleine (472) does not
find any in Ragtime. He believes the film lacking in character
motivation, narrative logic, and the evoking of popular legends.
Similarly, Robert Asahina (462) describes Ragtime as a disaster,
not explaining Tateh's success, unintentionally trivializing
Walker's cause for rebellion, and spending too much time on the
murder of Stanford White.

Among Ragtime's other detractors, Jack Kroll (444) finds it lacking a central vision, informed style, passion, and excitement.   Colin L. Westerbeck, Jr. (482) judges it as merely entertaining.   In his opinion, the characters are bearable because there are a number of them: audiences cannot dwell on any one's shortcomings.   Ragtime deals, he writes, "as lightly with history as it does with human relationships."   Michael Buckley (463) comments on the acting and calls the standoff sequence unexciting.   He finds the film interesting but flawed and ultimately depressing.   John Simon (476) describes Ragtime as an earnest, but conventional, social document, whose slight distortions of history are more annoying than the novel's wild ones.   Variety (448) disagrees with all these critics by giving the film high praise for all aspects of its production.

More positively, Robert Hatch (438) admires the film as well-constructed and acted, with a liberal social theme more sobering than the book, but attempting to "say" more than most epics.   Harlan Kennedy (443) describes Ragtime as a thinking man's disaster film, one of sociological rather than physical proportions.

David Thomson (481) describes Ragtime as a film about looking.   Bruce Williamson (483) similarly claims that the film is about cinema and rejects a simplistic liberal interpretation of its conclusion.

1984   Amadeus

Script: Peter Shaffer.   Director: Milos Forman.   Director of Photography: Miroslav Ondricek.   Editors: Nena Danevic and Michael Chandler.   Choreography and Opera Staging: Twyla Tharp. Music: Wolfgang Amadeus Mozart.   Music conducted by Neville Marriner.   Producer: Saul Zaentz.   An Orion Pictures Release. Players: F. Murray Abraham (Antonio Salieri), Tom Hulce (Wolfgang Amadeus Mozart), Elizabeth Berridge (Constanze Mozart), Simon Callow (Emmanuel Schikaneder), Roy Dotrice (Leopold Mozart), Christine Ebersole (Katerina Cavalieri), Jeffrey Jones (Emperor Joseph II), Charles Kay (Count Orsini-Rosenberg), Kenny Baker (Parody Commendatore), Lisabeth Bartlett (Papagena), Barbara Bryne (Frau Weber), Martin Cavani (Young Salieri), Roderick Cook (Count Von Strack), Milan Demjanenko (Karl Mozart), Peter Di Gesu (Francesco   Salieri), Richard Frank (Father Vogler), Patrick Hines (Kappelmeister Bonno), Nicholas Kepros (Archbishop Colleredo), Philip Lenkowsky (Salieri's Servant), Herman Meckler (Priest), Jonathan Moore (Baron Von Swieten), Cynthia Nixon (Lori), Brian Pettifer (Hospital Attendant), Vincent Schiavelli (Salieri's Valet), Douglas Seale (Count Arco), Miroslav Sekera (Young Mozart), John Strauss (Conductor), Karl-Heinz Teuber (Wig Salesman).   Academy Awards: Best Director (Milos Forman), Best Picture, Best Actor (F. Murray Abraham), Best Screenplay Adaptation (Peter Shaffer), Best Makeup, Best Sound, Best Art Direction, Best Costume Design.   Distributed by Thorn EMI/HBO Inc., 1370 Avenue of the Americas, New York, NY 10019 (212) 977-8990.

Plot Summary: Aging Antonio Salieri, ex-court composer and
favorite of Austro-Hungarian Emporer Joseph II, attempts to
commit suicide. He accuses himself for the murder of Wolfgang
Amadeus Mozart thirty-two years earlier and cries out to the late
composer's spirit for forgiveness.

At a private room in an insane asylum, Salieri later recounts his life for a young priest who comes to hear his final
confession. Salieri reveals his deep anger towards God for not
making his name as great as Mozart's. In actuality, Salieri
becomes a bitter man because he has no knowledge of spirituality.
When he was very young, he prayed for greatness in return for
sacrificing his physical pleasure. Shortly afterwards, his
father died of choking. Although the cause is clearly physical,
Salieri interprets the fatality as an answer to prayer. His
father's death allows him to get the musical training he desires,
and he subsequently rises to the height of popularity and royal
favor.

At the same time that Salieri was a boy, Mozart's father was
parading his gifted child before the crowned heads and holy
personages of Europe. Music was Mozart's life and identity, but
Salieri attributes his talent to a direct gift from God. When
his rival finally comes to Vienna years later, Salieri discovers
that Mozart freely indulges in all the physical pleasures that he
has denied himself. Moreover, Salieri's almost solitary recognition of Mozart's genius makes his own success feel like a curse.
Salieri believes that God is mocking him, and he therefore decides to seek revenge by destroying the Almighty's mouthpiece on
Earth, Mozart.

Salieri receives inspiration for his murder plot from the
relationship between Mozart and his father. Leopold Mozart
trains and guides his son almost from infancy and Wolfgang feels
guilt later in life when he defies his father's wishes in terms
of marriage and career choices. At a costume party, Salieri
witnesses the elder Mozart alternately loving and condemning his
son. Leopold Mozart wears a black mask with a comic face on one
side and a tragic one on the other that perfectly expresses how
quickly his attitude can change. It thus becomes clear that
Wolfgang has never been able to either fully please or escape the
control of his father. After Leopold's death, Salieri observes
how Mozart presents his father in a similar costume in his opera
Don Giovanni. Mozart calls up this father figure from beyond the
grave to accuse himself.

Seeing a possibility for tormenting Mozart, Salieri uses the
same costume that Leopold wore at the party to anonymously commission a Requiem Mass. In actuality, Salieri has already done
all that is necessary to assure Mozart's collapse. He uses
political manipulations to guarantee short runs for Mozart's
works and cut off his rival from lucrative appointments. Mozart
has not helped himself by insulting Salieri and every other
bureaucrat in a position to help him. If Mozart were to realize
his own failings and take steps to correct them, Salieri's plan
would never have a chance of success. Instead, he accepts the
masked figure as the source of his problems, allowing it to haunt
him. Similarly, Salieri views Mozart as a spiritual figure,
believing him to be God's chosen voice on Earth. Through his

plot, Salieri hopes to eventually claim Mozart's <u>Requiem Mass</u> as his own, thus gaining revenge against God. He never considers the option of learning from Mozart and using his political talents to promote instead of hinder his rival. Had he done so, Salieri might have achieved some measure of the immortality he desired. Thus, both men waste their talents through pettiness and superstition.

Salieri's use of the costume indicates an obvious change of identity. Mozart, meanwhile, is also transforming himself through alcohol and working to complete both the <u>Requiem</u> and <u>The Magic Flute</u> at the same time. He pursues the physical to the same degree that Salieri chases the spiritual and both are losing their identities in the process. Finally, Mozart collapses during a performance of <u>The Magic Flute</u>. Salieri takes Mozart back to his own quarters where he tricks his rival into reciting the remainder of the <u>Requiem</u> to him.

In the morning, Mozart's wife and son arrive. Constanze had left him after Mozart had ignored her pleas to be practical. Now, she returns just in time to see him die. She also takes the completed requiem and locks it away as the helpless Salieri looks on. At the end, Mozart is buried in a mass grave. The old Salieri rides in his wheelchair down a hall of lunatics. Declaring himself the high priest of mediocrity, he absolves them all. But Mozart's laugh rings out one more time to mock him still from beyond the grave.

Analysis: In <u>Amadeus</u>, Milos Forman once again presents the theme that individuals can achieve fulfillment despite the restrictions placed on them. He does so through the conflict of Antonio Salieri and Wolfgang Amadeus Mozart, both of whom fail to recognize their natural limitations and therefore waste their talents and energies in meaningless pursuits. Salieri feels cheated by God because he has devoted his life to serving the Almighty and has not been granted the musical talent that he sought. When he discovers that the vulgar Mozart does possess such ability, he devotes his energy toward destroying the man that he feels God has personally blessed.

Because of his great talent, Mozart does not feel that he should have to abide by the same rules or modes of conduct that have brought Salieri fame and fortune. Salieri was, after all, the most popular composer of his day and a favorite of Emperor Joseph II. Mozart pursues wine, women, and song. He justifiably rejects the shallow pretentiousness and high-minded ideals of offical church and state for life among the common people. His art moves from the opera hall to the vaudeville house. Unfortunately, his constant drinking helps send him to an early grave.

Both men did have alternatives. Salieri's frustration is due not merely to his lack of ability, but also to a lack of physical pleasure. When Salieri prays for talent, he is not really seeking to serve God. He wants greatness. He wants to be remembered. He desires everything that he is supposedly denying himself. Salieri sneaks about at a party, tasting desserts that have been put aside. He becomes jealous upon discovering that Mozart has made love to his vocal student, and he later attempts to seduce Mozart's wife. But in his music, Salieri hopes to

achieve his goals by writing on great spiritual and mythological
themes. When his work fails to achieve the greatness of Mozart's
despite his outward piety, Salieri turns to revenge against his
rival and God. He never considers the possibility of learning
from Mozart's method of drawing inspiration from actual life
rather than eternal themes or using his political skill to help
promote Mozart's work rather than hinder it. Instead, he devotes
himself to a murderous plot that does little more than cause his
own madness.

When Mozart dies, Salieri feels responsible. But, rather
than usurping some of Mozart's blessings, as he had hoped,
Salieri only lives on to see his own music forgotten while
Mozart's greatness is increasingly recognized. His spirit is not
able to overtake his rival's. At the end of the film, Salieri
rides down the hall of an insane asylum, granting absolution to
all the lunatics as the patron saint of mediocrity. His words
are as empty as his revenge. As he rides, Mozart's bizarre laugh
rings out once again. Mozart will eternally have the last laugh
on such pretentiousness. But, had he recognized his limits,
Salieri could have used his talents to achieve at least some
measure of greatness.

In contrast, Mozart openly seeks and indulges himself in
worldly pleasures because the splendor of the high courts of
church and state hold no appeal for him. From the time he was
three, Mozart's father trained him as a musician and composer and
paraded him before all the crowned heads and high priests of
Europe. Mozart developed his greatness before he even knew the
world. As an adult, he therefore rejects all of Salieri's world
and his father's wishes. He refuses to submit to the court's
attempt to put him in competition with inferior composers for an
important position. He continually insults Salieri without even
realizing it. In return, Salieri uses his political influences
to guarantee short runs for all of Mozart's operas.

To some extent, Mozart's actions are understandable and
excusable. After all, he did not have a childhood, and his work
is greater than that of any of his contemporaries precisely
because he does look to common humanity for his themes. While
Salieri lowers grand ideas to mediocrity, Mozart raises the mean
and average to greatness. In the end, however, Mozart only
reaches his goal of unity with the common man through burial in a
mass grave. By not showing the small amount of propriety
requested of him, Mozart wastes both his chance to have everything he wants and his talent.

Both men's troubles result from their misunderstanding of
what is spiritual. Salieri attributes both his father's death by
choking and the Emperor's yawning during Mozart's The Marriage of
Figaro to miracles because they both promote his fortunes at a
time when all had seemed lost. More foolishly, he believes
Mozart's talent comes directly from God when actually his nemesis
was blind to everything but music from the age of three.
Mozart's father made music his very being. When Mozart defies
his father's wishes in terms of marriage and career choices,
Salieri is able to exploit his guilt. He comes to Mozart in a
black costume with a mask that has a comic face on one side and a
tragic one on the other, which Mozart's father had once worn to

a ball. Salieri, who was also present, witnessed how the mask
perfectly expressed Leopold Mozart's assumption of a God-like
role, someone who could either fully love or condemn his son.
Later, when Mozart uses a similarly costumed figure in Don
Giovanni as a statement of judgment upon himself, Salieri sees
how Wolfgang accepts his father's authority. Salieri, therefore,
uses Leopold's costume to commission a requiem anonymously, and
Mozart allows the apparition to become a source of torment.

Both composers thus make the same mistake of attributing
human events to spiritual sources, and both suffer for their
confusion. Salieri's belief that Mozart is divinely inspired and
his decision to take revenge against God lead to his own madness.
Similarly, Mozart's vulnerability to Salieri's appearance as a
costumed figure comes from his inability to recognize his own
political failures as the true source of his problems. Thus,
Mozart continues drinking heavily in his pursuit of physical
pleasure as a source of escape from spiritual torment. When
Salieri is in disguise and Mozart is drunk, both have taken leave
of their true identities. Later, after his suicide attempt,
Salieri takes on the appearance of a priest with a white band
around his neck. But his words of absolution are empty.
Similarly, Mozart's union with the common man is only a meaningless one that he is able to achieve in death. A priest sprinkles
holy water over Mozart's grave during a rainstorm, once again
making the difference between the natural and the spiritual
difficult to distinguish.

Each composer presents a distinctly opposite problem. In
his life and work, Salieri represents the perfection of form
without substance. Mozart is all substance without form. Individually, they are similar to the lunatics in the asylum, many of
whom perform meaningless repetitive motions somewhat like
Salieri. Yet, they are also basic examples of humanity who are
capable of all of the bodily functions in which Mozart wallows.
They are simply unable to put their actions into meaningful
forms. But when Salieri and Mozart combine in the film's brilliant climactic scene, they produce music that rises above their
physical existence. Mozart, naturally, composes the music while
Salieri mechanically notes it down. The music provides hope by
rising above its origins in the morass of human existence, and it
demonstrates Milos Forman's point that spirituality has a
physical base.

Forman's camera in Amadeus functions similarly to the way it
did in The Firemen's Ball. It represents a distinct consciousness moving about freely in space and time and remaining somewhat
distant from the character. But the effect is now ironic because
despite the camera's seeming omnipotence, it remains dependent on
others to tell the story. Amadeus opens with the camera searching the dark winter streets of Vienna. When Salieri cries out
Mozart's name, it quickly finds his parlor. But there, it must
wait until Salieri's servant and valet open the old composer's
door to find him suffering on the floor from his suicide attempt.
The camera does not know the story. It must receive it from
Salieri just as he is dependent on the servant girl he sends to
spy on Mozart.

Forman reveals the camera's dependency on others during a scene from Mozart's The Magic Flute. He first shows the Queen of the Night singing in the middle of a series of dark rings that fill the screen like the nighttime sky. A short time later, another shot reveals that set standing in pieces backstage. This ironic role for the camera leaves responsibility for finding the film's substance with the viewer. The camera can present images of beautiful clothes, food, and people. But the viewer must recognize that the origin of the film's substance lies at a more basic level.

Forman also directly addresses the contemporary audience through his use of American actors speaking with their natural accents. Tom Hulce as Mozart provides the most obvious example. With his colored wigs, brash language, and anti-establishment attitudes, Hulce's Mozart appears very much like a modern punk musician. This fantasy blending of past and present enables Forman to comment directly to today's young rebels. Forman obviously admires Mozart's insistence on substance and relevance, but he is also warning punks about destroying themselves. In Emporer Joseph II, Forman presents a different kind of statement about art. The Emporer's decree that no opera may contain ballet forces Mozart to rehearse his dancers without music. Even Joseph recognizes that too much government interference can have a debilitating effect on art.

The artist's role is to enlighten the world. Thus, Forman uses candles to compare Salieri and Mozart as artists throughout the film. In the opening scene, Salieri has a small enclosed lantern next to him as he rides through the streets on a stretcher. At one point, he looks up when he hears some of Mozart's music. Forman cuts to the well-lit ballroom where people are dancing. Throughout the film, numerous lighted candles constantly surround Mozart while only unlit ones appear behind Salieri. The only time Salieri uses fire directly is to burn his cross. Another time, he blows out a candle after describing his vow to take revenge against God. Thus, he has become anti-artistic.

The camera defines its own artistic role at the end of Salieri's ride to the asylum. It stops at a long shot of the building as Salieri is carried inside. After the credits, the scene changes from dark to light. The camera will attempt to enlighten us, but the viewers must make the final interpretation. A key shot occurs as Mozart lays dying. Forman briefly shows the composer's son playing with some coins on the bed. To escape his father's fate, the boy must acquire some of his mother's practical knowledge of money's importance. Similarly, to truly rise above our limitations, we must first understand our basic nature. Mozart's music is proof that we can do so.

Survey of Criticism: Some critics, such as Robert Craft (596), objected strongly to the characterizations of Mozart and Salieri. Craft, for example, wants a more "accurate" depiction of Mozart's life. But he admits that when he saw the film, the audience was captivated enough by the music to stay in the theater all the way through the closing credits. Craft excuses Forman and Shaffer for making some understandably difficult dramatic choices, but

criticizes the costuming, music editing, and modernized dialogue.
Eva Hoffman (544) finds the film weak in attempting to actualize
and romanticize Mozart's life simultaneously without the same
distancing of seeing him only through Salieri's eyes, as was true
in the play. Hoffman feels that the film equates sexual and
creative liberation.

David Denby (537) insists on the truth about Mozart: he
knew how to behave around aristocrats. According to Denby,
Forman makes the Mozarts so ordinary, he travesties his own
material. Denby believes that the film does show Mozart as the
voice of God. Denby also interprets the film as saying that
Mozart's society was unworthy of him, but the modern age would
have had the taste to accept him. He accuses Forman of trying to
evoke "tearful breast-beating" over Mozart's death.

John Simon (554) finds the film improbable and crudely
Freudian and the direction heavy-handed. David Edelstein (538)
condemns the film as nothing more than a standard, but kinky,
biographical film. He criticizes it mainly for simplifying the
process of creation, showing both composers as men who never look
inward. He particularly dislikes the final scene where Mozart
and Salieri work together in writing down the Requiem Mass, not
understanding how Salieri could suddenly love the man he is
trying to kill. Pauline Kael (547) again finds Forman's work
confusing. Kael thinks that Forman and Shaffer agree with
Salieri's idea of genius being a gift of God, which denigrates
Mozart's talent.

Other critics, such as Vincent Canby, (508), Peter Travers
(556), and Joy Gould Boyum (532) disagree, praising the film as a
work that explores and celebrates genius. David Thomson (608)
provides the best response to Amadeus' attackers, working through
his own problems with the film until finally finding its justification in the last scene. Until that point, Salieri appears as
the more intelligent man, but Thomson finds in the conclusion
Forman's theme of the differences between form and substance.
His final decision is that Salieri is like a smooth Hollywood
operator who elevates superficiality and smothers true
creativity.

Works Cited

Altman, Charles F. "The Hollywood Musical." Wide-Angle Winter
    1970:10-17.

Conaway, James. "Milos Forman's America is Like Kafka's--
    Basically Comic." New York Times Sunday Magazine 11 July
    1971:8-12.

Cowie, Peter, ed. 50 Major Film-Makers. New York: A. S. Barnes
    and Co., 1975.

Dewey, Langdon. "The Czechoslovak Cinema: Go! Stop! Go! Go?"
    Film Autumn 1968:20-32.

Forman, Milos. "Closer to Things." Cahiers du Cinema in English
    January 1967:57-58.

Issari, M. Ali and Doris A. Paul. What is Cinema-Verité?
    Metuchen, NJ: Scarecrow Press, 1979.

Liehm, Antonin J. Closely Watched Films: The Czechoslovak
    Experience. White Plains, NY: International Arts and
    Sciences Press, Inc., 1974.

----------. The Milos Forman Stories. White Plains, NY:
    International Arts and Sciences Press, Inc., 1975.

----------. "Some Observations on Czech Politics and Culture in
    the 1960s." Czech Literature Since 1956: A Symposium. Ed.
    William E. Harkins and Paul I. Trensky. New York: Bohemia,
    1980:134-55.

Lipton, Leonard Joel. "A Critical Study of the Filmmaking Style
    of Milos Forman With Special Emphasis on His Contributions
    to Film Comedy." Ph.D. Dissertaion: University of Southern
    California, 1974.

Morden, Ethan. The Hollywood Musical. New York: St. Martin's
    Press, 1981.

Skvorecky, Josef. All the Bright Young Men and Women: A Personal
    History of the Czech Cinema. Toronto: Peter Martin
    Associates, Ltd., 1971.

----------. "The Birth and Death of the Czech New Wave." Take
    One 2.8 (November-December 1969):9-12.

Slater, Thomas J. "Milos Forman: An Interview, Part I." Post
    Script 4.3 (Spring/Summer 1985):2-15.

----------. "Milos Forman: An Interview, Part II." <u>Post Script</u>
5.1 (Fall 1985):2-16.

4. A Guide to the Annotated Bibliography

Milos Forman's professional career began in 1955, shortly after his graduation from film school, when director Martin Fric requested his assistance on the script of <u>Nechte to na mne</u> (<u>Leave it to Me</u>). But he did not begin receiving critical attention until ten years later, after he had completed three films as a director and Western writers had fully recognized the Czechoslovak New Wave. Since that time, Forman's life and work have been very thoroughly documented, but the references to those materials have been scattered through a wide variety of bibliographies and indexes. The following bibliography is the first to collect all of the major Forman materials (and a few hundred of the minor ones). Each citation is annotated for the guidance of other scholars and writers. The bibliography has several other features that should be useful as well.

First, the structure is primarily chronological with materials from books, newspapers, and periodicals listed separately and alphabetically within each year. This organization provides several benefits over a strict alphabetical listing of all sources. One advantage is that it allows scholars to see the growth and fluctuation of attention paid to Forman, both in terms of quantity and content. For example, the reader will notice that the number of sources begins increasing rapidly after 1965 but is slim during the years when no Forman film was released. In addition, scholars will be able to measure the changes in the critical reception to Forman's work from reading the annotations. In every case, the annotations attempt to restate the original writer's ideas with no judgment about their quality being given. Readers are free to watch the films and decide for themselves which opinions they feel are most valid. These annotations will also help writers refer to specific sources without actually having to obtain the material themselves.

Another benefit of this organization is that most of the sources relating to a specific film are all together. Users do not have to look through the entire list for references to a specific work. Therefore, anyone who wants to find most of the material relating to <u>Taking Off</u>, for example, very quickly, can look in the years 1970-72 and find it there. More thorough scholars will want to use the index to find the

scattered references that appear in later years. The bibliography will
also help those who want to trace the history of a project. For
example, Forman's involvement with Ragtime began in 1976, so stories
about his replacing Robert Altman as the film's director begin appearing
then. In this sense, the bibliography itself also functions something
like a biography. It should provide a basic sense of the shifts in
Forman's life and career.

The bibliography is limited by some necessary choices. Citations
derive from major periodicals, scholarly journals, and The New York
Times, The Los Angeles Times, The London Times (including The Sunday
Times, The Times Literary Supplement, and The Times Educational Supplement), The Washington Post, and The Christian Science Monitor newspapers. Reviews and other materials from regional and metropolitan
magazines are not included. There are occasional exceptions, such as
Leonard J. Berry's article in the Boston Globe (Sunday Magazine) (125).
But what has been included is generally what will be most accessible to
most researchers. Items about box-office returns (most often found in
Variety) have been largely excluded as well. The purpose of this work
is to focus on materials that contribute to an understanding of Forman
and his work. Several references to how well a film did over a number
of short periods seems unnecessary. Similarly, the books included
contain at least one good paragraph on Forman, usually more. Books that
only mention him in passing were excluded.

One drawback to any bibliography is that simply looking at the
individual entries will not reveal which are the most important. Cer-
tainly, any in-depth study of Milos Forman should begin with Antonin J.
Liehm's The Milos Forman Stories (213) and Josef Skvorecky's All the
Bright Young Men and Women: A Personal History of the Czech Cinema
(135). Liehm's book is the only volume entirely devoted to Forman
currently in existence. In it, Forman tells of his personal experiences
since childhood that have contributed to his artistic sensibility and
also stories about important events during his film career. Liehm
includes his reviews of Forman's films up through The Decathlon (1972)
and information about Czech culture that deepens the reader's understanding of Forman's background. Unfortunately, the work only covers
the years up through 1972. Liehm's interview with Forman in Closely

Watched Films: The Czechoslovak Experience (206) provides a good companion piece in which Forman discusses his ideas and situation during the late sixties. The entire work is also a valuable introduction to the history of Czech filmmaking, as is Skvorecky's book. Skvorecky, a Czech novelist, has known Forman since childhood and worked on screenplays with him twice. His comments are instructive about Forman's artistic development and integrity and his cultural background.

The only other works beside The Milos Forman Stories that provide an in-depth consideration of Forman's entire life and career are Leonard J. Lipton's 1974 dissertation, "An Examination of the Filmmaking Style of Milos Forman With Special Consideration of His Contributions to Film Comedy" (208), and Thomas J. Slater's 1985 dissertation, "Milos Forman: The Evolution of a Filmmaker" (569). Lipton includes a good deal of biographical information about Forman along with a detailed analysis of several aspects of his style. Slater's work is the only comprehensive study of Forman currently in existence and relates each of his films to its cultural and historical period. The work also traces the consistency and variations in Forman's themes and techniques from Competition (1963) through Amadeus (1984). Slater's two-part interview with Forman (606, 607) also covers the director's entire career from Amadeus back to the beginning.

Clearly, film scholarship could benefit from a new complete study of Forman. In the meantime, researchers will have to be satisfied with piecemeal approaches. Works such as Skvorecky's and Liehm's will always provide a valuable introduction to the important topic of Forman's development in relation to Czech culture and the history of that nation's film industry. Peter Hames' The Czechoslovak New Wave (562) and Politics, Art and Commitment in Eastern European Cinema, edited by David W. Paul (486), are two recent valuable contributions to this area of study. Hames considers Forman and all other New Wave directors in relation to both national and international trends. Paul's book contains essays about Eastern European and Czech cinema as a whole and one specifically about Forman by Antonin J. Liehm as well. Interestingly, both Liehm and Paul view Forman as becoming too much a part of the Hollywood system, too eager to please his audience, and too out-of-touch with his material in his American career.

Other important pieces on the New Wave and the history of Czech
filmmaking include Jiri Weiss's "Czech Cinema Has Arrived" (002),
Forman's own "Chill Wind on the New Wave" (064), and Robin Bates' "The
Ideological Foundations of the Czech New Wave" (335). Weiss was an
important director in the initial resurgence of Czech film in the late
fifties. His article explains the nationalized film industry and shows
why the New Wave was merely the continuation of an interrupted growth.
Forman's article also stresses the theme of continuation in an industry
threatened in the mid-sixties with the spector of commercialism. Bates
explains how the New Wave directors attempted to work within socialism.
Their attacks on the system were not intended as anti-socialist statements. Finally, Liehm's "Some Observations on Czech Culture and
Politics in the 1960s" (392) and his essay in V. V. Kusin's The Czechoslovak Reform Movement: 1968 (193) also add valuable information about
the cultural context for the New Wave.

Scholars can easily piece together a history of Czech filmmaking
along with a knowledge of the industry and its struggles during its
brief enjoyment of freedom in the sixties from a series of articles
beginning with Gideon Bachmann's "Is there really a new wave in Czech
films--and will it last?" (015) and Jaroslav Broz's "Grass Roots" (016).
Alex Madsen's "This Year at Marienbad" (069), Jan Zalman's "Question
Marks on the New Czechoslovak Cinema" (075), and the article "Will They
Listen to the Tales of Hoffmann?" (074) reveal the threat to the most
innovative Czech directors when the government began demanding that they
produce commercially successful films in 1967. A number of articles in
1968 summarize the success and decline of the New Wave before and after
the Russian invasion in August of that year. The most valuable work in
this regard is Alan Levy's So Many Heroes (391), which intimately
reveals Forman's relationship with his country's fortunes throughout the
late sixties. Time magazine's cover story for April 5, "Czechoslovakia:
Into Unexplored Terrain" (092), details Alexander Dubcek's reform policies and comments on the contributions of the cinema and other arts in
bringing him to power. Another article by Liehm, "A Reckoning of the
Miracle: An Analysis of Czechoslovak Cinematography" (098), and Langdon
Dewey's "The Czechoslovak Cinema: Go! Stop! Go! Go?" (093) provide a
final appreciation for this brief bright moment in film history.
Finally, Renata Adler's "Where Will They Work?" (080) and Joseph

Morganstern's "Fragile Freedom" (099) document the impact of the Russian invasion on the New Wave directors. In 1970, Alex Keneas described their first efforts in the West in "The Czechs in Exile" (129).

Besides Liehm and Skvorecky, another important chronicler of Forman's Czech career is Gordon Gow. In "Red Youth" (036) and "A Czech in New York" (162), Gow provides a concise analysis of Forman's evolution in terms of his work with actors and his use of satire. Besides these, Gow composed three other pieces about Forman as well. British filmmaker and critic Lindsay Anderson was one of the first Western writers to praise the new Czech films. In "Nothing Illusory About The Young Prague Filmmakers" (007) and "A Rationally Ordered Cinema Does Work" (008), both from May 1965, Anderson praises the Czech system and lauds Forman as the most important of the young directors. Other articles providing a valuable assessment of Forman's films and career changes in the sixties include John Peter Dyer's "Star-Crossed in Prague" (018), Bosley Crowther's "Czechs Consider Italian Film Deal" (022), Howard Thompson's "The Nude Boy Needed Three Days to Think It Over" (030), and Alan Levy's "Watch Out For the Hook, My Friend" (068). Used along with Liehm's The Milos Forman Stories, these pieces reveal useful production histories of Loves of a Blonde and The Firemen's Ball and tell the story of Forman's dealings with Italian producer Carlo Ponti. The most detailed analysis of these two films are Jean Collet's "Indiscretions" (063), Calvin Green's "The Proper Study of Man" (094), and David Wilson's "The Firemen's Ball" (104).

Because Forman's Czech films all received their first American screenings at the New York Film Festival, the New York Times critics were generally the first to review them. In 1966, Bosley Crowther devoted four lauditory reviews to Loves of a Blonde (023, 024, 025, 026), thereby probably going a long way toward establishing Forman's reputation in America. Judith Crist, "'Blonde' Sets Fast Pace at Festival" (021), was another early American commentator on Forman. Subsequently, she also praised Ragtime (434) and Cuckoo's Nest (282), though she found that to be a shallow film. Vincent Canby has commented on Forman's films several times beginning with Taking Off (140, 141, 215, 216, 252, 340, 341, 342, 418, 419, 508, 509). Although Canby generally appreciates Forman's work, he also usually finds the adaptations weaker than the original works. He has had unqualified praise

only for Taking Off and Hair. Canby's attempt to straddle the fence
between criticism and praise seems to reveal some confusion in his
thinking. A good example occurs in his pair of reviews about Cuckoo's
Nest (215, 216). In the second, Canby attempts to upgrade his assessment of the film, but he is not really able to put aside his original
interpretation.

Among Forman's other American reviewers, David Thomson (313, 481,
608) has generally been highest in praise and the most in-depth in his
analysis. Thomson always writes his pieces only after seeing the film
several times, which lends some extra weight to his opinions. Though
Molly Haskell (163, 231), Bruce Williamson (119, 483, 558) and Andrew
Sarris (045, 378, 451) have all been consistently positive in their
comments, Forman has not fared so well with a number of other critics.
Vernon Young (306, 386, 609) has been the most caustic. Young has a
great deal of rage against the sixties' youth counterculture and is
particularly angry at Forman for praising it in Cuckoo's Nest and Hair.
John Simon (169, 240, 380, 476, 554) tends to lambast Forman for exploiting shallow characters. Only in his review of Ragtime does Simon
allow Forman some excuses for what he sees as another failure. Pauline
Kael (234, 441, 547) generally agrees with Simon that Forman's characters lack depth. She does praise Cuckoo's Nest, but only because of the
acting.

Others have been fairly balanced in their reviews. Jack Kroll
(236, 372, 444) expresses a basic admiration for Forman's adaptations,
but finds Cuckoo's Nest and Ragtime lacking the power of the novels.
Robert Hatch (038, 164, 232, 438) found Loves of a Blonde, Taking Off,
and Cuckoo's Nest inventive but shallow, but then praised Ragtime for
sticking to the center of the novel and containing some powerful scenes.
John Coleman (201, 281, 359, 464, 594) finds Forman a talented and
entertaining director but provides little depth in his reviews. He
gives high praise to Cuckoo's Nest and Amadeus. Stanley Kauffmann
(166, 203, 235, 371, 442, 548) has probably commented on Forman's films
more than any other reviewer except Canby. Although Kauffmann has
always believed Forman to be overrated, he praises Hair and Amadeus as
fine directorial performances.

Milos Forman never likes to analyze his own work, but he has discussed his life, ideas, and methods in a number of interviews. Some of

the most valuable are the ones by Larry Sturhahn (241), Todd McCarthy
(374), Richard Conniff (533), James Blue and Gianfranco de Bosio (058),
Galina Kopanevova (097), Joseph Gelmis (122), and the issue of Dialogue
on Film (187). Forman gives a clear statement of his ideas about real-
ism in his article "Closer to Things" (065). Further insights into
Forman's screenwriting methods are available in Thomas Berger's "I Am
Not a Movie Person" (431) and in the several articles by and about Peter
Shaffer concerning his work on Amadeus (515, 524, 541, 553, 588, 601).
A valuable piece about Forman's work as an editor and the contributions
of his editors to Hair is Roy Huss' "The Man Who Cut Hair: Shaping
Character and Mood in the Editing Room" (409). Finally, scholars can
find detailed information about the contributions of Forman's veteran
director of photography Miroslav Ondricek in a pair of articles (480,
603).

These written works provide an adequate introduction to Milos
Forman's life and ideas, but, to make a complete assessment of the
artist, scholars ultimately need to turn to the films. The literature
reveals a remarkable degree of consistency and artistic integrity.
Readers will find a great many of Forman's statements repeated several
times. They will be able to trace the evolution in his method of working with actors. But the films show both change in Forman's technique
and his continual relevance, the factor that is the measure of his value
as an artist. Forman does not need to update his themes such as the
possibilities for freedom within a set of limitations and the responsibility of the individual. But, with each new film, he finds the appropriate techniques for highlighting certain aspects of the story that
make it peculiarly meaningful for its time. Hopefully, this bibliography will lead scholars toward materials through which they will be
able to develop their own understanding of Forman's message.

5. Bibliography

1955

Periodicals

001 "What is New in the Production of Feature Films: Leave It To Me."
     The Czechoslavak Film 8.6 (1955):1.

     Plot summary of the film by Martin Fric on which Forman assisted on
the screenplay.

1959

Periodicals

002 Weiss, Jiri. "Czech Cinema Has Arrived." Films and Filming 5.6
     (March 1959):8,34.

     An important piece, providing a broad view of the evolution of
Czech cinema up to the sixties. Weiss comments that during the war,
like several other Czech directors, he continued working in England and
was heavily influenced by British documentaries. Then, Italian neo-
realism inspired him, as it did Forman. Weiss regrets that the art of
screenwriting in Czechoslovakia is undeveloped, so filmmakers have to
rely on novels. The sixties produced the closer look at Czech society
that Weiss desires. They also confirmed his view that progressive
directors are not separated by generations or nationalities. Weiss also
includes comments on artistic philosophy and the structure of the film
industry.

1962

Books

003 Kesey, Ken. One Flew Over the Cuckoo's Nest. New York: New
     American Library, 1962.

     Novel that is the basis for Milos Forman's 1975 film of the same
title.

1964

Periodicals

004 "Cerny Petr." Variety   12 August 1964:6.

     Expert blending of professional and nonprofessional actors plus the
episodic nature give the film its freshness. Black Peter provides
insights into contemporary Czechoslovakia and timeless comments about
the universal issue of inter-generational conflict. Mostly reprinted in
"Black Peter," Filmfacts (periodical 1971).

1965

<u>Books</u>

005 Bocek, Jaroslav. <u>Modern Czechoslovak Film, 1945-1965</u>.
     Prague: Artia, 1965.

     Largely filled with stills from the most prominent films of the
years of nationalized cinema, Bocek also includes a short but insightful
essay, offering a unique perspective on Czechoslovak film. Bocek not
only outlines the twenty-year history of socialist Czech cinema but also
comments on its consideration of and relationship to history. Bocek
traces the changes in films about WWII from simple stories of heroism to
complex portrayals about the nature of integrity and decency in the
sixties. Of Forman's generation, Bocek says that they have a greater
understanding of history because they view it through individuals and
not vice-versa. This perspective reveals a deep understanding of the
relationship between man and his world, a knowledge of the ties between
the past and future, and a matter-of-fact acceptance of the human
condition.

006 Stephenson, Ralph. <u>The Cinema as Art</u>. Baltimore: Penguin Books,
     1965.

     Refers to the conclusion of <u>Black Peter</u> as an interesting use of
stopped action.

<u>Newspapers</u>

007 Anderson, Lindsay. "Nothing Illusory About The Young Prague Film-
     Makers." <u>London Times</u> 19 May 1965:8.

     The British are belatedly and inadequately recognizing that a great
number of good films have been coming out of Czechoslovakia. Though
some of the films are set in WWII, all have contemporary and universal
themes. The movement covers three generations, but the youngest, led by
Forman, is the most important. <u>Black Peter</u>'s incidental nature, fine
acting, and subjective camera contain all of their style's essential
ingredients. Could the British have something to learn from the Czech
system?

008 ------------. "A Rationally Ordered Cinema Does Work." <u>London
     Times</u> 20 May 1965:19.

     Explanation of requirements for the Czech film school and assur-
ances of work for its graduates. Czech directors are socialist in
ideology and communicate with their audience even in their most formal
work.

009 "Good Modern Film From Czechoslovakia." <u>The London Times</u> 30
     September 1965:16.

     Praises <u>Peter and Pavla</u> (<u>Black Peter</u>) as a film about youth that
deals not in sensationalism, but in nuances. The family and boy-girl

relationships are lovingly pieced together by a born miniaturist.
Forman presents reality without drawing conclusions.

010   Halberstam, David.   "Czechs Are Proud of Their Film Renaissance."
      New York Times 28 November 1965:141.

      Analysis of breakthrough in Czech filmmaking as related to the
Party's break with economic dogmas and the desire to compete with Polish
films.   Economic changes allowed artists cultural freedom which they
desired to flaunt in the face of Polish achievements during the fifties.

011   Pond, Elizabeth.   "Czech Films Going Up."   Christian Science
      Monitor 22 July 1965:6.

      Cites Black Peter as an example of honesty and novelty.

012   Roud, Richard.   "Forman's 'Peter and Pavla.'" Manchester Guardian 1
      October 1965:11.

      Many films present the awkward years of adolescent girls, but few
attempt to do the same for boys.   Forman's achievement is even more
impressive because his main character is not particularly witty or
intelligent, just average.   The style is not flashy, but brilliantly
constructed in the form of controlled improvisation.   Only Emberto
Olmi's Il Posto is similar, but Peter and Pavla (Black Peter) identifies
the audience with the main character much more closely.

013   Wright, Ian.   "Film Sculptor."   Manchester Guardian 1 October
      1965:11.

      Forman explains his method of blending professional and nonpro-
fessional actors, how using nonprofessionals helps preserve the script's
honesty, and how not letting them see it preserves their freshness.   He
feels his films may be too slow for Western audiences but would like to
make a film in England.

Periodicals

014   Arkadin.   "Film Clips."   Sight and Sound   Winter 1965-66:46.

      Forman's first two features, Black Peter and Loves of a Blonde, are
among the best coming out of East Europe because they are distinctly his
own, representing no artistic movement or trend.   Forman believes that
starting as a screenwriter is the best path to directing because the
person must first have something to say before putting it on film.   His
films touch a responsive chord because he always notes the blending of
happiness and sorrow and finds true drama not in the conflict of good
and evil but in that of two ideas about what is good.

015   Bachmann, Gideon. "Is there really a new wave in Czech films--and
      will it last?" _Film_ Autumn 1965:10-14.

      Unlike artistic breakthroughs in other Eastern Block countries, the
Czech New Wave may have substance because it is dealing with contemporary society right from the beginning instead of safe historical
themes. Milos Forman is the most interesting new director because he
seems the most concerned with the individual. He has fully embraced
cinema-verite, but he combines a graceful camera with tight control.
Socialist ideology has not been abandoned, and artists still face repri-
mands, but the Czechs are showing a glimpse of the reality of present-
day life in their country.

016   Broz, Jaroslav. "Grass Roots." _Films and Filming_ June
      1965:39-42.

      Chronological history of Czech filmmaking from 1937 to the begin-
nings of the New Wave. Broz highlights the top achievements of each
decade and characterizes the present as a time of filmmakers turning
towards the conditions of daily life.

017   Crawford, Stanley. "A Blonde in Love." _Film_ Winter
      1965-66:17-18.

      Favorably compares the film with Emberto Olmi's _Il Posto_, finding
Forman's work more original and satirical. The blending of humor and
pathos and comments on working class concerns in a socialist country
make it one of the year's best films.

018   Dyer, Peter John. "Star-Crossed In Prague." _Sight and Sound_
      Winter 1965-66:34-35.

      Dyer concludes that although Forman's general type of social
commentary in _Black Peter_ and _Loves of a Blonde_ is probably the most
acceptable in a socialist society, the director is probably doing
exactly what he wants. Forman's films are comparable to Karel Reisz's
documentaries about British youth, but Forman achieves much more with
his naturalistic constructions using amateur actors. Forman is the
master of using significant pauses for thematic and comic effect, but he
never does so by rebuking the character. He respects people's shyness
more than any other director.

019   Taranstova, Lydie. "The Man Who Likes to Sleep: An Exclusive
      Interview With Milos Forman." _Film World_ 2.2 (1965-66):30-31.

      Comments on Forman's productions, achievements, and marriages.
Also mentions his plans for a film, _Jonas and the Tingle-Tangle_, as a
sequel to _The Audition_.

1966

Newspapers

020   Crawford, Corine. "Iron Curtain Lifts on Czech Movie Image." Los Angeles Times 19 June 1966:"Calendar,"9.

Director Jan Kadar (The Shop on Main Street) discusses the history of Czech filmmaking, de-centralization of the industry in the sixties, his salary, and the differences between his work and Forman's.

021   Crist, Judith. "'Blonde' Sets Fast Pace at Festival." New York World Journal Tribune 13 September 1966:52.

Forman finds the universal in small details. He is not conde-scending, though he knows the foolishness of his young characters. He sees the vulnerability beneath their outer scruffiness. Mostly reprinted in Filmfacts (periodical, 1966).

022   Crowther, Bosley. "Czechs Consider Italian Film Deal." New York Times 6 June 1966:51.

Closing of a deal between Czechoslovakia and Italy to share resources in the production of films for world-wide distribution. Italian producer Carlo Ponti has spoken with several Czech directors including Jan Kadar and Elmar Klos (a team) and Forman. Kadar and Klos are skeptical about the impact of international influences on quality. Ponti wants Forman to direct one film a year for him but has no commitment.

023   ------------. "Film Festival: Off to a Sparkling Start." New York Times 13 September 1966:51.

Funny, human, and comprehending in a curiously inarticulate way. Like Black Peter, Loves of a Blonde senses and shies away from the problems of youth. Like life, it is inconclusive. Mostly reprinted in Filmfacts (periodical, 1966).

024   ------------. "It's More Than Mere Chance." New York Times 12 June 1966:II:1,24.

Praises the variety, skill, and boldness of recent Czech films including the light comedy of Black Peter and Loves of a Blonde. Attributes part of the Czech success to increased freedom and a good film school.

025   ------------. "Screen: Czech Charmer." New York Times 27 October 1966:55.

Loves of a Blonde is a simple, but delightful film. Inconclusive, but hopeful and realistic. The performances are all excellent.

026   ------------. "Speaking Now of 'Loves.'" 30 October 1966:2:1,5.

Loves of a Blonde compels the audience to identify with its teen-agers in ways that American films do not. Forman uses subtle editing techniques to dispense with narrative points while revealing the characters' psychological conditions. Forman blends comedy and pathos in taking a realistic look at the natural urges of ordinary people and elicits both humor and compassion.

027 "A Czechoslovak Slap." New York Times 8 October 1966:3.

Communist Party mildly rebuked writers and filmmakers for dwelling on disillusionment, pessimism, and indifference to serious social problems and stated it would not tolerate any ideology that hampers socialism.

028 Neuerbourg, Hanns. "Czechs Seeing Red Over Film Laurels." Los Angeles Times 27 December 1966:IV:24.

The Communist Party hierarchy, displeased with the award-winning films Czech directors are making, plans to gain strict ideological control. Director Jan Kadar of the Oscar-winning Shop on Main Street does not fear any such moves on the government's part.

029 Thompson, Howard. "For the Czechs, More Bravos?" New York Times 14 August 1966:II:9,12.

Notes that Loves of a Blonde will open the New York Film Festival, one of four Czech entries included.

030 ------------. "The Nude Boy Needed Three Days to Think it Over." New York Times 23 October 1966:2:13.

Forman discusses the actual incidents that were the basis for Loves of a Blonde, the reasons for its becoming the top moneymaking Czech film ever, changes in the Czech film industry since Stalin's death, his young stars' embarrassment about their nude scene, his family history, and his impressions of New York.

Periodicals

031 Alpert, Hollis. "Film Festivals—1966." Saturday Review 8 October 1966:91-92.

Suggests Loves of a Blonde achieves its noted "freshness" and "gentleness" because it does not try to challenge Party ideology. Forman's depiction of a friendly factory manager would be loved by the state. Mostly reprinted in Filmfacts (periodical, 1966).

032 "Andula's Dream." Newsweek 19 September 1966:112.

Films were meant to be like this. Forman puts real life on the screen but makes the viewer feel more sympathy and happiness than what would exist in reality. His comedy is a part of the characters and not pinned on to them.

033 "The Eyes Have It." _Time_ 23 September 1966:74-75.

Loves of a Blonde successfully smashes all sex comedy formulas.
Forman works with such subtlety that he seems to have not realized his
own power. Reprinted in The National Society of Film Critics on Movie
Comedy (Williamson, Bruce, "The Loves of a Blonde," book, 1977). Mostly
reprinted in Filmfacts (periodical, 1966).

034 "Film Clips." Sight and Sound Winter 1966-67:49.

Basically, a plot summary of Competition, which had not yet been
seen in the West. Although flawed, the reviewer feels it is character-
istically Forman.

035 Gill, Brendan. "Women in Love." New Yorker 5 November 1966:197-99.

Like the early Chaplin, Forman views his characters with such
sympathy that he does no harm in constantly making fun of them. Loves
of a Blonde is a pleasant comedy that asks the audience only to recognize what a difficult time youths have.

036 Gow, Gordon. "Red Youth." Films and Filming 12.5 (February 1966):
     32-33.

Forman's first two features, Black Peter and Loves of a Blonde,
have thrust him to the forefront of international filmmaking. He gives
a new, universal appeal to the old theme of parent-adolescent conflict
because his teenagers are basically obedient and only mildly rebellious.
Forman's skillful observation comes from his personal background, his
use of nonprofessional actors, and his subtle control, which allows for
improvisation.

037 Hartung, Phillip J. "Czechmates." Commonweal 11 November 1966:
     166-67.

In Loves, Forman directs his cast expertly and gives his young
characters universal qualities. But the film does not have the depth
and scope of Ivan Passer's Intimate Lighting.

038 Hatch, Robert. "Films." The Nation 14 November 1966:526.

Loves of a Blonde is an endearing but artless film. The long
ballroom sequence has little to do with the main plot.

039 Hooper, Mary. "Forman." Film Spring 1966:34-35.

Description of Czech film industry, worker's unions, and salary
levels. British film producer Raymond Stross feels that the Czechs need
to use Western movie stars to survive, but Forman disagrees. His method
of working with nonprofessional actors helps him create films of universal appeal. To Forman, Czech film is at an ideal point: free from
ideological pressure and not yet engulfed by commercial pressure.

040 Knight, Arthur. "My Favorite Blonde." Saturday Review 22 October
1966:48.

Loves of a Blonde succeeds because it has a freshness and spontaneity lacking in most American films. Forman understands and enjoys
both sides of the generation gap though he finds the distance between
them to be insuperable.

041 Kotlowitz, Robert. "Films Worth Seeing." Harper's December 1966:
137-38.

Loves of a Blonde is almost perfect. Forman takes the serious
topic of young women attempting to escape restricted lives and shows it
with humor.

042 "Laterna Magika." Tulane Drama Review Fall 1966:141-49.

Description of the combination of film and theater that Forman
assisted with at the 1958 Brussels World's Fair. Scenarist Josef
Svoboda, later an Oscar-winner for Amadeus, describes it as theater's
attempt to capture the way contemporary people view landscape.

043 Liehm, Antonin J. "Success On The Screen." Survey: A Journal of
Soviet and Eastern European Studies 5.1 (April 1966):12-20.

Historical explanation of Czech filmmakers' attempts to continue
the high standards established in the late thirties but interrupted
first by the Nazis and then by the Stalinists. Liehm feels the success
will continue because it includes directors of at least two generations,
all with a similar commitment and a dedication to exploring contemporary
reality while remaining open to international influence. A significant
problem is to produce enough entertainment for the masses while continuing artistic developments.

044 "Loves of a Blonde." Filmfacts 9.22 (15 December 1966):285-86.

Contains credits, a plot summary, and lengthy excerpts from reviews
in Variety (periodical, 1965), Time and Saturday Review (periodicals,
1966), and the New York Times and New York World Journal Tribune
(newspapers, 1966).

045 Sarris, Andrew. "Films." Village Voice 10 November 1966:27.

Though a bit smug and conservative, Loves of a Blonde possesses a
likable sincerity. Forman gets a fine performance from Hana Brejchova,
but he has suffered from too much praise from American critics.

046 "Spotlight on Prague." Newsweek 18 July 1966:93-94.

The Oscar for Jan Kadar and Elmar Klos's The Shop on Main Street
confirms that the Czechs have produced the latest important wave of
filmmaking. Given freedom and responsibility by the government and
backed by an intellectual-controlled film industry, Czech directors are
turning out films in a variety of styles that all share the qualities of
honesty and sensitivity. Though most audiences want mindlessness, the

Czechs have found moviegoers who are tired of simplicity. Allurement from Western studios is threatening the wave, but the Czechs have created a number of great moments in film and are still showing strength.

047 Still, Ronald. "Films at the Philharmonic." The Christian Century 2 November 1966:1340-41.

Loves of a Blonde proves Forman's talent as an interpreter of common humanness.

048 "Sweet Light from a Dark Casino." Time 29 June 1966:44.

Account of the Karlovy Vary Film Festival in Czechoslovakia, brief history of Czech film industry, and mention of several Czech directors and their films. The best Czech films combine cinematic experimentation, thematic audacity, and wry humor. Also mention of Forman's contract with Italian producer Carlo Ponti.

049 Walsh, Moira. "Loves of a Blonde." America 17 December 1966:812-13.

The film gives an unflattering but accurate view of young people as lacking values and motivation that is relevant not only behind the Iron Curtain. It encourages people to examine themselves and feel compassion for the unfortunate. The Catholic Review Board should not have given it a "condemned" label, but the nude scene is unnecessarily lengthy and graphic.

1967

Books

050 Broz, Jaroslav. The Path of Fame of the Czechoslovak Film. Prague: Ceskoslovensky Filmexport, 1967.

Discussion of the growth of Czech film over a seventy year period, 1896-1967. Broz places film within the contexts of social and political changes, the nationalization of the film industry, technical developments in filmmaking, and the contributions of major directors in Czech film history. Czech film gained international recognition in the sixties because it finally got in tune with worldwide developments in the arts. Comments on Forman are limited to quoting lauditory reviews of Loves of a Blonde from the American press. Broz states that the newest generation of filmmakers is looking forward to expanding within the socialist system.

051 Simon, John. Private Screenings. New York: Macmillan Co., 1967.

In Loves of a Blonde, Forman focuses on the ordinary for too long, missing the inherent absurdity revealed in Black Peter.

Newspapers

052   Caruthers, Osgood.   "Prague's Haunting Cultural Dilemma."   Los
Angeles Times 5 March 1967:"Calendar,"1,14.

Announces that Communist Party leaders in Czechoslovakia are looking for ways to make orthodox ideology appealing to young people and to
put greater restrictions on artists. Limits still exist, though all
areas of art are experiencing great freedom.

053   Lukas, J. Anthony.   "The Case of a Runaway Flower Child."   New
York Times 19 October 1967:1,52.

A follow-up to Lukas's article about Linda Fitzpatrick in which
another New York parent discusses his fourteen-year-old runaway daughter. The hippie movement was attracting a number of young adolescent
girls to Greenwich Village.

054   -------------.   "The Two Worlds of Linda Fitzpatrick."   New York
Times 16 October 1967:1,53.

Story of the last weeks of Linda Fitzpatrick, daughter of a wealthy
spice importer murdered one week earlier in Greenwich Village along
with a hippie boyfriend. Forman saw enough humor in the generational
conflict between Fitzpatrick and her parents to become inspired to make
Taking Off.

055   Madsen, Alex.   "Czechs Tugging on Ideological Movie Reins."   Los
Angeles Times 30 July 1967:"Calendar,"11,17.

Reprint of Madsen's "This Year at Marienbad" (periodical, 1967).

056   Thomas, Kevin.   "Forman--A Czech in Love With Lotus Land."   Los
Angeles Times 21 April 1967:14:1,12.

Forman discusses his relationship with Italian producer Carlo
Ponti, the plans for his next film, The Americans Are Coming, his fondness for working with nonprofessional actors, and his love of Hollywood
history.

Periodicals

057   Bachmann, Gideon.   "Miracle in Prague."   Atlas July 1967:54-58.

Describes the production conditions and the degree of government
censorship in Czech films. Though they are not necessarily political or
anti-regime, the new Czech films are all humanist, taking non-escapist
views of reality and presenting affirmations of life.

058   Blue, James and Gianfranco De Bosio.   "Interview with Milos
      Forman."   Cahiers du Cinema in English February 1967:53-54.

      Extensive discussion of Forman's work with nonactors, how he
chooses people who trust him, what tricks he uses with them to get the
emotions he wants, and what filming techniques he uses to relax them and
capture the best performances.

059   Broz, Jaroslav.   "Czechoslovakia: New Ideas, New Names, New
      Successes."   Film World 3.1 (1967):28-30.

      Brief mention of some of the top Czech directors and their films.

060   Broz, Martin.   "Conversation With A. M. Brousil."   Young Cinema and
      Theatre 3 (1967):29-32.

      Antonin Brousil, head of Prague's Academy of Dramatic Arts, which
includes the film school, discusses the role of professional standards,
theory, a broad humanistic approach, and well-known artists as teachers
at the school.   He also discusses the school's contributions to the
philosophy of the New Wave.

061   ------------.   "Introducing the Prague Film School FAMU." Young
      Cinema and Theatre 3 (1967):24-28.

      Presents the structure of the film school and lists the accom-
plishments of its graduates.

062   Clouzot, Claire.   "Loves of a Blonde."   Film Quarterly 21.1 (Fall
      1967):47-48.

      Forman touches on the painful spots of adolescent searching and
discovery and explores them with accuracy and tenderness.   Though funny,
Loves is not essentially a comedy with contrived situations designed for
laughter such as Georgy Girl.   It is based on actual situations and uses
non-professional actors.   The American version contains the additional
scene of Mila being duped by his girlfriend, which reveals American
tastes and misleads the audience.

063   Collet, Jean.   "Indiscretions."   Cahiers du Cinema in English
      February 1967:55-57.

      In Loves of a Blonde, Forman invades his characters' dreams, cap-
turing the indiscretions which reveal them most fully.   All the time, he
very obviously presents the camera as voyeur, causing embarassment for
the audience.   We are conscious of seeing and hearing what we should
not, and we recognize these words and actions as the substance of the
film and of life.

064   Forman, Milos. "Chill Wind on the New Wave." Saturday Review 23
      December 1967:10-11,41.

     Writing in the context of having escaped Stalinist restrictions and
now facing the threat of commercial standards, Forman reviews the history of the Czech film industry. He emphasizes the importance of tradition to a national culture. The Czech film school, established in
1945, created a number of talented directors who were ready when
Stalinism began to crumble. The new threat of commercialism is unfair
because Czechoslovakia hardly has enough people to make films profit-
able, and the most artistic films make all their money outside the
country.

065   ------------. "Closer to Things." Cahiers du Cinema in English
      January 1967:57-58.

     Forman argues that the film is always greater than its auteur. He
wants to believe that an actor is actually the character he is playing,
even if that cannot be verified. Forman therefore values the films that
look honestly at the surface of things. Cinema must begin looking at
the minute to discover the energy for exploring the infinite.

066   Fraser, Graham. "Loves of a Blonde." Take One February 1967:24.

     Forman subtly studies his ordinary characters with sympathy and
sensitivity, revealing their deceits, self-deceptions, and conflicts.
The viewer feels both detachment and close affection towards them.

067   Gilliatt, Penelope. "Czech Wave in New York." New Yorker 1 July
      1967:54.

     Czech films are basically honest self-expressions that also incor-
porate a public dimension. They assume that their audiences want the
truth, and they use humor without being derisive. Gilliatt discusses
several directors and their works, not including Forman.

068   Levy, Alan. "Watch Out for the Hook, My Friend." Life 20 June
      1967:77-86.

     Forman discusses his childhood, film school, working conditions in
Czechoslovakia, and takes Levy on a tour of a concentration camp. Levy
discusses Competition, Black Peter, Loves of a Blonde, and Forman's
dealings with blustery Italian film producer Carlo Ponti.

069   Madsen, Alex. "This Year at Marienbad." Sight and Sound Autumn
      1967:176-77.

     Young avante-garde Czech filmmakers such as Vera Chytilova and Jan
Nemec are facing government repression, though international fame is
keeping them in demand. Forman is forgiven because he brings in money,
but even he is probing deeper with The Firemen's Ball. He has no in-
tention of leaving the country to work and may be filming The Americans
are Coming with Jerry Lewis. Czech filmmakers plan on making a united
appeal to the government.

070 Sarris, Andrew. "The Movers." Saturday Review 23 December 1967:10.

Brief note about how Forman's career began and his affinity with teenagers. Sarris notes a similar improvisatory quality in both Black Peter and Loves of a Blonde.

071 ------------. "Two Cheers For the Czechs." Village Voice 20 July 1967:21,31.

Cites some of the basic aspects of Czech films. They contain dry wit, poeticize the commonplace, frequently use urban pastoral, and show an intolerance for bourgeois neurosis. Refers to Forman as a major minimalist.

072 Techine, Andre. "The Smile of Prague." Cahiers du Cinema in English February 1967:55-57.

Mainly about Black Peter but also including Loves of a Blonde. Forman has a simplicity of watching things around him and letting them go, but underneath that he weaves a subtle dream. His narrative appears chronological and spontaneous, but actually he is examining every moment as if trying to hold on to them. The narrative becomes circular, and sarcastic laughter gives way to a smile. Forman's cinema speaks from that smile.

073 Vogel, Amos. "The Humanists of Prague: The Young Czech Cinema." Village Voice 15 June 1967:33,36-37.

Briefly summarizes Prague's culture and history and cites Kafka, nationalization, and the film school as the most important ingredients of the New Wave. Socialist-realist films are not made any longer. The filmmakers consist of symbolist-allegoricallists and realists (including Forman), who are no less radical because they also provide truth and spontaneity. The question of whether or not they will be able to continue to confront their reality without hindrances is one facing artists all over the world.

074 "Will They Listen to the Tales of Hoffmann?" The Economist 4 February 1967:407.

Czech film and theatre have always provided an outlet for what cannot be expressed in print. However, the state is now cutting back on its subsidies, and Mr. Karel Hoffmann, newly-appointed minister of culture, will probably try to enforce artistic adherence to the Party lines. But, he will be working with a very difficult group to control.

075 Zalman, Jan. "Question Marks on the New Czechoslovak Cinema." Film Quarterly Winter 1967-68:18-27.

Zalman defines the New Wave as consisting of three groups, those with a style based on cinema-verité methods (including Forman), those providing a modern adaptation of critical realism, and those breaking

with all past rules of filmmaking, but with each group sharing techniques and a manner of thinking. The pressures on the New Wave in 1967
were both economic and ideological. In order to persecute the most
experimental of the young filmmakers, the industry was breaking from the
basis for its nationalist organization by demanding that new productions
be aimed towards box-office success. Zalman here details a problem that
Forman refers to in his "Chill Wind." Ideologically, the state began to
give its highest awards to the oldest generation of directors, whose
films had the most traditional narrative structures. Although Zalman
does not discredit these films, he argues that the most experimental
filmmakers are also working within a national cultural tradition and are
the most progressive force in Czech films. Zalman particularly praises
Jan Nemec, Vera Chytilova, and Ester Krumbachova. He provides synopsis
and interpretations for several films by these and other directors. He
also defines the difference between Forman and Ivan Passer, whom Zalman
says is more cruel in revealing the emptiness of the aims of bourgeois
life. The whole crisis rested on the unanswered question of what the
relationship between art, society, and society's institutions should be
within socialism.

1968

Books

076 Cowie, Peter, ed. "Hori, Ma Panenko (Like A House on Fire)."
     International Film Guide, 1969. New York: A. S. Barnes and Co.,
     Inc., 1968:57.

     Forman shows that there is pain behind every laugh and that good
intentions often produce failure.

077 ------------. "Milos Forman." International Film Guide, 1969.
     New York: A. S. Barnes and Co., Inc. 1968:12-15.

     See "Cowie, Peter," book entry in 1975. This article is exactly
the same except that it does not include Taking Off or Visions of Eight.

078 Zalman, Jan. Films and Film-makers in Czechoslovakia. Prague:
     Orbis, 1968.

     Forman combines the simplicity of Chaplin with the cinema-verite
techniques of Godard in Competition, Black Peter, and Loves of a Blonde.
Unlike the Theatre of the Absurd, which reveals reality through absurdity, Forman shows the absurd face of reality. His unconventional
method of examining reality instead of relying on comic formulas has
revealed the artistic value of banality.

Newspapers

079 Adler, Renata. "Film Festival: A Muted Comedy and a Deeply Moving
     Documentary From Czechoslovakia." New York Times 30 September
     1968:60.

     The Firemen's Ball is a beautiful film about moral stupidity--
people devoted to saving lives fail each other through insensitivity.
Forman's skill for being bitter, clear, and funny all at once indicates
a possible comic renaissance. Reprinted in Adler's A Year in the Dark
(1969). Mostly reprinted in Filmfacts (periodical, 1969).

080 ------------. "Where Will They Work?" New York Times 22
     September 1968:2:1,18.

     Discussion of Czech directors meeting in Paris shortly after the
Russians' invasion, planning to begin work elsewhere or eventually go
back, and watching their whole world turn inside-out. French filmmakers
Claude Berri and Francois Truffaut went to great lengths to help them.
Reprinted in Adler's A Year in the Dark (1969).

081 "The Firemen's Ball." New York Times 1 September 1968:80.

     A triumph that establishes Forman as one of the major directors of
our times. Adds allegory to his usual anecdote.

082 Hamilton, Thomas J. "Some Film People Have Left Prague." New York
     Times 8 September 1968:4.

     Comments on exit of several Czech directors. Forman's friends
believe his denunciation of the Russian occupation over Czech television
will make it impossible for him to return for some time.

083 "The Miracle of Four Years Ago That Promises to Last." London
     Times 16 August 1968:9.

     In this ironically-titled article (first of two parts), the writer
recounts the beginnings of the Czech New Wave in 1962-64 and critical
reactions at that time. The article states the basis of the film
"miracle" as existing in the national film industry's history and the
temporary absence of both commercial and ideological pressures. The
writer would clearly like to see a similar situation in England.

084 Taylor, John Russell. "Film Comedy With a Bite." London Times 21
     November 1968:16.

     The Firemen's Ball is both a hilarious comedy and a cruelly accu-
rate portrait of human foibles.

085 "The Times Diary: Czech Film Directors Speak." London Times 27
     September 1968:10.

     Forman and Ivan Passer, in New York, state that there has been no
repression of the Czech film industry yet since the Russian invasion,
and they both hope to return to work there.

086   "The Times Diary: Czech Film Exodus Averted." London Times 27
      April 1968:8.

      Forman says he is hopeful about the move towards democractic
socialism in Czechoslovakia under Dubcek. The previous year, 1967, was
one of heavy ideological pressure. He believes artists paved the way
for political change.

087   Weiler, A. H. "A Czechoslovak Trio." New York Times 4 July
      1968:13.

      Comments on The Audition as a good example of Forman's work,
reminiscent of American musical youth.

088   ------------. "'Dropping Out' with Milos Forman." New York Times
      20 October 1968:215.

      This piece, written while The Firemen's Ball was playing New York,
refers to an early title for Taking Off. Forman indicates that the
film will focus on the runaway teenage girl and states that he then
plans to return to Czechoslovakia to film Josef Skvorecky's novel The
Cowards.

Periodicals

089   Bond, Kirk. "The New Czech Film." Film Comment 5.1 (Fall
      1968):70-79.

      By "new," Bond means films that have gone beyond the "ordinariness"
of Loves of a Blonde into new narrative techniques that define film as
poetry.

090   Clurman, Harold. "Films." Nation 14 October 1968:379-82.

      Article about films at the New York Film Festival. Briefly refers
to The Firemen's Ball as unassuming and affectionate, but without
condescension.

091   "Competition." Variety 31 January 1968:6,22.

      Competition represents the essence of Forman's technique, but age
will limit its box-office. Forman again follows teenagers facing conflicts between youth and tradition, viewing all involved with objec-
tivity and sympathy. Why Do We Need All Those Brass Bands? is superior
to the film's other half, The Audition.

092   "Czechoslovakia: Into Unexplored Terrain." Time 5 April
      1968:26-30,34.

      Summary of Czech political history and a short biography of the
leader, Alexander Dubcek, who was most instrumental in producing the
"Prague Spring" of 1968, which lasted from January until the Russians
invaded in August. During that time, Czechs enjoyed political freedom
and freedom of expression otherwise unknown behind the iron curtain.

The country's artists and intellectuals set the climate for reform.   One paragraph is devoted to Loves of a Blonde.

093   Dewey, Langdon.   "The Czechoslovak Cinema: Go! Stop! Go! Go?" Film Autumn 1968:20-32.

Includes a brief political history of the Czech film industry and discussions by Forman and Ivan Passer about the value of film school and the practical basis for using nonprofessional actors.

094   Green, Calvin.   "The Proper Study of Man."   Film Society Review October 1968:29-36.

Five East European features at the current New York Film Festival, though entirely different aesthetically, demonstrate a profound similarity in forcing viewers to consider Man himself.   Forman's The Firemen's Ball is the most perfectly structured of the films and demonstrates the director's masterful control of timing.   Forman captures unrepeatable moments to demonstrate the ludicrousness of the characters' aspirations, but his satire is never taunting.   The film represents a definite maturity over Loves of a Blonde.

095   Hartung, Philip J.   "Fun at the Fest."   Commonweal 18 October 1968:87-88.

The Firemen's Ball includes some fine satire on man's selfishness, but it is mainly cynicism without warmth.   Part of a report on the New York Film Festival.

096   Kauffmann, Stanley.   "The Long Weekend."   New Republic 19 October 1968:28,40.

Color and a thin layer of artiness do not cover the low level of obvious humor in The Firemen's Ball.   Part of a report on the New York Film Festival.

097   Kopanevova, Galina.   "Two Hours With Milos Forman."   Ceskoslovensky Film: Foreign Film Bulletin 15 November 1968:1-12.

Subjects covered include the evolution of Forman's style based upon inexperience and the need to simplify things when working with nonactors, where he finds his nonprofessional actors, his methods of collaboration with co-writers Ivan Passer and Jaroslav Papousek, his experience with the Magic Lantern and love of jazz, methods of working with nonprofessional actors, similarities with Western filmmakers, experiences with The Firemen's Ball, an explanation of the cruelty in that film, and his first perceptions about the problems of working in America.

098 Liehm, Antonin J. "A Reckoning of the Miracle: An Analysis of Czechoslovak Cinematography." Film Comment 5.1 (Fall 1968):64-69.

Liehm argues that the New Wave has now developed into a stable film culture, the measure of which is the films of the previous five years. Neither filmmakers nor audiences will ever be able to return to the standards of socialist realism. Liehm divides the critically successful directors between those (including Forman) concerned with realism and those concerned with ideas. He wrote the piece shortly before the Russian invasion.

099 Morganstern, Joseph. "Fragile Freedom." Newsweek 2 September 1968:66-67.

Expresses concern for and reviews history of the Czech New Wave, now threatened by the Russian invasion. With Black Peter and The Firemen's Ball, Forman stood prominently at both the beginning and end of this amazingly brief movement. Borrowing methods from everywhere, the New Wave produced films that were human and nonjudgmental.

100 ------------. "Weird, Wonderful Festival." Newsweek 7 October 1968:96-97.

Notes The Firemen's Ball as more of an appreciation of man's foibles than a political allegory. Part of a report on the New York Film Festival.

101 Polt, Harriet R. "The Firemen's Ball." Film Quarterly 22.2 (Winter 1968-69):56.

A hilarious film that exposes all of mankind's worst traits, but everybody at the ball still has a good time. Forman's one fault is that he tends to carry jokes too far.

102 Schickel, Richard. "Unsung Heroes of Screen '68." Life 20 December 1968:8.

The Firemen's Ball teeters uncannily between farce and tragedy but has an odd strength. The firemen represent bureaucratic blunderers, but Forman's insights on human nature push the film beyond politics.

103 "The Way the Ball Bounces." Time 6 December 1968:109.

The Firemen's Ball must play on three levels, pre-Dubcek, during Dubcek, and post-Dubcek, but it succeeds on each. Mostly reprinted in Filmfacts (periodical, 1969).

104 Wilson, David. "The Firemen's Ball." Sight and Sound Winter 1968-69:46.

The film can be read as a political allegory, but Forman's basic concern is compassion for humanity. Here, he focuses on the old as victims. He achieves his humor through perfectly timed shifts of mood.

1969

Books

105 Adler, Renata. <u>A Year in the Dark: Journal of a Film Critic</u>. New
     York: Random House, 1969.

     Contains reprints of her articles "Film Festival: A Muted Comedy"
and "Where Will They Work?," both from 1968 (newspaper).

106 Hibbin, Nina. <u>Eastern Europe: An Illustrated Guide</u>. New York:
     A. S. Barnes and Co., 1969.

     Brief biographical information about Forman, with a list of his
productions included.

107 Ragni, Gerome and James Rado. <u>Hair: The American Tribal Love-Rock
     Musical</u>. New York: Pocket Books, 1969.

     Text of the original play that served as the basis for Milos
Forman's 1979 film of the same name.

Newspapers

108 Champlin, Charles. "Oscar Nominee 'Firemen's Ball' Will Screen."
     <u>Los Angeles Times</u> 1 April 1969:IV:1.

     Though less natural than <u>Loves of a Blonde</u>, <u>The Firemen's Ball</u> is a
vastly amusing film about ordinary people.

Periodicals

109 Armstrong, Marion. "Unpretentious Fun." <u>The Christian Century</u> 19
     February 1969:258.

     Summary of episodes in <u>The Firemen's Ball</u>. Armstrong looks for no
meanings.

110 Bocek, Jaroslav. "Triumphs of Good Over Evil." <u>Film World</u> 5.1
     (January-March 1969):19.

     Brief outline of three distinct types of filmmakers that were part
of the Czech New Wave: the realists (Forman), the allegorical (Jan
Nemec), and the combination of the two (Evald Schorm). Bocek sees the
Forman style as the most politically limited.

111 Chavan, Prabhakar. "New Czech Cinema: Some Observations."
     <u>Close-Up: The Magazine of the Film Forum</u> 4 (1969):9-11.

     Comments on the influence of international art trends, Kafka, and
realism on Czech film in the sixties. Also gives examples of suicide as
a solution for human weakness and the blending of comedy and tragedy
being used as themes.

112 Columne, Benjamin. "Illuminating the inner world: the sixth New York film festival." The Catholic World February 1969:177-81.

Forman's healthy cynicism in The Firemen's Ball demonstrates how avarice limits and cripples man's simplicity. His group of young girls who drop out of a beauty contest comments too cutely on innocence untarnished by possessiveness.

113 "The Firemen's Ball." Filmfacts 11.23 (1 January 1969):417-19.

Includes credits, a plot summary, and lengthy excerpts from New York Times (newspaper, 1968), Time (periodical, 1968), and Variety (periodical, 1968).

114 Gow, Gordon. "The Firemen's Ball." Films and Filming February 1969:41,44.

Forman uses individuals to satirize a communal state of mind. Since the characters embody universal attributes such as selfishness and age, we must laugh or else despair. The comedy is therefore therapeutic.

115 "New Wave Directors of Czechoslovakia." Film World 5.1 (January-March 1969):25-26.

Encyclopedic entries including picture, birthdate, film titles, and awards.

116 Schrader, Paul. "Fireman's Ball" (sic). Cinema 5.2 (1969):46-48.

Although not yet fully appreciated because he works in comedy, Milos Forman has developed a style so unique that his films can only be compared with each other. Firemen's Ball is a tour-de-force, using one sustained dance hall sequence, Pinter-like dialogue that is more funny and haunting than Pinter's, and a camera style blending neo-realism with cinema-verité. Emerging from a life of tragedies, Forman creates black humor based on the lives of simple people that is still compassionate.

117 Skvorecky, Josef. "The Birth and Death of the Czech New Wave." Take One 2.8 (1969):9-12.

Brief history of the Czech film industry and outline of factors contributing to the "miracle" of the sixties: nationalization, a good film school, and the repression of the fifties and reactions against it by audiences and filmmakers alike. Following a brief thaw in the late fifties, the optimum situation finally occurred. Forman's unique style, based on collaboration, improvisation, and work with non-professional actors, is typically Czech in its combination of sensitivity and satire. Also, a brief commentary on other major Czech directors of the sixties.

118   Tuten, Frederic.   "The Firemen's Ball, 'tableau of greed.'" Vogue
      January 1969:68.

Forman satirizes the firemen and villagers without bitterness or
self-righteousness. It is a universal story, wisely told.

119   Williamson, Bruce.   "Movies." Playboy   January 1969:34.

The Firemen's Ball is a cynical and hilarious view of a bureaucracy's attempts to distribute rewards. Forman avoids pathos or geri-
atrics. He threatens to revive the golden age of screen comedy single-
handedly. The film's one flaw is that it has no central characters.

120   Zalman, Jan.   "Revolution in Czechoslovak Cinema." Film World 5.1
      (January-March 1969):11-13.

Part of an entire issue devoted to the Czech New Wave, Zalman
argues concisely and effectively that the new Czech films are based upon
national traditions in filmmaking. Czech film became innovative during
the thirties, but then showed only intermittent signs of strength during
the next two decades. Still, a stable production and distribution
system was established. The sixties directors were highly diversified
in terms of age and style, but, contrary to Western beliefs, all aimed
toward the goal of strengthening socialism.

                              1970
Books

121   Crist, Judith.   The Private Eye, The Cowboy, and the Very Naked
      Girl. New York: Holt, Rinehart, and Winston, Inc., 1970.

Cites Loves of a Blonde, a compassionate picture that makes unappealing people seem very attractive, as the fourth best film of 1966.

122   Gelmis, Joseph.   The Film Director as Superstar. Garden City,
      NY: Doubleday and Co., Inc., 1970.

In his introduction to this 1968 interview, Gelmis discusses the
dominant humanism in the Czech New Wave films and the attributes of the
Prague film school, where all of the movement's directors were trained.
There, students worked directly with a professional for four years and
reviewed hundreds of classic and contemporary films from around the
world. In the excellent interview, Forman tells detailed stories about
the benefits of being an unpressured film student, free to make mistakes, working with nonprofessional actors, and the making of each of
his Czech films. He also relates how his financial difficulties with
The Firemen's Ball and refusal to add eight minutes to it nearly earned
him a long prison sentence. The interview ends with Forman discussing
the problems of working in English for his first American film.
Reprinted in Whittemore and Cecchetini, Passport to Hollywood (book
1976).

123   Skvorecky, Josef. The Cowards. New York: Grove Press, 1970.

Novel about the experiences of a group of apolitical jazz-loving young boys during the last years of the war and the anti-German atrocities that take place in their small town. Forman wanted to film the story at both the end of the 50s and of the 60s.

124   Zvonicek, Stanislav. 25 Years of Czechoslovak Socialist Cinematography and Its Prospects. Prague: Czech Film Institute, 1970.

An interesting example of the ideas governing the "reform" of the Czech film industry in the early seventies. Zvonicek charges that the members of the New Wave distorted history, picked facts out of context, and misinterpreted social processes in order to benefit themselves. The movement started positively in 1962-64, but then ceased being new and pushing the culture forward. The young directors began offering nothing but unrelenting criticism and casting their eyes towards foreign bank accounts. Zvonicek admires Competition and Black Peter but finds Loves of a Blonde and The Firemen's Ball too critical. He goes so far as to highly praise the films of the early fifties, cited by most others as the period in which Stalinist oppression did the most damage to the Czech film industry. Clearly, those times were returning. For Zvonicek, art must show man's progress towards communism.

Newspapers

125   Berry, Leonard J. "Czech Director Survives Baptism of Hollywood Fire." Los Angeles Times 17 May 1970:"Calendar,"56.

Recounts Forman's problems with Paramount and explains the freedom Universal gave him for making Taking Off. Also discusses his casting of the film, working with nonprofessionals, and the differences between the American and Czech film industries.

126   ------------. "Milos Forman On His Films." Boston Globe (Sunday Magazine) 16 August 1970:31-36.

Recounts the origins of all of Forman's Czech films, plus Taking Off. A great deal of material about working with nonprofessional actors. Forman comments that getting into filmmaking is easier in Czechoslovakia, but the potential rewards are much smaller.

127   Lichtenstein, Grace. "The Loves of a 'Loser.'" New York Times 12 July 1970:D11,28.

Forman discusses his problems with getting financing for Taking Off (how Bob Evans of Paramount rejected his script and demanded $140,000 paid back) and how he got the idea and did research for the film. Forman claims the film will be much like his Czech pictures: a simple story about losers. He keeps his script from his actors because he is afraid of what they will think about it.

Periodicals

128 Forman, Milos. "How I Came to America to Make a Film and Wound Up
     Owing Paramount $140,000." Show February 1970:38-40,86-88.

In 1967, Milos Forman came to America to make a film. He met with
Paramount executives Charlie Bluhdorn and Bob Evans, who both told him
that they loved his script and wanted to make the picture. He met with
an agent who told him that he would soon be rich. But Bluhdorn and
Evans did not tell him that Paramount had no money for new projects.
The agent did not mention anything when he suddenly became a producer.
When Forman decided to leave Paramount, they told him that he owed the
amount of money stated in the title. Eventually, Joe Levine and Sidney
Lumet stepped in as financier and producer to try to save him (they
eventually failed), but Forman ends his article on a very bitter note.
He says that filmmaking in America is a big mystery to him and no fun.
He is not surprised at the vast quantity of mediocre films that America
produces every year. Reprinted in Forman, et. al., Taking Off (book,
1971).

129 Keneas, Alex. "The Czechs in Exile." Newsweek 27 July 1970:70-71.

Forman, Ivan Passer, and fellow director Jan Kadar talk about the
problems of working in America following the Russian invasion of Czechoslovakia. Troubles with getting financing for Taking Off and some
elements of the production are mentioned.

130 Polt, Harriet R. "Getting the Great Ten Percent: An Interview
     With Milos Forman." Film Comment Fall 1970:58-63.

Forman felt that his comedy was universal in nature. The situations in his Czech films could be transplanted into America. His
heroes were losers as were the heroes of many American films in the late
60s. But Forman thinks of his films as life experiences. They have to
be fun, and the making of Taking Off was not much fun for him. He talks
here about his struggles with English and Hollywood, his favorite
American films, and finding and working with non-actors. Reprinted in
Forman, et. al., Taking Off (book, 1971).

1971

Books

131 Dewey, Langdon. Outline of Czechoslovakian Cinema. London:
     Informatics, 1971.

Encyclopedic review of Czech cinema from 1898-1970, arranged
chronologically, with individuals discussed apparently in order of their
appearance on the scene. The notes on Forman include brief biographical
information, plot summaries of each Czech film, and a brief mention of
camera style, adeptness at casting, and use of improvisation. Forman
shows ironic humor, penetrating observations, and compassion.

132   Forman, Milos, John Guare, Jean-Claude Carriere, and John Klein.
      Taking Off. New York: The New American Library, Inc., 1971.

An illustrated screenplay that adds insight to the film by commenting on the characters and actions. The book also includes reprints of
Harriet R. Polt's interview ("Getting the Great Ten Percent") and
Forman's "How I Came to America." Forman adds a postscript to his
article here. Levine and Lumet eventually backed out of the production.
Only after Forman's friend Mike Hausman helped him get the budget down
to $850,000, the unions made salary concessions, and Forman acted out
the entire script for Universal studio chiefs was the production finally
started. During filming and editing, Forman had a great relationship
with Universal, and he ends this piece sounding much more optimistic.

133   Pickard, R. A. E. Dictionary of 1,000 Best Films. New York:
      Association Press, 1971.

Includes a brief plot summary, short commentary, and partial
credits for Loves of a Blonde, listed under Blonde In Love.

134   Rice, Susan. "Taking Off." International Film Guide, 1972. Ed.
      Peter Cowie. New York: A. S. Barnes and Co., 1971:263-64.

Taking Off succeeds where other youth films fail because Forman
does not patronize nor make villains out of either the parents or their
children. Masterfully edited, the films' irony involves the failure of
material values and the hypocrisy of adults.

135   Skvorecky, Josef. All the Bright Young Men and Women: A Personal
      History of the Czech Cinema. Toronto: Peter Martin Associates,
      Ltd., 1971.

Skvorecky recounts his experiences with Forman in boyhood, as a
co-screenwriter in the late 50s, and as a possible actor in Loves of a
Blonde. He emphasizes Forman's integrity throughout his life, his
willingness to risk everything for his principles, and his struggles
with both Czech and American critics who have viewed his films as too
cruel. Skvorecky's comments describe how Forman's Czech films shed new
light on his country. Cinema-verité was only a starting point from
which the use of non-actors remains.

136   Szulc, Tad. Czechoslovakia Since World War II. New York: The
      Viking Press, 1971.

Provides a detailed account of the role of the arts during the
sixties.

137   Whyte, Alistair. New Cinema in Eastern Europe. London: Studio
      Vista, 1971.

Comments on some of the common characteristics of Black Peter,
Loves of a Blonde, and The Firemen's Ball--Forman's use of dance hall
sequences to observe social traits, and his social satire combined with
personal compassion.

Newspapers

138 Berry, Leonard J. "Buck Henry Rises to Surface, Finds That It's Glaring." Los Angeles Times 25 April 1971:"Calendar,"20.

Mainly discusses Henry's writing career. Forman comments that he chose Buck Henry for the lead in Taking Off because of the actor's woeful expression. It produces compassion, which is good for comedy.

139 Bragg, Melvyn. "A Good Week for Comedy." London Times 3 September 1971:8.

Taking Off is Forman's best film. The story is new but fundamental. The comedy is hilarious but poignant. Performances are excellent.

140 Canby, Vincent. "A Man in Pursuit of Laughter." New York Times 18 April 1971:Entertainment Section:1,32.

Taking Off is an unusual film because its characters do not do anything unusual. They never have any big moments. Forman seeks the immediate laugh without consciously addressing any great issues, but he does not exploit his characters either. The film maintains a detached affection that shows us the characters without fully revealing them.

141 ------------. "The Screen: 'Taking Off.'" New York Times 29 March 1971:40.

Forman specializes in gentle comedy in the midst of bleak circumstances. Although the characters often act foolish, he views them with affection. The editing trick of juxtaposing two apparently unrelated scenes to comment on each other is artful, but perhaps not as meaningful as it appears. Forman casts excellently in terms of actors and faces.

142 Champlin, Charles. "A Comedy of Discomfort." Los Angeles Times 9 April 1971:IV:1.

As in his Czech films, Forman shows average characters in depressing situations in Taking Off. But they manage to survive, and they are funny. Forman's first American film seems crueller than his earlier ones with some of the situations more contrived. Buck Henry, as Larry Tyne, gives an amazing performance and often shows more compassion than Forman does. Mostly reprinted in "Taking Off," Filmfacts, 1971, (periodical).

143 Conaway, James. "Milos Forman's America Is Like Kafka's—Basically Comic." The New York Times Magazine 11 July 1971:8-12.

Details about the creation of Taking Off and Forman's adjustment to life in America. At this time, Forman was living in New York's Chelsea Hotel, a refuge for poverty-stricken artists. But he was anticipating a success, looking forward, and guarding against overconfidence. Conaway

analyzes Forman's view of families and synopsizes his two failed projects, The Americans Are Coming and Bulletproof. Also valuable are
stories of Forman's days living in the East Village, discovering the
comedy and tragedy of American life while researching Taking Off.

144   DeMott, Benjamin. "Ha! Ha! Dad's Nude, Mom's Drunk." New York
        Times 16 May 1971:D11.

Taking Off is a very funny film. However, though other reviewers
have seen it as gentle and compassionate, it is really just one more
example of how parents seek their own comfort first and lack any ability
to show sustained concern for their children. Rather than being compassionate, Forman uses every visual aspect of the film to show their
emptiness.

145   Greenspan, Roger. "Screen: 'Black Peter.'" New York Times 21 July
        1971:17.

The film is more appealing than when viewed six years earlier
because Forman's style now seems more original than imitative. Without
being too assertive, Forman presents a human comedy of brotherhood, a
tale about summer in a small town, amateur musical aspirations, and the
way people stumble on through life without being able to say what they
mean. Mostly reprinted in "Black Peter," Filmfacts (periodical, 1971).

146   Grenier, Cynthia. "Americans Sweep Prizes at Cannes Fete." New
        York Times 28 May 1971:20.

Notes Taking Off winning a special jury prize.

147   Hochman, Sandra. "Milos Forman Went Czeching Up on Our Generation
        Gap. . . ." New York Times 18 April 1971:D13.

Taking Off's main problem is that it will date quickly, though it
is funny and accurate. The film is concerned with how to define paradise and the search for a meaning of life that sets people free. The
youth-rock culture finally achieves sainthood.

148   Klemesrud, Judy. ". . . Lynn Went Along as Mom." New York Times
        18 April 1971:D13.

Summary of the life and career of Lynn Carlin, who plays Lynn in
Taking Off. Carlin liked working with Forman because he allowed her to
just play the role without analyzing it and feels that the film is a
tragedy, revealing the lack of morals that causes problem youngsters.

149   "Milos Forman: 'Everything I Have Heard Said About America in My
        Life is the Truth.'" London Times 9 June 1971:9.

Forman discusses making Taking Off with a minimum budget but a
maximum of freedom. Hippies were a popular topic, and Easy Rider's
success made this type of film possible. Talks about renting a theatre
to audition amateur girl singers and the power of agents.

150   Sweeny, Louise. ". . . and Czech Forman makes his first U.S.
      film." Christian Science Monitor 2 April 1971:4B.

      Taking Off fails because it reflects attitudes in 1968 that have
changed in 1971. Also, Forman's rhythm is too slow for the story's
humor.

151   Thomas, Kevin. "How Milos Forman's 'Taking Off' Almost Didn't."
      Los Angeles Times 9 May 1971:"Calendar,"16.

      Forman talks about the origins of Taking Off, casting and writing
the film, his struggle to have it produced, the differences between
small and large countries, and why some critics see his work as compassionate while others find it nasty. Forman sees Taking Off as a
mystery involving the question "Who murdered the family?" He plans for
his next film to be Bulletproof.

152   Taylor, John Russell. "Kozintsev's Lear: Distinction is Not
      Enough." London Times 5 October 1971:17.

      Briefly praises Taking Off.

Periodicals

153   Alpert, Hollis. "Parental Perplexity." Saturday Review 27 March
      1971:50.

      Taking the framework of an average teenage rebellion movie, Forman
adds warmth and understanding to make Taking Off valuable entertainment.
Mostly reprinted in "Taking Off," Filmfacts (periodical, 1971).

154   Benoit, Shelley. "Prototype For Hollywood's New Freedom." Show
      March 1971:24-26.

      Producer Ned Tanen describes his new unit at Universal, designed to
provide directors with small budgets and unlimited freedom, and the
financing of Taking Off.

155   "Black Peter." Filmfacts 14.20 (1971):521-22.

      Contains a plot summary, credits, and lengthy excerpts from reviews
originally published in Newsweek (periodical, 1971), New York Times
(newspaper, 1971), New York Daily News, and Variety (periodical, 1964).

156   Boyd, George N. "Unmotivated." Christian Century 15 September
      1971:1093.

      Because we cannot understand the characters' motivations in Taking
Off, we cannot laugh with them or benefit from them. The characters are
not believable and have no self-discoveries. The blending of pathos and
comedy does not work.

157   Brudnoy, David. "Iris' Head, Eric's Knee, Milos' Gap." National
      Review 27 July 1971:822-23.

Enough good scenes to make the film worth seeing, but Taking Off
relies too much on caricature, and some scenes are just plain wrong.
Reprinted in Whittemore and Cecchettini, Passport to Hollywood (book,
1976).

158   Cocks, Jay. "Low-Altitude Flight." Time 5 April 1971:86.

Forman relies on caricatures and bile and is overly condescending.
His exploiting of the teenagers in the audition sequences is crude.
Reprinted in Whittemore and Cecchettini, Passport to Hollywood (book,
1976), David Denby's Film 71/72 (book, 1972), and mostly reprinted in
"Taking Off," Filmfacts, 1971 (periodical).

159   Crist, Judith. "Doesn't Anybody Play Parcheesi Anymore?" New York
      5 April 1971:52-63.

Forman accurately captures American family relationships, and he
has an honest appreciation for youth. The opening sequences of Taking
Off are superb, but certain aspects of the parental characters do not
mesh.

160   Geist, Kenneth. "Taking Off." Show May 1971:52.

Forman maintains his droll Czech style in this anthropological
comedy. Using the audition here like he used the dances in his Czech
films, Forman reveals the ludicrous aspects of contemporary culture and
American adults. Buck Henry is outstanding.

161   Gilliatt, Penelope. "A Fist, with the Hand Itself." The New
      Yorker 3 April 1971:107-08.

Forman sees American adults as ludicrous, but he sees them sym-
pathetically. They are bound by simple conventions that they cannot
escape, even though they feel obligated to continually try. Forman
shows that the generation gap is based on human issues and not major
ones. Reprinted in Whittemore and Cecchettini, Passport to Hollywood
(book, 1976), David Denby's Film 71/72 (book, 1972), and in Gilliatt,
Unholy Fools (book, 1973).

162   Gow, Gordon. "A Czech in New York." Films and Filming 17.12
      (September 1971):20-24.

Forman discusses his reasons for coming to New York to film, why he
likes the city, and the basis for Bulletproof. Gow details specific
scenes from Forman's Czech films to illustrate both his gentle handling
of family tensions and his broadening satire in each picture. Forman's
comments provide insight to how he views New York in Taking Off.

163   Haskell, Molly. "Downfall parents." <u>Village Voice</u> 1 April
      1971:71,74.

Though <u>Taking Off</u> lacks the details of characterization that Forman
achieved in his Czech films, it combines comedy and satire without being
either too emotional or too derisive. Forman is expert in capturing
characters at points of emotional weakness and using editing to comment
on the distances between the parents and teenagers in his films.

164   Hatch, Robert. "Films." <u>The Nation</u> 19 April 1971:508-09.

In <u>Taking Off</u>, Forman oversimplifies the generation gap problem,
but he also reduces the pressures of contemporary conflicts. If he did
not treat everything as a joke, he could be a great director. Reprinted
in Whittemore and Cecchettini, <u>Passport to Hollywood</u> (book, 1976).

165   Houston, Penelope. "Festivals 1971: Cannes." <u>Sight and Sound</u>
      Summer 1971:136-38.

<u>Taking Off</u> is not so much an American film as a Forman film made in
America. Forman and cameraman Miroslav Ondricek have amazingly assimi-
lated American locations back to Czechoslovakia.

166   Kauffmann, Stanley. "An Apology." <u>New Republic</u> 24 April 1971:22,
      33.

In <u>Taking Off</u>, Forman tries to tell his generation gap story
through pictures, mainly close-ups, rather than words. He creates a
very middle-European view of New York as a place with an inflexible
class structure. The characters' motivations are sketched too lightly
to understand. Forman has some cinematic talents, but little control
over them. Lynn Carlin gives the only noteworthy performance.

167   Rowen, Bob. "Taking Off On the KEM." <u>American Cinemeditor</u> 21.3
      (Fall 1971):16-20.

Editor John Carter discusses how Forman insisted on his using a KEM
for his work on <u>Taking Off</u>. Carter reveals how he adjusted to the new
machine, its advantages over his old tools, and how he edited some of
the scenes.

168   Schickel, Richard. "Parents and kids without ogres." <u>Life</u> 2 April
      1971:12.

In <u>Taking Off</u>, Forman looks with compassion at both sides of the
generation gap, suggesting that Americans are tied up in problems they
cannot understand. The parents lead such a single-minded pursuit, they
never notice all the dangers they might fall prey to and willingly give
up their bourgeois attitudes if it will help them gain understanding.
Forman resists ridiculing them when they are vulnerable. The film's R
rating, barring the audience that could most benefit from it, is its
worst aspect.

169   Simon, John.   "Forman Against Man."   The New Leader 3 May
      1971:24-26.

Forman uses every opportunity to mock both the parents and the
young people in Taking Off and proclaim his own superiority. The acting
is terrible, and the whole film is an ugly and pointless exercise that
does not even have the courage of its most satiric convictions. Forman
pulls back whenever he has the chance to make a really devastating
point. Forman is morally deficient and only an imitation artist. His
followers are dupes and fools.

170   "Taking Off."   Filmfacts XIV.4 (1971):61-65.

Full credits, synopsis, summary of criticism, and lengthy excerpts
from reviews by Hollis Alpert (Saturday Review), Paul D. Zimmerman
(Newsweek), Jay Cocks (Time), and Charles Champlin (Los Angeles Times),
all 1971.

171   Westerbeck, Colin L., Jr.   "Lovers and Other Dangers."   Commonweal
      21 May 1971:261-63.

Watching average parents go crazy while reflecting all the worst
aspects of the youth counterculture in Taking Off is neither funny nor a
powerful insight. Forman merely exploits untalented young people in the
audition scenes.

172   "What Directors Are Saying."   Action   November/December 1971:22.

Forman is quoted as saying he enjoys all the technical and human
resources available to him in America, though he has increased anxieties
as well.

173   Wilson, David.   "Taking Off."   Sight and Sound Autumn 1971:221-222.

Taking Off is easily Forman's most enjoyable film. He takes a
bemused and tolerant look at his vulnerable characters, all selfishly
searching for their identities. Forman subtly explores the area between
what is said, what is meant, and what is understood. Reprinted in
Whittemore and Cecchettini, Passport to Hollywood (book, 1976).

174   Zimmerman, Paul D.   "Forman in the U.S.A."   Newsweek   5 April
      1971:92-93.

Taking Off includes many good moments, and the protagonists are
typically average people. However, Buck Henry and Lynn Carlin are
miscast, and the resolution of their marriage does not work. Reprinted
in Whittemore and Cecchettini, Passport to Hollywood (book, 1976), and
mostly reprinted in "Taking Off," Filmfacts, 1971 (periodical).

175   ------------.   "Games Young People Play."   Newsweek 2 August
      1971:75.

Milos Forman's Black Peter shows the director's humanist neutrality
and compassion for his characters, a fine understanding of young people,

and a natural documentary style.   Mostly reprinted in "Black Peter,"
Filmfacts   (periodical, 1971).

1972

Books

176   Cawkwell, Tim.   The World Encyclopedia of Film.   London: Studio
     Vista, 1972.

    Brief filmography and biographical notes.

177   Denby, David, ed.   Film 71/72.   New York: Simon and Schuster,
     1972.

    Contains reprints of Penelope Gilliatt's and Jay Cocks's reviews of
Taking Off (periodicals 1971).

178   "Forman, Milos."   Current Biography, 1971.   New York: The H. W.
     Wilson Company, 1972:138-40.

    Biographical article detailing Forman's family life, his experi-
ences at film school and in work with other Czech directors during the
fifties, the backgrounds to his own projects through Taking Off, his
thematic concerns, and his critical reception in the United States.

179   Froug, William.   The Screenwriter Looks at the Screenwriter.   New
     York: The Macmillan Company, 1972.

    Buck Henry talks about what Forman achieves by not letting his
actors memorize their lines.   The result is that actors must "behave"
because there are no important events to react to.   No scenes are designed to sum up the actions or cause an emotion.   Henry discusses one
scene from Taking Off in particular.   Reprinted in Whittemore and
Cecchettini, Passport to Hollywood (book, 1976).

180   Manvell, Roger, ed.   The International Encyclopedia of Film.   New
     York: Crown Publishers, Inc., 1972.

    Cites Forman as the dominant figure of the Czech New Wave in the
"Czechoslovakia" entry.   The entry on Forman comments on The Audition as
looking forward to some of his favorite themes, his other Czech films as
combining acute observation with a sense of the ridiculous, and Taking
Off as retaining much of his characteristic human sympathy.

181   Sadoul, Georges.   Dictionary of Filmmakers.   Berkeley: University
     of California Press, 1972.

    Brief entry on Forman's biography, style, and main themes through
Taking Off.

182   -------------. Dictionary of Films. Berkeley: University of
California Press, 1972.

Brief entry on Loves of a Blonde comments that Forman's consistent
vision of life and people can produce a full picture of humanity from a
small anecdote.

183   Willis, John. Screen World 1972. New York: Crown Publishers,
Inc., 1972.

Contains stills and full production credits from Taking Off.

Newspapers

184   "Directors to Do Film on '72 Olympics." Los Angeles Times 10 May
1972:IV:21.

Announcement of the directors scheduled to contribute to Visions of
Eight.

185   "Filming the Olympics." Washington Post 4 June 1972:G9.

Producer David Wolper reveals plans for filming the Olympics.
Forman's topic is not yet known.

186   Weiler, A. H. "Milos Forman Takes Off Again." New York Times 17
December 1972:II:19.

Paul Zimmerman talks about the script for The Autograph Hunter,
co-written with Forman and planned for production in 1973. Zimmerman
later used the idea as the basis for Martin Scorsese's King of Comedy.

Periodicals

187   "Milos Forman, Ingrid Thulin." Dialogue on Film 3 (1972):1-14.

In a group interview, Forman discusses the advantages and dis-
advantages of working with professional and nonprofessional actors,
aided in his remarks by Lynn Carlin (Lynn Tyne in Taking Off). Forman
discusses the origins of the film, the filming of the audition
sequences, and his work with his director of cinematography, Miroslav
Ondricek.

188   "Shooting the Olympics." Newsweek 11 September 1972:85.

Summary of producer David Wolper's plans for Visions of Eight and
his reasons for making the film. Forman refers to the decathlon as the
most heroic of all the events.

189   Zimmerman, Paul D. "A Last Look at 1971's Movies." Newsweek 3
January 1972:33.

Refers to Taking Off as a charitable look at America's generation
gap that delivers belly laughs with style.

1973

Books

190   Casty, Alan.   _Development of the Film: An Interpretive History._
      New York: Harcourt, Brace, Jovanovich, Inc., 1973.

      Forman's Czech films comment with humor and sympathy on the
pathetic pettiness of life and the frailties of bureaucracy. _Taking Off_
has more humanity than most fashionable films about the generation gap.

191   Gilliatt, Penelope.   _Unholy Wits, Comics, Disturbers of the Peace._
      New York: Viking Press, 1973.

      Contains a reprint of her review of _Taking Off_ from the April 1971
New Yorker.

192   Hooker, Charlotte S.   "The Feature Films of Milos Forman: A
      Bibliography of the Literature." ERIC Document ED087053:1973.

      A listing of dictionaries, encyclopedias, yearbooks, books, and
articles containing material about Forman and his films.

193   Kusin, V. V., ed., _The Czechoslovak Reform Movement: 1968._ Santa
      Barbara, CA: Clio Press, 1973.

      A collection of symposium essays, including one by Antonin J. Liehm
describing the important role played by Czech film and literature in the
reform movement and how artists were able to form organizations to
protect their own interests.

194   Robinson, David.   _World Cinema: A Short History._ London: Eyre
      Methuen, 1973.

      Cites Forman as the most significant talent of the Czech New Wave.
His Czech films showed the absurdity and dignity of the average individual and became increasingly sombre and symbolic throughout the sixties.

Newspapers

195   Allen, Neil.   "Decathlon Finds Its Voice in Beethoven's Ninth."
      London Times 3 August 1973:12.

      Praises _Visions of Eight_ for its lack of commentary and Forman's
The Decathlon for finally giving proper tribute to the event.

196   Champlin, Charles.   "Olympics as an Art Form." _Los Angeles Times_
      17 August 1973:IV:1.

      Visions of Eight reminds viewers that there is more to sports than
winning. Forman's segment will be the most disputed because of its
hilarious and unrespectful comedy.

197 Greenspan, Roger. "The Screen: New 'Visions of Eight' Studies
     Olympics." New York Times 11 August 1973:25.

     The film as a whole is unable to deal with the killing of eleven
Israeli athletes by Arab terrorists during the Games. Forman speeds up
everything in his satiric segment on the decathlon, the worst in the
film.

198 English, Priscella. "Visions of Humor From Milos Forman." Los
     Angeles Times 11 November 1973:"Calendar,"24,35.

     Forman explains his theme in The Decathlon of the event being just
like life. He was interested mainly in the athlete's faces. He sees
humor as universal and valuable as a means of dealing with problems.
Totalitarians lack the ability to laugh at themselves. Forman also
discusses his reliance on Buck Henry during the filming of Taking Off,
his screenplay for The Autograph Hunter, and the nature of self-irony
versus self-pity. Self-irony requires action.

199 Sweeny, Louise. "Screen Poetry." Christian Science Monitor 11
     August 1973:18.

     Forman uses music for comic effect in The Decathlon and does not
take the subject too seriously.

Periodicals

200 Brudnoy, David. "Obsessions 3." National Review 12 October
     1973:1127.

     Visions of Eight provides a beautiful view of athletes not
available in televised sports.

201 Coleman, John. "Game Pie." New Statesman 7 September 1973:324.

     Visions of Eight is an aimless and characterless film that is too
much self-conscious art about athletes in motion. Milos Forman's The
Decathlon is mere self-parody that provides amusing relief.

202 Fabricant, Gerry. "Visions of 8." Show October 1973:32-35.

     Mainly about producer David Wolper's inspiration for and organiza-
tion of the project. Also comments on Forman's research for The
Decathlon.

203 Kauffmann, Stanley. "On Films." New Republic 15 September
     1973:22,33.

     On the whole, Visions of Eight is remarkable. But Milos Forman's
The Decathlon is so full of hokey camerawork and so devoid of sympathy
that it quickly becomes a detestable bore. Reprinted in Kauffmann's
Living Images (book, 1975).

204 Plimpton, George. "Olympic Visions of Eight." <u>Sports Illustrated</u>
     27 August 1973:30-35.

     Brief description of David Wolper's organization of the project.
Forman's focus changed from a twelve-minute film of a rifleman's trigger
finger to the high jump to the decathlon. <u>The Decathlon</u> is full of
startling personal tricks. Forman skillfully uses music as a supporting
structure.

205 "Visions of Eight." <u>Variety</u> 30 May 1973:12.

     Forman juxtaposes music and sports, sometimes gratuitously, for the
purposes of comic relief in <u>The Decathlon</u>.

                              1974
Books

206 Liehm, Antonin J. <u>Closely Watched Films: The Czechoslovak
     Experience</u>. White Plains, NY: International Arts and Sciences
     Press, Inc., 1974.

     A collection of interviews with Czech directors, including a
two-part discussion with Forman, Liehm discusses factors contributing to
the New Wave. Forman, in the first part, just back from America, the
Oscars, and dealing with Carlo Ponti, talks about the problems of being
successful and maintaining artistic integrity. In the second half,
recorded late in 1969, he discusses the problems of writing his first
American film and how business considerations sap emotions from Western
films that artistic freedom would seem to allow them. The Czech situation had been ideal, and, though art will not triumph there either,
Forman wants to make one film in America and then return.

207 Stoil, Michael Jon. <u>Cinema Beyond the Danube: The Camera and Its
     Politics</u>. Metuchen, NJ: The Scarecrow Press, Inc., 1974.

     A study of the history and political content of Eastern European
cinema. Includes a lengthy definition and examples of Soviet socialist
realism. In brief comments on Czech film, Stoil cites the national
culture as one that has long emphasized a humanistic look at the daily
lives of ordinary people. Forman's <u>Black Peter</u> and <u>Loves of a Blonde</u>
provide clear examples of realistic films combining satire with sympathy
for youth looking for romance in a cold society.

Dissertations

208 Lipton, Leonard J. "A Critical Study of the Filmmaking Style of
     Milos Forman with Special Emphasis on His Contributions to Film
     Comedy." Ph.D. Dissertation: University of Southern California,
     1974.

     Lipton compares scenes from Forman's films to similar ones from
films by Charlie Chaplin and Harold Lloyd to demonstrate Forman's use of
American silent comedy techniques such as the chase scene and the

"topper." He discusses how Forman develops the thematic importance of his comedy through his use of nonprofessional actors, his screenwriting process, his cinematography, editing, and other aspects of filmmaking. Lipton then compares Forman's work with other highly-regarded contemporary comedies to demonstrate how his work gets the viewer emotionally involved and relates closely to the daily situations of average people.

Periodicals

209   "Laff With, Not At, Mental Patients." Variety 12 April 1974:7.

Producer Michael Douglas discusses working with Oregon state officials and his desire for independent financing so the major studios will not take control away. History of the project given. Distribution is waiting the signing of the lead actor.

1975

Books

210   Cowie, Peter. "Milos Forman." 50 Major Film-makers. New York: A. S. Barnes and Co., 1975:88-91.

Brief biography and analysis of Forman's style through accounts of all of his films from Competition (1963) through The Decathlon (1973). Cowie stresses Forman's ability to capture the universal within individual people and moments. The youngsters and old people in his Czech films become representative of the way society abuses people of those age groups. His middle-aged characters are stubborn, except in Taking Off (1971) where they resign themselves to a low spot in the social world. Forman reveals a lot by focusing on private expressions in public settings.

211   Doctorow, E. L. Ragtime New York: Random House, 1975.

Novel that is the basis of Milos Forman's 1981 film of the same title.

212   Kauffmann, Stanley. Living Images. New York: Harper and Row, 1975.

Contains a reprint of his Visions of Eight review from the September 15, 1973 New Republic.

213   Liehm, Antonin J. The Milos Forman Stories. White Plains, NY: International Arts and Sciences Press, Inc., 1975.

Forman recalls personal stories about his life and work, and Liehm provides reviews for each film from Competition through Taking Off. Forman also comments on various aspects of filmmaking. Many insights into life and work in Czechoslovakia.

Newspapers

214   Arnold, Gary.   "Pain, Not Laughter, Rules the Roost in 'Cuckoo's
      Nest.'"   Washington Post   17 December 1975:C1,C15.

      Forman's emphasis on realism makes his work more somber than Ken
Kesey's novel. This approach creates an ensemble atmosphere that Jack
Nicholson and Louise Fletcher do not dominate despite their fine performances. Brad Dourif is particularly good in making his cliched
character human.

215   Canby, Vincent.   "'Cuckoo's Nest'--A Sane Comedy About Psychotics."
      New York Times   23 November 1975:II:1,15.

      Forman succeeds because he refrains from creating a simple analogy
between the institution and society and does not emphasize social
themes. The ending is awkward and the presentation of hospital prac-
tices is questionable. Nicholson sets the tone and illuminates the
performances of all the others. Reprinted in The National Society of
Film Critics on Movie Comedy, 1977 (book).

216   ------------.   "Nicholson, the Free Spirit of 'Cuckoo.'"   New York
      Times 20 November 1975:52.

      Nicholson and Louise Fletcher give excellent performances, as do
many others, and Forman is at his best when he uses comedy to challenge
our notions of sanity. But the attempt to explain America in terms of a
mental institution does not work. The ending is unbelievable.

217   Champlin, Charlie.   "'Cuckoo's Nest' Revisited."   Los Angeles Times
      21 November 1975:IV:1.

      On second viewing, the ensemble performance and Jack Nicholson's
acting in particular are even more astounding than with the first attendance. Nicholson plays McMurphy as a man who knows he is putting up a
large facade and occasionally reveals the emptiness behind it. A long
close-up of Nicholson at the end of the party scene is a key shot in the
film.

218   ------------.   "Nicholson Hatches Gold Ego in 'Nest.'"   Los
      Angeles Times 16 November 1975:"Calendar,"1,28.

      Jack Nicholson and Louise Fletcher powerfully reveal their charac-
ters in Cuckoo's Nest's clash of the individual versus authority. The
ensemble performance provides a sense of watching characters and not
actors. Forman produces a moving combination of comedy and tragedy in
the party sequence especially.

219   Davidson, Bill.   "The Conquering Antihero."   New York Times Sunday
      Magazine 12 October 1975:18-36.

      Discusses Jack Nicholson's life and career from poverty and low-
budget films in the fifties and sixties to stardom in Easy Rider (1971)
and his desire to direct. Nicholson prepared for his Cuckoo's Nest role

by totally losing himself in the life of the mental ward two weeks
before shooting.   Forman praises him highly, saying it is impossible to
tell whether he is sane or insane in the film.   Comments also on
Nicholson's hero-worship and his rebellion against being labelled an
anti-hero type.

220   Denby, David.   "'Cuckoo's Nest' is Just an Adolescent Fantasy."
      New York Times   21 December 1975:II:17.

Ken Kesey's novel equated insanity with moral weakness and sexual
repression, and the movie preserves these notions.   Both are mysoginist
in presenting men who need to defeat an oppressive feminine spirit to
gain their freedom.   Forman exploits the patients for grotesque comedy
and Nicholson shows no irony in his hero role.   The movie is dangerous
as an appeal to adolescent fantasies about rebellion as an answer.

221   Donnelly, Tom.   "Getting a 'Chameleon' to Show His Colors."
      Washington Post 7 December 1975:G1,G7.

At a group interview, Jack Nicholson tells what he learned about
mental institutions while making Cuckoo's Nest, how he copes with his
celebrity status, his conception of McMurphy as someone who will fight
for his fellow man, and his desire to work on films that are interesting but not necessarily commercial.

222   Harmetz, Aljean.   "The Nurse Who Rules the 'Cuckoo's Nest.'"   New
      York Times   30 November 1975:2:13.

Discussion of Lousie Fletcher's life and career.   Her isolation as
a child, growing up with deaf parents, led to her career choices and
ability to handle the isolation of her role as Nurse Ratched.   She
portrays Ratched's monstrousness with subtlety and humanness.   Forman
selected her after accidentally seeing her in Robert Altman's Thieves
Like Us.

223   Levine, Richard.   "A Real Mental Ward Becomes a Movie 'Cuckoo's
      Nest.'"   New York Times 13 April 1975:2:1,15.

Discussion of activities on and off the Cuckoo's Nest set, the
film's public relations director trying his best to put a good face on
life in the mental ward, and reactions of patients who decide that the
film people are not as crazy as they had suspected.   Also, discussion of
filming process and scenes eventually not used.

224   Lichtenstein, Grace.   "Telluride Festival in Colorado Forms a Peak
      for Movie Buffs."   New York Times 2 September 1975:34.

Forman professes his admiration for the festival because of its
lack of hype.

225   Sterritt, David. "Jack Nicholson's latest: boisterous but
      humane." Christian Science Monitor 4 December 1975:43.

      Forman's focus on faces shifts the film from lyrical to horrifying
and emphasizes compassion for the men suffering in Cuckoo's Nest's
mental institution. The film sometimes accepts McMurphy's lunacy too
willingly.

226   "What 'Sting' or 'Godfather II' in the Holiday Package?" Washing-
      ton Post 14 December 1975:G5.

      Brief production history and plot summary of Cuckoo's Nest. Forman
mutes the novel's humor and poetry, achieving an emotionally powerful
sense of intimacy.

Periodicals

227   Barbaro, Rick. "Loves of a Blonde." Cinema Texas: Program Notes
      9.4 (Fall 1975):61-65.

      Forman uses simplistic characters and an unobtrusive filming style
to comment on people's common needs for escape, love, dignity, and
freedom. Politically, the film argues for a liberal communism, but
Forman's focus is mainly on the individual. Forman enjoyed working in
Czechoslovakia until 1968, when he became disenchanted. Loves shows he
is more against callousness and selfishness than stupidity, and he is
for tolerance and understanding.

228   Cahill, Tim. "Knocking Around the Nest." Rolling Stone 4 December
      1975:48-54,87-88.

      Jack Nicholson and others talk about the problems of keeping their
sanity on the Cuckoo's Nest set and the similarities of the patients to
people in the outside world. These problems make distinguishing sanity
from insanity difficult. Michael Douglas tells why he chose Forman to
direct, and Douglas and Forman discuss selecting cast and crew. Having
good public relations during filming was important, and two bad incidents did occur. During filming, Nicholson discovered that some of the
hospital's most brutal methods are justified. But out of these
depressing conditions, Forman has created an optimistic film about the
triumph of the human spirit.

229   Cowie, Peter. "One Flew Over the Cuckoo's Nest." Focus on Film
      23.6 (Winter 1975):4-5.

      Forman opens and closes the film with images of freedom and fills
it completely with pain and suffering in between, proving in the process
that he has mastered the American idiom. Forman's theme is not new, but
his ability to observe individual foibles and turn the audience's
laughter from the patients to the hospital staff and, ultimately, to get
viewers to question themselves makes his films outstanding. His opposi-
tion of Jack Nicholson's crazy individualism against Louise Fletcher's

well-mannered oppressiveness produces the film's biggest irony: McMurphy is finally being punished because he is normal.

230   Eyles, Allen.   "Milos Forman."   Focus on Film   23.6 (Winter 1975):5.

    Biographical sketch including the comment that Forman's current project is Someone is Killing the Great Chefs of Europe.

231   Haskell, Molly.   "Nicholson Kneads a Fine Madness."   Village Voice 1 December 1975:136,126-27.

    Jack Nicholson is nothing short of miraculous as R. P. McMurphy. He performs his virile male hero role with too much ironic self-awareness to be offensive.   Fletcher displays Nurse Ratched as a traumatized human being, and Forman naturally handles the ensemble acting excellently.   Only the message, a struggle of the hip versus the dull, is ordinary.   Forman talks about the therapeutic effects of the filming for patients of the Oregon State Hospital, his dislike of a subjective camera viewpoint, and his Nurse Ratched as a dangerous authoritarian, fearful of losing her power.   Partially reprinted in Film Review Digest Annual (book, 1976).

232   Hatch, Robert.   "Films."   Nation 29 November 1975:573-74.

    Cuckoo's Nest is entertaining and inventive but has no depth.   Too much of a fairy tale to be useful as an attack on mental institutions, but one wonders why hospital superintendent Dr. Dean Brooks allowed his institution to be presented so horrifically.   Partially reprinted in Film Review Digest Annual (book, 1976).

233   Jacobson, Harlan.   "Lag In Filming Lunacy Symbolism."   Variety 26 November 1975:21.

    Production history of Cuckoo's Nest related by co-producers Michael Douglas and Saul Zaentz.   Story began in early sixties when actor Kirk Douglas (star of the stage version) attempted to contact Milos Forman in Czechoslovakia about directing the film but failed.   In the early seventies, Douglas sold the rights to his son Michael, who got together with Zaentz at Fantasy Records.   Zaentz supplied original capital.   Later, United Artists came in on the production.   Ken Kesey wrote a script that was rejected, but Zaentz gave him a part of the production anyway. Forman entered as director because he and the producers agreed the film should have a realistic production.

234   Kael, Pauline.   "The Bull Goose Loony."   The New Yorker 1 December 1975:131-36.

    High praise for Jack Nicholson and Louise Fletcher.   Both give excellent, understated performances.   Forman wisely gives the story a realistic setting, but he is callous in presenting the men as inept and insensitive.   The film is good, but lacks the visual energy a Scorsese could have given it.   Reprinted in Kael's When the Lights Go Down (book, 1980).

235 Kauffmann, Stanley. "Jack High." New Republic 13 December
     1975:22-23.

     Cuckoo's Nest is warped, sentimental, and dangerous. The analogy
of the mental hospital with society is simplistic and burdensome, But
Jack Nicholson is tremendous as McMurphy, handling a wide range of
emotions. Milos Forman treats the material sensitively, giving it a
perfect texture and casting expertly.

236 Kroll, Jack. "You're All Right, Jack." Newsweek 24 November
     1975:113-113A.

     Forman necessarily simplifies Cuckoo's Nest, giving it shape and
clarity. He creates an effective comedy of manners, but loses the
terror, black humor, and complexity that made the novel a riveting
allegory. But Jack Nicholson gives his greatest performance, and
Forman directs the cast superbly. Partially reprinted in Film Review
Digest Annual (book, 1976).

237 "One Flew Over The Cuckoo's Nest." Variety 19 November 1975:18.

     Cuckoo's Nest succeeds in being potent and contemporary despite
being loaded with irrelevant themes. Performances and production are
excellent.

238 "Oregon Mental Hospital Site For Mike Douglas Film Of 'Cuckoo'
     Play." Variety 29 January 1975:28.

     Production history of Cuckoo's Nest and mention of Hal Ashby as
previous choice for director. Douglas says Forman was selected because
of his talents for black comedy and naturalism.

239 Schickel, Richard. "Aborted Flight." Time 1 December 1975:68.

     Cuckoo's Nest attempts only to please its viewers and capture the
surfaces of asylum life. The film shows none of Ken Kesey's understanding of the subtleties of revolutions and revolutionaries. The
characters lack the depth and dramatic power that they have in the
novel.

240 Simon, John. "Unholy Writs." New York 1 December 1975:80-83.

     Forman's adaptation of Cuckoo's Nest lacks the mythic power of the
novel. Forman is somewhat humane in his approach, but his characters
lack clear motivation for their blatant actions. The film needs to be
both more plain and more subtle.

241 Sturhahn, Larry. "One Flew Over the Cuckoo's Nest: An Interview
     With Milos Forman." Filmmaker's Newsletter December 1975:26-31.

     Forman discusses how he works with writers, casts, and crews,
mainly in terms of Cuckoo's Nest. Much information here about lighting,
sound, casting, scheduling, and editing. Forman also explains his
considerate attitude towards his characters. He first assumes they are
good and then lets reality take over.

242   Walker, Beverly.   "Cuckoo's Nest."   Sight and Sound   44.4
      (1975):216–17.

Notes on the production of the film and how Forman handled the
issues of depicting mental illness and coping with cinematographer
Haskell Wexler.   Forman defined mental illness as the inability to
adjust to ever-changing, unwritten social rules; thus, it is a social
disease.   He was forced to fire Wexler, who did not appreciate a comic
approach to the material.   Forman also differed with screenwriter
Lawrence Hauben, who wanted a less realistic approach.   Walker also
discusses the behavior of Jack Nicholson on the set, the selection and
acting of the rest of the cast, and Forman's handling of the part of
Nurse Ratched.

                                  1976

Books

243   Armes, Roy.   The Ambiguous Image: Narrative Style in Modern
      European Cinema.   Bloomington: Indiana University Press, 1976.

Forman is part of a group of filmmakers who began working in the
context of divergence from traditional narrative forms in the early 60s.
These directors all have a strong knowledge of film, and their works
often relate more to other films than to reality.   They explore new
relationships between film and reality through their self-reflexive
films.   Nevertheless, Forman's attraction by Hollywood reveals his
basically traditional nature, placing him outside the scope of modern-
ity.   His films, though funny and skillful, lack the questioning of
cinema itself evident in the work of other modernist directors.   Taking
Off provides a good example.

244   Bauden, Liz-Anne, ed.   The Oxford Companion to Film.   New York:
      Oxford University Press, 1976.

Brief biographical entry on Forman.   Cites Competition as exemplifying his main themes and methods: a focus on generational conflicts, an implicit social criticism, an unrelenting eye for detail and
posturing, a rooting in Czech tradition of black humor, a use of other
art forms, and a use of cinema-verité influences in incorporating non-
actors and documentary footage.   Entry on cinematographer Miroslav
Ondricek tells how his association with Forman began in 1958.

245   Mast, Gerald.   A Short History of the Movies.   Indianapolis, IN:
      The Bobbs-Merrill Co., Inc., 1976.

Brief history of Czech cinema and comments about how Forman's
comedies examine the follies of youth and boredom of adults in three
important social settings: the dance hall, the kitchen, and the
bedroom.

246 "One Flew Over the Cuckoo's Nest." Film Review Digest Annual 1976.
     Millwood, NY: KJO Press, 1976:243-47.

     Includes production credits and excerpts from reviews in the
     Saturday Review, Film Information, Women's Wear Daily, New York, the New
     York Post, the Christian Science Monitor, the Los Angeles Times, the
     Village Voice, Newsweek, the Nation, the Sunday Times (London), The
     Times (London), Films in Review, Take One, and the Monthly Film
     Bulletin.

247 Sherman, Eric. Directing the Film: Film Directors on Their Art.
     Boston: Little, Brown and Company, 1976.

     Forman talks about how Taking Off came to be focused on the adults,
     how he likes to work with at least two co-writers, how he works with
     nonprofessional actors, and how a director of photography is preferable
     to a cameraman.

248 Thomson, David. A Biographical Dictionary of Film. New York:
     William Morrow and Co., Inc., 1976.

     Cites Forman's influences as Italian neo-realism, Karel Reisz,
     Lindsay Anderson, and American silent comedy, as well as cinema-verité.
     Forman fit spontaneity into traditional narratives. His Czech films
     show a love for his characters without exploring them or their environ-
     ment too deeply. Taking Off avoids the cliches of most American genera-
     tion gap films, but Forman's very skill makes his affection for the
     characters seem forced.

249 Whittemore, Don and Philip Alan Cecchettini. Passport to
     Hollywood. New York: McGraw-Hill, 1976.

     One chapter about Forman. Original essay includes insightful
     comments about the economic and ideological factors behind the rise and
     fall of the Czech New Wave. Biographical information about Forman's
     life and early career. Remarks on Black Peter focus on Forman's con-
     centration on the family, adolescence, and sexuality, his departure from
     socialist realism, and the unavoidable political dimensions to the work.
     The authors mention Cuckoo's Nest as a departure in terms of using
     mainly professional actors, a different cinematographer, and a novel as
     the basis for the work. But they spend most of their time discussing
     Taking Off. These remarks include descriptions of how Forman researched
     and wrote the script, his filming methods, what he discovered from his
     research, and his balancing of documentary realism with comic absurdity
     in an intriguing manner that never reveals a simplistic answer to the
     situation. Remainder of the chapter includes a reprint of the Joseph
     Gelmis interview and several reviews of Taking Off.

250 Willis, John. Screen World 1976. New York: Crown Publishers,
     Inc., 1976.

     Contains stills and full production credits from Cuckoo's Nest.

Newspapers

251   Burke, Tom. "Forman: 'Casting is Everything.'" New York Times 28
      March 1976:2:1,15.

Forman discusses selecting actors for Cuckoo's Nest who were
naturally crazy but would not try to accentuate it, working with Jack
Nicholson and Louise Fletcher, and the importance of winning an Oscar.

252   Canby, Vincent. "Can a Director Grow on Foreign Soil?" New York
      Times 2 May 1976:2:13.

Comments that Forman seems to have found a place in America, but
Taking Off and Cuckoo's Nest lack the resonance of his Czech films.

253   "Five Oscars for Film About Mental Hospital." London Times 31
      March 1976:6.

Includes comments by Nicholson and Forman upon winning their
Oscars for Cuckoo's Nest.

254   Gussow, Mel. "Easy Actor's Road Was Hard Riding." New York Times
      2 January 1976:16.

Brief review of Jack Nicholson's career and his desire to create an
entirely new character with each role. For Cuckoo's Nest, he became so
involved with patients that recognizing any member of the cast as sane
was difficult by the end. Nicholson drew on his experience of working
with schizophrenics for the role and did not realize the huge transi-
tions within scenes that it required when he first read the script.

255   Higham, Charles. "How 'Ragtime' Led to Discord." New York Times
      26 September 1976:2:1,15,39.

Description of the disputes between Dino DeLaurentiis (producer),
Robert Altman (original director), and E. L. Doctorow (author) over the
filming of Ragtime. DeLaurentiis fired Altman and hired Forman after
the success of Cuckoo's Nest, which angered Doctorow. The author was
also angry about reports that Coalhouse Walker, Jr., a black rebel, was
to be the film's central figure. Forman denies those reports, and
DeLaurentiis states that he and Doctorow are working on a new outline of
the film together.

256   "An Irish Winner." London Times 23 September 1976:13.

Notes that Cuckoo's Nest is all-time box-office champion in Eire.

257   Kermode, Frank. "Men, women, and madness." The London Times
      Literary Supplement 19 March 1976:318.

Forman's alteration of Cuckoo's Nest's narration from the schizophrenic Chief Bromden to an "objective reality" makes the film a
simplified myth. Forman does away with symbols and attaches the film to
the characters' faces, which are worth taking seriously. Other than
that, the film follows a crude sexual and spiritual mythic structure.

258   Ledbetter, Les.   "Kesey, at Oregon Farm, Mulls Over Screen Rights."
      New York Times 31 March 1976:26.

Cuckoo's Nest author complains that producer Michael Douglas broke
a verbal agreement with him about his percentage of the film's gross
income and amount of control over the adaptation. His novel was about
Chief Bromden's struggle for manhood and America as a conspiracy. Both
topics were cut out of the film, and Kesey planned to sue for a higher
percentage plus damages. The failure of any of the film's Oscar winners
to thank him ruined their chance to avoid a suit.

259   Lichtenstein, Grace.   "He Refuses to be an 'Ugh-Tonto' Indian."
      New York Times 6 June 1976:2:13.

Will Sampson, who played Chief Bromden in Cuckoo's Nest, talks
about his life and career, mostly as a painter. Sampson changed his
character by convincing Forman that Bromden was an educated man with
perfect diction. Forman and Jack Nicholson praise him as a natural
actor.

260   Lindsay, Robert.   "'Cuckoo's Nest' Wins Top 3 Oscars."   New York
      Times 30 March 1976:38.

Reports mainly on Jack Nicholson's and Lousie Fletcher's reactions
upon receiving their awards for Best Actor and Best Actress.

261   Murphy, Mark.   "Backstage at the Oscar Aftermath."   Los Angeles
      Times 31 March 1976:IV:1,16.

Forman's appearance with his twin sons, whom he had not seen in
five years, provides a touching moment. Cuckoo's Nest leads Jack
Nicholson and Louise Fletcher answer questions about their feelings.
Describes the press situation at the Oscars.

262   Norvaez, Alfonso A.   "Oscar Winners Return For Passaic Festivi-
      ties." New York Times 1 May 1976:59.

Forman accompanies Cuckoo's Nest co-producer Saul Zaentz and associate Bernard Lieberman at ceremonies honoring them in their hometown.

263   Norman, Philip.   "King Leer." The Sunday Times (London) 15
      February 1976:32.

Brief biography of Jack Nicholson, his struggles to succeed, and
his significance now that he has.

264   Powell, Dilys.   "Rebel Behind Bars." The Sunday Times (London) 24
      February 1976:35.

Cuckoo's Nest is a film about power and those who have failed to
escape from it. Forman is thinking about his former Czech colleagues in
the film, though he has now become an international director. Partially
reprinted in Film Review Digest Annual (book, 1976).

265   Robertson, Nan. "The Fletchers: Family That Heard the Silent
      Thanks." New York Times 5 April 1976:36.

   Account of the lives of Louise Fletcher's parents, both deaf since
childhood, their struggles in raising four children, and their reactions
to her winning an Oscar for Cuckoo's Nest.

266   Robinson, David. "Pleasures and Perils of Pastiche." London Times
      27 February 1976:11.

   Basically, a plot summary of Cuckoo's Nest. Forman blends comedy
and tragedy as skillfully as in his Czech films and uses the hospital as
a metaphor for society.

267   Shales, Tom. "'Cuckoo's Nest' Flies With Top Four Oscars."
      Washington Post 30 March 1976:131,137.

   Forman, Jack Nicholson, Louise Fletcher, and the film all win.
Forman also gets to see his sons for the first time in five years. Full
account of the ceremonies.

268   ------------. "The Nesting of a Golden 'Cuckoo' Egg and Other
      Reel-Life Stories." Washington Post 18 April 1976:K1,K5.

   Although Cuckoo's Nest was already a huge success before the
Oscars, United Artists' marketing strategy was timed perfectly to capi-
talize heavily after the awards. Due to its subject (mental illness),
the film began with limited engagements and built a critical reputation.
Then, UA produced 165 additional prints and booked broadly after the
popular success. Theater owners grumbled about the percentage split,
but most willingly accepted the terms.

269   Sterritt, David. "Jack Nicholson." Christian Science Monitor 31
      March 1976:14.

   Nicholson discusses the benefits of his many years working in
B-pictures, how he identifies with his characters but wants to be
thought of as separate from them, and how he tries to portray a totally
unique character in each new film. He liked his role in Cuckoo's Nest
as McMurphy because the film has a very human appeal.

270   ------------. "Louise Fletcher--Before and After the Oscars."
      Christian Science Monitor 12 May 1976:29.

   Fletcher discusses why she chose to not work for eleven years from
1962-1973, how her looks were a disadvantage when she started her career
in the fifties, why she chooses to work now, how she and Forman con-
ceived of Nurse Ratched as a well-intentioned character, and how she
hopes for good roles in the future.

271   ------------. "Oscar-winning director stresses faces, not camera
      tricks." Christian Science Monitor 1 April 1976:26.

   Forman mentions that he was unaware of Cuckoo's Nest's reputation
when he decided to make the film. He finds the story and characters

much like those of his other films, but chooses not to analyze himself. Forman expresses his preference for believable characters in under-standable stories and his admiration for the American film industry.

272   Thackrey, Ted, Jr. "Oscars Fly to 'Cuckoo's Nest.'" Los Angeles Times 30 March 1976:1,3.

Announcement of Academy Awards winners including responses by Forman, Jack Nicholson (Best Actor), and Louis Fletcher (Best Actress).

273   "The Times Diary." London Times 10 February 1976:14.

Jack Nicholson, in London to promote Cuckoo's Nest, says it may be the only serious film of the year. Producer Michael Douglas made the right contacts to bring it to the screen. A psychiatrist felt it showed American treatments to be as bad as Russian.

274   Warga, Wayne. "'Cuckoo's Nest' Tops Oscar List." Los Angeles Times 18 February 1976:IV:2:11.

Lists all nominations.

275   Wordsworth, Araminta. "Watch how they react." Times Educational Supplement 5 March 1976:86.

Some will object to the idea of laughing at mental patients, but Milos Forman has once more made a successful and funny film about the effects of institutions on the human spirit in Cuckoo's Nest. Although the film is handsome and never boring, it is not outstanding. The performances by Jack Nicholson and Louise Fletcher really carry it.

276   Zion, Sidney. "2 Who Flew Over the Cuckoo's Nest." New York Times 16 May 1976:I:10-11.

Account of co-producer Saul Zaentz and associates Bernard Lieberman telling of childhood memories at ceremonies honoring them in Passaic, NJ, their hometown.

Periodicals

277   "Adaptors Honor Adaptors, Ignore Original Authors; 'Kesey Will Get His Share.'" Variety 7 April 1976:6,40.

Ken Kesey, author of Cuckoo's Nest, argues he has not received 5 percent of box-office gross from the film and is further piqued that no Oscar winner except Forman mentioned him. Producer Saul Zaentz replies that Kesey never submitted an acceptable script and does not understand what he was promised. Zaentz claims that no one involved with Cuckoo's Nest has been paid yet.

278   "After His 'Cuckoo' Smash Milos Forman No Longer Now On a 'Rain
      Czech.'" Variety 3 March 1976:5.

      Forman explains he is trying to choose a new project and complains
that too many reports falsely state he is working on a specific film.

279   Byron, Stuart. "The Industry: Martyr Complexes." Film Comment
      July/August 1976:29-30.

      Author Ken Kesey (Cuckoo's Nest) seems to be actively pursuing a
martyr status. His complaints about not getting enough money from the
movie neglect the fact that sales of the novel skyrocketed with the
film's popularity, and Kesey was fortunate in being allowed even a
minimal share of film profits.

280   "Cloudcuckooland for the Oscars." Time 12 April 1976:58,61.

      Account of how Michael Douglas took over production from his father
Kirk and got Jack Nicholson to play McMurphy, how Forman selected Louise
Fletcher for the role of Nurse Ratched and acted so detached on the set
that few actors mentioned him at the awards ceremony, and how Ken Kesey
believes he was cheated.

281   Coleman, John. "You All Crazy?" New Statesman 27 February
      1976:269-70.

      Cuckoo's Nest is remarkable, entertaining, and as good as anything
Forman has ever done. Doing away with Chief Bromden as narrator was
right, and the details are all amusing. A problem is that the patients
are all too passive and available for comedy. Also, Forman should have
pursued the near-complicity between McMurphy and Nurse Ratched.

282   Crist, Judith. "The Movies: Kubrick as Novelist." Saturday
      Review 10 January 1976:61,64.

      Cuckoo's Nest all fits together well. The performances are fine.
There is just nothing below the surface. Forman just shows another free
spirit beaten down by the system and laughs at the mentally ill besides.
Partially reprinted in Film Review Digest Annual (book, 1976).

283   "'Cuckoo': Before and After Win." Variety 14 April 1976:3.

      Cites the improvement in box-office for Cuckoo's Nest in several
major markets after winning five Oscars.

284   Dawson, Jan. "Milos Forman's One Flew Over the Cuckoo's Nest: A
      Conflict of Styles." Take One 5.1 (1976):28-31.

      Forman captures the surface of the novel, but not its spirit. The
comedy merely clashes with the realism of the sets, and the violent
episodes are unexplainable in the context of the comedy. Partially
reprinted in Film Review Digest Annual (book, 1976).

285   Farber, Stephen.   "Americana, Sweet and Sour."   The Hudson Review
      Spring 1976:95-98.

Forman handles Cuckoo's Nest better than any macho American
director could have.   The realism provides a sense of claustrophobia,
and the characters have real depth.   Unfortunately, all the story's good
points remain based on Ken Kesey's rampant sexism.

286   "Forman Funds Due; UA In His Future; 'Hair' As Nostalgia."   Variety
      17 March 1976:4,50.

Forman expresses concern about Czech authorities allowing his sons
to come to America for the Academy Awards ceremonies.   He views Hair as
a sentimental piece because of his early interest in the show but feels
that now the play can be handled objectively.   Also, Forman is talking
about a project with producer Dino DeLaurentiis and considering scripts
for two other films.

287   "Forman May Lens 'Lord' As His Next Pic Project."   Variety 10
      November 1976:22.

Brief notice, stating that Forman was working on a screenplay of
the novel At Play in the Fields of the Lord with Jean-Claude Carriere
(who co-scripted Taking Off) in Paris.

288   Gallo, William.   "One Flew Over the Cuckoo's Nest."   Film Heritage
      11.4 (Summer 1976):43-45.

Milos Forman, Lawrence Hauben, and Bo Goldman have successfully
transferred the rebellious spirit and tragic heart of Ken Kesey's original novel to the screen.   McMurphy shows that the system can be beaten,
and Jack Nicholson is astounding in the role.   Brad Dourif as Billy
Bibbit is also excellent.   Only the humanizing of Nurse Ratched is
difficult to understand.

289   Graybeal, David M.   "On Finding the Cuckoo's Nest."   The Christian
      Century 4-11 August 1976:688-89.

Graybeal explains all the similarities between McMurphy and Christ,
stating that audiences love the movie because they have just been told
the story of salvation once more.

290   Humphries, Reynold and Genevieve Suzzoni.   "One Flew Over the
      Cuckoo's Nest."   Framework 11.5 (Winter 1976/77):23-24.

Cuckoo's Nest is a dangerously irresponsible and anti-intellectual
film, encouraging its audience to strongly sympathize with the individual against the institution.   It shows madness as having distinct
physical characteristics that can be solved with specific physical
actions if the castrating intellectuals do not interfere.

291   Kindred, Jack.   "Ballyhooics of 'Cuckoo' Four."   Variety 3 March
      1976:28.

Jack Nicholson, Milos Forman, Michael Douglas, and Saul Zaentz
answer philosophical and social questions about Cuckoo's Nest in
Hamburg, Germany. Zaentz denies the film was made under a tax shelter
scheme. Also a description of past and future Saul Zaentz productions.

292   McCormick, Ruth.   "One Flew Over the Cuckoo's Nest."   Cineaste
      VII.3 (1976):42-43.

Along with Bo Goldman and Lawrence Hauben, Milos Forman has
achieved a rare successful transformation of novel into film and
eliminated most of the sexism and racism of the original work. The film
is more inspirational than political and slightly less progressive than
the book in dampening the parts in which the men work together to
achieve their rebellion. Cuckoo's Nest is achieving great success
because it can appeal to any political perspective and it says nothing
new.

293   McCreadie, Marsha.   "One Flew Over the Cuckoo's Nest."   Films in
      Review January 1976:53.

Though unsurrealistic, the film is just as unsettling as the novel.
Performances are excellent. Partially reprinted in Film Review Digest
Annual (book, 1976).

294   McMurtry, Larry.   "O Ragged Time Knit Up Thy Ravell'd Sleeves."
      American Film. December-January 1976-77:4-5.

E. L. Doctorow should not worry about the quality of the film to be
made from his novel Ragtime because his work is completed and safe.
Producer Dino DeLaurentiis now has the problem of re-selling an already
oversold work, and his commercial considerations will probably ensure
that the film will be poor. The real tragedy from all this hype is that
money rather than quality has become the standard for art.

295   McVay, Douglas.   "One Flew Over the Cuckoo's Nest."   Film March
      1976:8.

Forman brilliantly presents the question of what is sanity, made
ambiguous by Jack Nicholson's performance.

296   Milne, Tom.   "One Flew Over the Cuckoo's Nest."   Monthly Film
      Bulletin February 1976:32-33.

Amidst raucous activities, Forman slowly builds a cold anger
against the oppressive system, despite Randle Patrick McMurphy's questionable tactics against it. Forman successfully transforms Ken Kesey's
surrealistic narration by giving the hero's role to Chief Bromden at the
conclusion after McMurphy proves his destructiveness and receives a
lobotomy. Cuckoo's Nest aptly demonstrates Forman's conviction that
insanity is the inability to adjust to ever-changing, unspoken social
rules and shows the Chief as representing a last bastion of freedom at
the conclusion. Partially reviewed in Film Review Digest Annual (book,
1976).

297   Murphy, Robert. "No Politics, Please. This is Comedy." Village
      Voice 26 July 1976:109.

      Murphy emphasizes the humanness of Forman's films. Cuckoo's Nest
was new for Forman because he was forced to deal with tragedy and a
recognizably evil character, Nurse Ratched. Murphy feels that Forman
strayed from author Ken Kesey's political commentary, but Forman insists
that he kept the novel's essence. Forman asserts that his first
priority is to entertain.

298   Myers, Lee and Hugh T. Kerr. "One Flew Over the Cuckoo's Nest: A
      Psycho-Symbolic Review." Theology Today October 1976:285-90.

      As a Christ-figure, McMurphy brings the good news that adherence to
the law is not necessary for redemption. For those in the helping
professions, the film challenges whether they are offering clients a
chance to experience life or just a new set of rules to go by.

299   Rainer, Peter. "Movies." Mademoiselle February 1976:64,66.

      Ken Kesey's Cuckoo's Nest appealed to a sixties' generation that
wanted the right to do what they pleased and believed that society is
insane. Milos Forman turns the story into a folksy fable that has
little of the novel's impact. Jack Nicholson's performance quickly
becomes tiring, and McMurphy's conflict with Nurse Ratched is almost
completely missing.

300   Reed, Rex. "Movies: 'One Flew Over the Cuckoo's Nest.'" Vogue
      February 1976:80.

      Jack Nicholson gives his finest performance in this warm and won-
derful film. Thought-provoking and with some shocking moments. Forman
guides the action with precision, giving the film an unusual rhythm.

301   Schonauer, David. "Interview: Milos Forman." Mademoiselle August
      1976:231.

      Forman talks about his laziness, his dislike of politics, an inci-
dent in Cuckoo's Nest drawn from real life, and the basic importance of
telling a good story and makes brief comments on several other subjects.

302   Thomas, Bob. "Milos Forman: Award Winner." Action 11.3 (May/June
      1976):7-10.

      Review of Forman's American career, including adjusting to this
country and his experiences with Taking Off. Also discusses the history
of his involvement with Cuckoo's Nest, the casting of Louise Fletcher as
Nurse Ratched, his work on the set with Jack Nicholson and cinematographer Haskell Wexler, and his editing of the film.

303   Van Nostrand, Jillian. "One Flew Over the Cuckoo's Nest: a por-
      trait of despair in one dimension." Film Criticism 1.1 (Spring
      1976):23-26.

      The film is exquisitely directed and acted, which poses a problem.
For the viewer is too emotionally involved to make the necessary intellectual response to the film's depiction of mental illness and its
suggestion of escape as the only answer. Its fault is in the empty
characterizations of the patients, who have no background and therefore
can gain no direction. McMurphy's rebellion is against emptiness but
for nothing, and he is too obviously meant to be the hero in every
instance.

304   VanWert, William. "One Flew Over the Cuckoo's Nest: An Ariel View
      of the Nest." Jump Cut Summer 1976:51-52.

      Rather than provide a critical perspective on Kesey's original
work, Forman maintains all of its racist and sexist implications and
even takes away the dignity afforded to Native Americans in the novel.
McMurphy appears as a self-sacrificing hero. The smooth editing, Jack
Nicholson's performance, and the camaraderie between the patients all
involve the audience emotionally in this elegy to ravishing white male
sexual prowess.

305   Wood, Michael. "No, But I Read the Book." New York Review of
      Books 5 February 1976:3-4.

      Forman encourages masterful performances out of Fletcher and
Nicholson and successfully transforms Kesey's macabre scenario into a
realistic setting. All of which leads to the question of how much we
allow ourselves to be oppressed. When characters believe they are sane,
they look sane. But, ultimately, Forman's optimism is too simplistic,
and he fails to hide the sexism and racism at the story's center.

306   Young, Vernon. "Nobody Lives Here Any More." The Hudson Review
      Summer 1976:259-65.

      Forman has always exploited his characters for humor, and he does
it again (in Cuckoo's Nest) while also exploiting every known American
guilt and neurosis. Popular and critical response indicates that
Americans have no confidence in their own democracy.

1977

Books

307   Canby, Vincent. "One Flew Over the Cuckoo's Nest." The National
      Society of Film Critics on Movie Comedy. Ed. Stuart Byron and
      Elizabeth Weis. New York: Grossman Publishers, 1977:205-07.

      Reprint of review originally published in the New York Times on 23
November 1975.

308   Cowie, Peter. Eighty Years of Cinema. New York: A. S. Barnes and
      Co., 1977.

      In Loves of a Blonde, Forman reveals the growth of a young girl's
maturity without rancor or self-consciousness.   In One Flew Over the
Cuckoo's Nest, Forman's vision is wry and provincial and he challenges
the audience that is tempted to sympathize with his hero.

309   Ebert, Roger.   "The Firemen's Ball."   The National Society of Film
      Critics on Movie Comedy.   Ed. Stuart Byron and Elizabeth Weis.   New
      York: Grossman Publishers, 1977:256-57.

      Forman trusts his audience to know what is funny.   His characters
are victims of human nature, representing all the times when we have the
best intentions but things go completely wrong.   Then, do we laugh or
cry?

310   Liehm, Antonin J. and Mira Liehm.   The Most Important Art: Eastern
      European Film After 1945.   Los Angeles: University of California
      Press, 1977.

      Summary of important developments in the post-war cinemas of each
Eastern European nation.   Liehm introduces the Czech films of the sixties by commenting on the economic basis for their development.   He
characterizes Forman as a director who looked at all the details of
Czech life and produced a cruel portrait of the country that had never
been seen before.   In The Firemen's Ball, Forman used his method to
satirize the entire socialist system.

311   Scavullo, Francesco.   Scavullo on Men. New York: Random House,
      1977.

      Forman discusses his attitudes on a number of personal issues such
as women, sex, food, hobbies, death, and money.

312   Skvorecky, Josef.   "Eine Kleine Jazzmusick."   White Stones and Fir
      Trees; An Anthology of Contemporary Slavic Literature   Cranbery,
      NJ: Associated University Presses, 1977:351-64.

      Short story that was to be the basis for Forman's first directorial
effort in 1960 before President Antonin Novotny personally intervened to
cancel the project.   It tells about the struggles of a group of teenage
jazz band members during the Nazi occupation.

313   Thomson, David.   America in the Dark: Hollywood and the Gift of
      Unreality.   New York: William Morrow and Co., 1977.

      Cuckoo's Nest contains many shocking and negative portrayals, yet
it intelligently presents the struggle of the oppressed human spirit
against dominating institutions.   Unfortunately, the film's success
identifies it with institutions and seems to sap its energy.

314   Williamson, Bruce. "The Loves of a Blonde." The National Society
        of Film Critics on Movie Comedy. Ed. Stuart Byron and Elizabeth
        Weis. New York: Grossman Publishers, 1977:255-56.

        Reprint of review originally appearing in Time, 1966. See "The
Eyes Have It" (periodical).

Newspapers

315   Krebs, Albin. "Notes on People." New York Times 8 January
        1977:17.

        Reports on an out-of-court settlement between author Ken Kesey and
producers Michael Douglas and Saul Zaentz entitling Kesey to 2.5 percent
of gross from the film of Cuckoo's Nest.

316   ------------. "Notes on People." New York Times 26 March 1977:17.

        Notes Cuckoo's Nest winning for Best Picture, Best Director, Best
Actor, Best Actress, and Best Supporting Actor in British Academy
Awards.

Periodicals

317   Combs, Richard. "Sentimental Journey." Sight and Sound 46.3
        (Summer 1977):153.

        In his American films, Forman has worked throughout the seventies
with stories set in the sixties. His investigations for these films
produces their real drama, which involves the personal and social forces
working beyond the character. A character such as Randle Patrick
McMurphy in Cuckoo's Nest is powerful because he is ambiguous. These
films also take Forman back to his origins. Taking Off and Cuckoo's
Nest reminded him of Czech situations. At this point, Forman is
struggling with Hair. He also discusses some experiences while working
on Vital Parts with Thomas Berger.

318   "Forman On 'Hair' For United Artists; Dances By Tharp." Variety 12
        October 1977:6.

        Announcement of Forman to direct and Twyla Tharp to choreograph
Hair along with names of cast and other production people.

319   McCreadie, Marsha. "One Flew Over the Cuckoo's Nest: Some Reasons
        for One Happy Adaptation." Literature/Film Quarterly 5 (Spring
        1977):125-31.

        McCreadie credits the film's success to its retention of important
characters, settings, and the same emotional tone. She also mentions

the similarity of certain dialogue and events. For her, these similarities alone were enough to create a "happy adaptation." She makes no
suggestion about the themes of the novel and film and why each work was
tremendously successful in vastly different eras.

320 Safer, Elaine B. "'It's the Truth Even If It Didn't Happen.' Ken
     Kesey's One Flew Over the Cuckoo's Nest." Literature/Film
     Quarterly 5 (Spring 1977):132-41.

     Safer finds the film simpler than the novel because it does not
employ surrealism or characters of mythic stature. Instead, she feels
that Forman reduces complex psychological ideas to the level of slapstick comedy.

                                1978
Books

321 Haskell, Molly. "Kesey Cured: Forman's Sweet Insanity." The
     Modern American Novel and the Movies. Ed. Gerald Peary and Roger
     Shatzkin. New York: Frederick Ungar Publishing Co., 1978:266-71.

     Reprint of Haskell's "Nicholson Kneads a Fine Madness," originally
published in Village Voice (periodical, 1975).

322 Jarvie, I. C. Movies as Social Criticism: Aspects of Their Social
     Psychology. Metuchen, NJ: The Scarecrow Press, Inc., 1978.

     Taking Off is one of several films from the early seventies that
shows the middle-age years of marriage as routine and boring, prompting
a guilty search for fulfillment outside of it. Larry Tyne does so, but
remains a basically decent person. The only pressure on the marriage
comes from society.

323 Shale, Richard. Academy Awards. New York: Frederick Ungar
     Publishing Co., 1978.

     Reference book listing nominees and winners for the awards' first
fifty years.

Newspapers

324 Camp, Patricia. "Moviemakers Revive the 1960s on the Mall."
     Washington Post 16 April 1978:C1,C2.

     People involved in the crowd scenes for Hair filmed at the Lincoln
Memorial (mostly students attracted through the local media) tell their
reasons for coming and their memories of the 60s.

325   Fordin, Hugh and Robin Chase.   "Hollywood Puts On Its Dancing Shoes
      Again."   New York Times 25 June 1978:II:1,8.

Mentions Hair as one of several new movies including dance,
reflecting heightened fascination with physical beauty, and the problems
and history of filming dance.

326   Goodwin, Michael.   "Thousands Dance and Others Fume as 'Hair' is
      Filmed in Central Park."   New York Times 1 May 1978:B3.

Residents near Central Park complain about rock bands entertaining
extras early in the morning.   Filming took place two weeks after the
passage of a New York ordinance prohibiting large gatherings in the
Park, but Mayor Koch allowed it and personally congratulated the crowd
for its behavior.   Producer Lester Persky comments on the film being
over budget and differing from the stage version.

327   Krebs, Albin.   "Notes on People."   New York Times   14 February
      1978:32.

Announcement that Forman and Frantisek Daniel, former Czech film
producer, have been appointed co-directors of the Film Division of the
Columbia University School of Arts.   Daniel states their desire to
create a major film art school.

328   "1960's Return as 'Flower Children' Mass in Capital."   Los Angeles
      Times 16 April 1978:16.

Account of filming scenes in front of the Lincoln Memorial, featur-
ing a crowd of college students mixing styles from the sixties and
seventies.

329   Taran, Kenneth.   "'Hair' Today."   Washington Post 14 April 1978:B1,
      B7.

Mention of the musical numbers being filmed in Washington, D.C. and
call for extras.   Forman discusses his desire to film Hair since seeing
its very first performance.   Producer Lester Persky believes it will not
be as dated as it would have been if filmed in 1968.

330   Taylor, Clarke.   "'Hair' Restyled for a Film Setting."   Los Angeles
      Times 17 January 1978:IV:10.

Producer Lester Persky expresses his desire to make Hair a fresh
and relevant production, looking back at young revolutionaries who did
not realize what they were doing.   Comments on the changes being made
and reviews the careers of screenwriter Michael Weller and star Treat
Williams.   Also comments on the production schedule and locations.

Periodicals

331   "Forman, Daniel Full Profs Now At Columbia U." _Variety_ 15 February
      1978:4,28.

      Announcement of Forman and former Prague Film School director
Frantisek Daniel as co-chairs of Columbia's film school along with brief
biographical notes.

332   Morrison, Donald. "In Manhattan: Reliving the '60s." _Time_ 22 May
      1978:13-14.

      Account of extras for _Hair_ gathering in Central Park and assistant
director Michael Hausman's attempt to film them while keeping all signs
of the 70s out.

333   "The Yellow Brick Road to Profit." _Time_ 23 January 1978:80-81.

      The writer notes that most critics and even star John Savage have
reviled _Hair_. Cast morale was low during the filming. Forman defends
his work as revealing the contradictions and humor of the sixties.

                              1979

Books

334   Bates, Robin. "The Ideological Foundations of the Czech New Wave."
      The Emergence of Film Art, 2nd edition. Ed. Lewis Jacobs. New
      York: W. W. Norton and Co., 1979:494-505.

      The Czech New Wave did not fundamentally attack socialist realism;
at least, not until they had brought it up-to-date with historical
truths. The filmmakers accepted socialism as a basic tenet, and the
true doctrine of socialist realism, while it became corrupted by the
state, calls for an honest exploration of reality with the goal of
social unity in mind. The Czech New Wave films thus demonstrate an
underlying unity both in society and among themselves. Comparing
Forman's Czech films such as _Loves of a Blonde_ and _The Firemen's Ball_
with his American films such as _Taking Off_ and _Cuckoo's Nest_ demonstrates this point. The Czech films do not contain the same degree of
familial separation and social rebellion. Only after updating socialist
realism did Czech film move into more subjective visions.

335   Katz, Ephraim. _The Film Encyclopedia_. New York: Thomas Y.
      Crowell, 1979.

      Brief biographical entry citing Forman's forte as ironic comedy
about ordinary people in their daily lives, with the generation gap as a
frequent theme.

336   Osborne, Robert. <u>50 Golden Years of Oscar: The Official History of the Academy of Modern Picture Arts and Sciences</u>. Ernest E. Schwork, 1979.

Includes references to awards won by <u>Cuckoo's Nest</u>.

Newspapers

337   Arnold, Gary. "Milos Forman in the Light of 'Hair.'" <u>Washington Post</u> 1 April 1979:G3.

Forman interviewed at a benefit premiere for <u>Hair</u> in D. C. He believes that ex-hippies and pro-government people were probably not as far apart as they believed. They all wanted peace. Insightful comments about Forman's work with nonactors and his use of an actual judge, psychiatrist, and MP in the film. Also, comments about finding Cheryl Barnes to sing "Easy to Be Hard" and Michael Weller to co-write. Forman believes there are strong similarities between working under capitalism and socialism and hopes to bring his twin sons to America.

338   Bennetts, Leslie. "At a Party for 'Hair,' No Tears for the 60's." <u>New York Times</u> 14 March 1979:C14.

Account of lavish post-premiere party held in an abandoned New York warehouse focusing on the lack of political concerns among the film's actors and the guests.

339   Buckley, Tom. "At the Movies." <u>New York Times</u> 6 April 1979:C8.

Forman gives a lot of credit to Michael Weller for <u>Hair</u>'s critical success. The script had to provide a story line and some distance from the naive notions of the original production. Forman describes how he met and hired Weller.

340   Canby, Vincent. "The Age of Aquarius Lives--'Hair' Is 'Stylish, Satisfying.'" <u>New York Times</u> 25 March 1979:II:17.

Forman and Michael Weller made <u>Hair</u> one of the most satisfying musicals in years by being neither too reverent nor too free with the original work. Forman draws the audience into the story by making the country boy, Claude, the focus as he encounters the bedazzling world of Central Park in the mid-sixties. Though <u>Hair</u> thus becomes an extension of reality, Forman does not ignore or attempt to instruct about Vietnam. He simply refers to it directly.

341   ------------. "Film: 1969 Relived in 'Hair.'" <u>New York Times</u> 14 March 1979:C15.

Except for the staging of the title song and some editing of the dance numbers, the film is a delight. Forman makes the 60s live without bogging down the film in realism. The comedy and songs are lively, and the film makes no effort to be contemporary.

342 ------------. "'Small' and 'Personal' Were Hallmarks of Excel-
     lence." New York Times 30 December 1979:II:1,15.

     Hair makes a well-worn property seem fresh, integrates music and
dance successfully, and treats the sixties without condescension. It
should have done better at the box office.

343 Champlin, Charles. "A Debut For 'Hair's' Latest Do." Los Angeles
     Times 4 March 1979:"Calendar,"28.

     Forman and other United Artists executives attend a sneak preview
of Hair in Denver where the audience response is excellent. But they
still realize they have to make people want to see it. Forman comments
about his long-term interest in the project and about the temperamental
nature of screenwriters.

344 ------------. "'Hair' Comes to the Screen." Los Angeles Times 15
     March 1979:IV:1,25.

     Besides being the best musical since Cabaret, opened up magnifi-
cently in the outdoors by Forman and cinematographer Miroslav Ondricek,
Hair is a reminder of the importance of social commitment and of the
sorrowful backdrop that Vietnam played to the sixties.

345 Chin, Tony. "He Didn't Get Into a Role, But Under It." New York
     Times 1 June 1979:C14.

     A brief review of Treat Williams' life and career. His own hair
was woven for his role in Hair.

346 Martin, Judith. "This 'Hair' Is Restyled Becomingly." Washington
     Post (Weekend) 30 March 1979:26.

     The dance choreography of Twyla Tharp and cinema choreography of
Forman lift the film to the level of art. It is fresh American folk-
lore. Forman criticizes the hippies and shows tolerance for the adults.
The film is important as a symbolic separation of America's innocence
and aggressiveness.

347 Maslin, Janet. "Critic's Notebook: What's Happened To Movies That
     You See For Fun?" New York Times 8 June 1979:C8.

     Hair should have been fun, but the hippies in it are pathetic and
unlikable characters who have nothing to celebrate. The production
numbers are all botched.

348 Shales, Tom. "Blast From the Past--Tripping to the '60s With
     'Hair.'" Washington Post 26 March 1979:131,133.

     Cynical account of all those celebrating Hair's premiere on the
eve of Anwar Sadat and Menachem Begin signing the Mid-East Peace Treaty.
Everyone present said they loved the movie even though they probably
never loved the hippies.

349 Sterritt, David. "The Americanization of Milos Forman." <u>Christian
     Science Monitor</u> 24 May 1979:18.

Forman defends <u>Hair</u> as not being nostalgic because hippie influences in style are still visible, and the film contains the timeless
theme of young people searching for identity. Like Forman's previous
two American films, <u>Hair</u> focuses on characters on the fringes of society
and contains no identifiable villains.

350 ------------. "Movie 'Hair' ignores changes since Sixties."
     <u>Christian Science Monitor</u> 29 March 1979:19.

Forman goes to excess with his aggressive camera style, fragmenting
the choreography and drawing out the script. <u>Hair</u> presents the idea
that the hippies actually did achieve a revolution and drifts into
tastelessness at times.

Periodicals

351 Aitken, Will. "Hair: Buddy-film throwback." <u>Take One</u> May
     1979:13-14.

The original play was more about sex than about Vietnam. The movie
captures neither. Women are used only as extras. Forman creates only a
randomly structured film that makes little sense.

352 Asahina, Robert. "Cinematic Delusions." <u>New Leader</u> 9 April
     1979:20-21.

Forman did not know what kind of movie he was making in <u>Hair</u> or
what its effect on the audience would be. The colors contrast more than
the values and the "straights" appear more appealing than the hippies.
The music and choreography are also terrible.

353 Auster, Al. "Hair." <u>Cineaste</u> Spring 1979 IV.3 (Spring
     1979):55-56.

In <u>Hair</u>, Forman regains his touch and gives the musical a look it
hasn't had in about thirty years. Miroslav Ondricek's camera helps
Forman use light to turn Central Park into Oz. The cast is excellent,
and Forman's theme of the gains and losses of rebellion help the work
maintain relevance.

354 Blake, Richard A. "Selective Memory." <u>America</u> 7 April 1979:286.

<u>Hair</u> is literally breathtaking and good fun if one can forget the
turbulent times it glosses over. Thematically, Forman is merely continuing his attacks against institutions.

355 Brown, Geoff. "Hair." <u>Monthly Film Bulletin</u> July 1979:146-47.

Forman only hurts his dated material by treating it enthusiastically. Long list of production credits and short plot summary included.

356 "Cagney, At 80, May Return In 'Ragtime.'" <u>Variety</u> 26 December 1979:1,62.

Confirms that Cagney has signed to appear, states that shooting is scheduled while financing is being sought, and reviews previous false starts on the project in 1976 and '77.

357 Cameron, Julia. "Milos Forman and 'Hair': Styling the Age of Aquarius." <u>Rolling Stone</u> 19 April 1979:82-85.

Forman discusses his desires from the early sixties to work in America, his desire from the late sixties to film <u>Hair</u>, his life in the early seventies at New York's Chelsea Hotel (home for many artists), and his gentle attacks on hypocrisy in his films.

358 ------------. "Twyla Tharp Lands on Her Feet." <u>Rolling Stone</u> 19 April 1979:85.

Cameron praises the dancing in <u>Hair</u> as blending perfectly into the film and making the viewer feel like dancing. Tharp explains her ideas about choreographing for the camera, making dance accessible to an average viewer, and making the film a fable. She did not want an acid-trip sequence of unbelievable visions.

359 Coleman, John. "Tripping Up." <u>New Statesman</u> 20 July 1979:101-02.

Given an open screen instead of a restrictive theatre, <u>Hair</u> loses its rebellious charm. Forman squanders his talent on an uncritical nostalgic exercise. Forman and photographer Miroslav Ondricek offer some marvelous images of America and memorable musical numbers, but the self-righteous hippies are not admirable.

360 Denby, David. "'Hair' Transplanted." <u>New York</u> 19 March 1979:62-63.

The film does not try to re-create a love festival, but instead plunges the audience back into the issues and tensions of the 60s. Forman is notably unromantic in presenting the hippies, while his ending could serve as a metaphor for the fate of the decade's most noble efforts. But this very focus on issues makes the film too heavy-spirited. The camera destroys the choreography and other scenes disrupt the rhythm of the numbers. Ultimately, there is nothing new or profound.

361   "Dialogue on Film: Michael Douglas." American Film July–August
      1979:29–38.

Douglas, the producer of Cuckoo's Nest, discusses his basis for
hiring Forman, the artistic reasons for replacing Haskell Wexler as
cinematographer with Bill Butler, the weakness of Ken Kesey's original
script, and the hiring of Will Sampson as Chief Broom.

362   Douglas, Michael. "Douglas Replies." American Film September
      1979:8–9.

Cuckoo's Nest producer Douglas responds to statement by original
cinematographer Haskell Wexler about the shooting of the film. Douglas
states that he did contribute to decisions about the lighting, that
Wexler did much work on the film but not as much as he claims, and that
Wexler was dismissed for artistic and not political reasons. Douglas
also discusses the advantages of filming on location.

363   Edelman, Rob and Eric Bradford. "Hair: Two Views." Films in
      Review 14 May 1979:313–14.

Edelman complains that the hippie characters lack identity. Forman
never explores the roots of their character or culture, and his contrast
of hip and straight lifestyles is vague and abstract. Bradford feels
that Forman has made the freshest musical of the seventies. He opens up
the story to make it a celebration of life and love and give new relevance to "Let the Sun Shine In." The script and choreography are
excellent, but the casting of John Savage and Treat Williams is the most
important element.

364   Gilliatt, Penelope. "Fuzz." The New Yorker 16 April 1979:142–43.

Hair succeeds, but it is not properly exhilerating because it
recognizes that the basis of true exuberance is difficult to locate. As
in Black Peter and The Firemen's Ball, Forman focuses on insecure people
attempting to cope with important personal problems under the pressures
of history.

365   Goldstein, Richard. "Hair Cuts." Village Voice 5 February
      1979:37.

Twyla Tharp expresses some bitterness that much of her choreography
was cut from the final version of Hair, but says she understands that
her work had to come second to the director's vision. Forman admits
they had some creative debates, but says he had to emphasize the narrative.

366   "Hair." Variety 14 March 1979:21.

Some excellent qualities as a musical, but the film is neither
relevant nor nostalgic. Screenplay (returning to the outline for Joe
Papp's original Broadway production), choreography, casting, and technical qualities are all excellent. Box-office prospects shaky.

367   "Hair: The Film."   USA Today   July 1979:64.

Forman's film is as meaningful and enjoyable as the original play was in its day because he looks behind the flowers and beads and blends the music and story well.   The clash of hippies and adults is gentle instead of violent.

368   "Hair: The Second Dawning."   American Film   March 1979:29-31.

Outlines Forman's twelve-year desire to make the film and the problems that delayed it that long.   Also includes a brief plot description and information about where Forman located the main cast members.

369   Harvey, Stephen.   "The Party's Over."   Inquiry   14 May 1979:30-32.

Despite being the best film musical in years, Hair lacks purpose. It dumbly celebrates all the counterculture cliches.   Michael Weller's script is particularly weak.

370   "Here's 'Hair'!   At Last It's a Movie."   Life   March 1979:40-44.

Producer Lester Persky has taken a chance with producing the dated show and hiring the Czech director before Cuckoo's Nest had brought him fame.   Forman is glad for the distance from the sixties, which offers a better perspective.   The original score has only been livened a little, but the characters have been given much more depth.

371   Kauffmann, Stanley.   "Ex-Champions."   The New Republic   14 April 1979:40-41.

Hair's power has increasingly diminished with the advances of its success and age.   The lack of late 60s social pressures make it a limp work.   The hippies are more obnoxious than appealing.   But Forman, cinematographer Miroslav Ondricek, and choreographer Twyla Tharp keep the film at an imaginative level slightly above reality, an achievement few other recent films can match.

372   Kroll, Jack.   "Aquarius Reborn."   Newsweek   19 March 1979:102-03.

Hair abounds in high spirits and energy, capturing an important aspect of the American mood during the war years.

373   "Legit Shocker, Now PG Picture."   Variety   28 February 1979:6.

Comments on lack of group nudity or swearing in Hair, reflecting a change in public attitudes from the late sixties when the play was first produced.

374   McCarthy, Todd.   "Milos Forman Lets His Hair Down."   Film Comment   March 1979:17-21.

Forman discusses the casting, filming, and editing of Hair, the continued relevance of the story, particular problems of making a musical, a rumored dispute with choreographer Twyla Tharp, the early

progress of Ragtime and problems of working with a large budget, and the
failure of Taking Off and other difficulties in adjusting to America.

375 Pulleine, Tom. "Hair." Sight and Sound Autumn 1979:261-62.

The opening sequence promises to open up the show from the stage
play. But, thereafter, too many conflicting elements are jostling
against each other. The film has very little political consciousness,
and Forman never questions the hippies' self-confidence.

376 Quart, Leonard and Albert Auster. "Milos Forman in America." USA
Today July 1979:41.

Cites Hair as a reappraisal of the reality and mythology of the
1960s. Forman uses the script and music to question the hippies as much
as to celebrate them. The theme becomes the gains and losses of liberation. Forman's most human and complex American film. He gives the
musical a charm it has not had since the great MGM films of Minnelli,
Donen, and Kelly. Central Park becomes Oz, full of wonders and horrors.

377 Rich, Frank. "A Mid-60's Night Dream." Time 19 March 1979:88,90.

Forman and screenwriter Michael Weller handle the material perfectly, and Hair succeeds on every level. Weller's dialogue is sparse
but accurate and keeps the plot moving right through the musical numbers. Forman dominates through perfect editing of the songs and dances.
He treats all of the characters fairly. And, in the end, he re-opens
all the serious issues of the Vietnam era and resolves the plot while
still keeping the music going strong.

378 Sarris, Andrew. "A Rather Hairy Issue." Village Voice 26 March
1979:49,98.

Hair possesses magnificent singing and dancing, but the performers
can never escape from Forman's confining camera and the plot has no
point. Forman's outlook is basically pessimistic.

379 Segers, Frank. "'Talk Art, Not Tax Shelter'; Persky's Fave Topic
Now: 'Hair.'" Variety 4 April 1979:8.

Producer Lester Persky discusses the early bright box-office promise of Hair, his struggle from 1972 to 1978 to film it after acquiring
the rights from Michael Butler, Milos Forman's drive to obtain a fresh
and naturalistic approach to the material, and the selling of the project to United Artists. The film cost $12 million and would require $30
million to break even.

380 Simon, John. "Timely and Untimely." National Review 11 May
1979:633-34.

First, Hair should have never been made. Second, Forman makes
several major mistakes. His camera obliterates Twyla Tharp's choreography, and the cast is terrible. The viewer roots for the Establish-
ment when Forman wants them to cheer for the hippies.

381   Stern, Harry.   "Milos Forman: Moment to Moment with the director
       of <u>Hair</u>."   <u>Esquire</u>   8 May 1979:82-83.

       Forman discusses his life cycle: endlessly intense work followed
by promotional tours followed by extreme boredom. Then, work again.
This promotional tour is different because Michael Weller is already
writing the script for <u>Ragtime</u>. <u>Hair</u> is struggling at the box-office.

382   Webster, Ivan.   "'Hair'--Washed, Cut, and Restyled Badly."   <u>Encore</u>
       16 April 1979:45-46.

       <u>Hair</u>'s makers have no understanding of the sixties, and Forman has
no idea of how to film song and dance. The hippies attacked middle-
class values, not the upper-class, as is shown in the film. Forman
substitutes shock cutting for choreography, and what he does show of
Twyla Tharp's dances is not impressive anyhow. The characters, except
for John Savage's, are repulsive. The performances by Dorsey Wright and
Cheryl Barnes are particularly bad. <u>Hair</u> is a bad sign, because if
Hollywood can no longer make light-hearted musicals, it may not be able
to address serious issues either.

383   Westerbeck, Colin L., Jr.   "Hair Today."   <u>Commonweal</u>   25 May
       1979:305-06.

       <u>Hair</u> made nonconformity safe, and Forman makes <u>Hair</u> safe. Avoiding
any possibly disturbing issues, Forman simply accentuates everything
positive. Twyla Tharp's choreography is the only redeeming quality, but
Forman's editing obstructs our view of the dancing.

384   Wexler, Haskell.   "Wexler on <u>Cuckoo's Nest</u>."   <u>American Film</u>
       September 1979:8.

       Original cinematographer on the film, Wexler refutes earlier state-
ments by producer Michael Douglas that he was dismissed from the production for artistic reasons. Wexler describes his work on <u>Cuckoo's Nest</u>,
denies that Douglas had any artistic input on the lighting, and states
that he left for artistic reasons.

385   Williamson, Bruce.   "Movies."   <u>Playboy</u>   June 1979:36.

       Forman turns <u>Hair</u> from a dated novelty into a timeless American
classic, a fable about the endless energy of youth.

386   Young, Vernon.   "Film Chronicle: Trash and Poetry."   <u>Hudson Review</u>
       Autumn 1979:411-17.

       <u>Hair</u> is a shoddy production, probably the trashiest film of the
year, with no unifying style. The original show was sick and the film
has no charm at all.

1980

<u>Books</u>

387 Bodeen, De Witt. "One Flew Over the Cuckoo's Nest." <u>Magill's</u>
     <u>Survey of Cinema</u> English Language Films, First Series, Vol. III.
     Ed. Frank R. Magill. Englewood Cliffs, NJ: Salem Press,
     1980:1265-67.

     Forman's gentle handling makes telling the difference between the
     sane and insane difficult. The cast is excellent, especially Jack
     Nicholson and Louise Fletcher. Story of the production and plot summary
     also provided.

388 Edmunds, I. G. and Reiko Meimura. <u>The Oscar Directors</u>. San Diego:
     A. S. Barnes and Co., Inc., 1980.

     Includes a short synopsis of <u>Cuckoo's Nest</u> which draws as much
     from the novel as from the film.

389 Kael, Pauline. <u>When the Lights Go Down</u>. New York: Holt,
     Rinehart, and Winston, 1980.

     Contains a reprint of her essay, "The Bull Goose Loony," from 1
     December 1975 (periodical).

390 Kauffmann, Stanley. <u>Before My Eyes</u>. New York: Harper and Row,
     1980.

     Contains a reprint of his <u>Cuckoo's Nest</u> review from the December
     13, 1975 <u>New Republic</u>.

391 Levy, Alan. <u>So Many Heroes</u>. Sagaponack, NY: Second Chance Press,
     1980.

     Personal account of the Prague Spring and afterwards. Levy, a
     reporter for <u>Life</u>, lived in Prague during the sixties. Forman served as
     his guide into Czech life. Levy includes much about government-artist
     relationships.

392 Liehm, Antonin J. "Some Observations on Czech Culture and Politics
     in the 1960s." <u>Czech Literature Since 1956: A Symposium</u>. Eds.
     William E. Harkins and Paul I. Trensky. New York: Bohemia,
     1980:134-55.

     Explains how Czech literature and theatre, once given the chance,
     began to re-create itself in the late fifties and throughout the six-
     ties, producing a liberal climate that brought about political change in
     1968. Includes comments on the importance of the Semafor Theatre,
     setting for Forman's <u>The Audition</u>.

393   Liehm, Antonin J. and Dragomir Liehm.   "Czechoslovak Cinema of the
      60s."   Cinema: A Critical Dictionary   Vol. I.   Ed. Richard Roud.
      New York: The Viking Press, 1980:244-52.

      The Liehms quickly trace the growth of Czech films following Josef
Stalin's death in 1953 and comment on all the major directors, charac-
terizing Forman's films as ones that make small matters into important
subjects and reveal their creator as a significant social critic.

394   Michael, Paul, ed.   The Great American Movie Book.   Englewood
      Cliffs, NJ: Prentice-Hall, Inc., 1980.

      Includes complete credits and a still from Cuckoo's Nest.

395   Steinberg, Cobbett S.   Film Facts.   New York: Facts on File, Inc.,
      1980.

      Includes listings of great moneymaking films, awards, and favorite
films of various critics and other film people. Most references are to
Cuckoo's Nest.

396   Willis, John.   Screen World 1980.   New York: Crown Publishers,
      Inc., 1980.

      Contains stills and full production credits from Hair.

Newspapers

397   Blau, Eleanor.   "New York Production Halts."   New York Times   22
      July 1980:III:7.

      Notes that movie actors' strike threatens start of Ragtime's
filming in New York.

398   Borderer, William.   "Mailer, Dying for a Part in 'Ragtime.'"   New
      York Times   17 December 1980:C25.

      A number of plot details and a description of how Norman Mailer got
the role of Stanford White. Also, information about constructing the
Morgan Library and New York City street set at a cost of $1 million.

399   Buckley, Tom.   "At the Movies: Brad Dourif's long association with
      'Ragtime.'"   New York Times   7 November 1980:C6.

      Brief account of Dourif's career. The actor was first hired for
the role of Younger Brother by Robert Altman in 1976. Dourif feels the
film states much about American radicalism and anarchism.

400   Champlin, Charles.   "Top 10 Films For '79 . . . And Then Some."
      Los Angeles Times   6 January 1980:"Calendar,"1,28.

      Hair kept the spirit of the original stage version and was moving
as a film and as a reminder of a forceful young generation.

401   Harmetz, Aljean. "Will Cagney Return in 'Ragtime'?" New York
       Times 7 May 1980:C26.

       Reviews history of the project through producer Dino DeLaurentiis'
firing of Robert Altman and hiring of Forman, speculates that Cagney
probably will perform, and states scheduled dates for shooting. Film-
ways, formerly American International Pictures, is financing the film in
a quest for legitimacy.

402   Hinds, Michael de Courey. "From 'Ragtime' to Riches for Owners of
       1880's Home." New York Times 28 August 1980:III:1,6.

       Account of art director Patrizia von Brandenstein's search for and
detailed restoration of Victorian era mansion to serve as the suburban
family's home in Ragtime and agreements with the home's actual owners.
Working with set decorator George De Titta, Sr., von Brandenstein
designed the home to reflect the fictional Mother's tastes.

403   "Hollywood Counts Strike Costs." New York Times 31 July
       1980:III:15.

       Notes that Ragtime filming is continuing under agreement with
unions to abide by any strike settlement.

404   Mailer, Norman. "Letters: Mailer on 'Ragtime.'" New York Times
       24 December 1980:III:6.

       Mailer states that his wife was added to cast of Ragtime and did
not replace another extra at his request as reported by William Borderer
on 17 December 1980 (newspaper).

405   "New Jersey Journal." New York Times 5 October 1980:XI:3.

       Description of filming of Atlantic City scenes for Ragtime at
Spring Lakes, NJ.

406   Shepard, Richard F. "Filming of 'Ragtime' Restores 1906 to Block
       on E. 11th Street." New York Times 28 July 1980:C12.

       Drug-ridden, crime-infested neighborhood receives new hope with
renovations made by film company. Ragtime art directors chose the block
for its intact period architecture and lack of business. Rapport
between company and community was excellent.

Periodicals

407   Delon, Michael. "Milos Forman: A Two-Part Interview." Film May
       1980:6-7.

       Forman discusses his work at Columbia University, his selection of
projects, including Leave It To Me, his casting methods, his reasons for
being a filmmaker, and his concern for good dialogue.

408 ------------. "Milos Forman: Part 2." _Film_ June 1980:6-7.

Forman discusses the origins of Firemen's Ball, Cuckoo's Nest, and Hair, problems during the filming of Hair, his relationship with Ivan Passer, his disinterest in politics, his major influences, the blending of comedy and tragedy in his work, and how he lives between projects.

409 Huss, Roy. "The Man Who Cut Hair: Shaping Character and Mood in the Editing Room." _Film/Psychology Review_ Summer-Fall 1980:297-302.

Stan Warnow, one of Hair's three editors, describes the construction of four scenes--Claude's acid trip, Dionne and Jeannie (Cheryl Barnes and Annie Golden) at a gas station, the "Black Boys/White Boys" number, and the dancing horses. Each required subtle changes to provide effective meaning. Warnow also discusses the problems of editing to music and the amount of freedom Forman allowed. Hair is Forman's personal vision.

410 "1911: East 11th Street." _Sight and Sound_ Winter 1980-81:36-37.

Mainly stills showing the period details for Ragtime. Notes also tell of the work done and the use of neighborhood people in the crew.

1981

Books

411 Morden, Ethan. _The Hollywood Musical_. New York: St. Martin's Press, 1981.

Morden credits Forman for reviving both Broadway adaptations and narrative musicals with Hair. It failed at the box office because it plunged back into a time that most viewers wanted to forget.

412 Shaffer, Peter. _Amadeus_. New York: Harper and Row, Inc., 1981.

Play that is the basis for Milos Forman's 1984 film of the same title.

413 Taubman, Leslie. "Hair." _Magill's Survey of Cinema_ English Language Films, Second Series, Vol. II. Ed. Frank N. Magill. Englewood Cliffs, NJ: Salem Press, 1981:966-68.

A celebration of discovery and friendship. Cinematography, choreography, and music are exhilarating.

Newspapers

414 Arnold, Gary. "The Faulty Steps of 'Ragtime.'" _Washington Post_ 18 December 1981:C1,C9.

Forman and Weller attempt to weave three stories together from the beginning, but lose two of them halfway through. The Coalhouse Walker saga must then carry on alone, but the audience already knows the outcome. Only performances by Moses Gunn (as Booker T. Washington) and James Cagney save the last half of the film. Forman emphasizes the novel's theme of white guilt, which was in vogue in 1975 when the novel was published, but no longer.

415   Bennetts, Leslie. "The Swift, Magical Rise of Elizabeth McGovern."
      New York Times 27 November 1981:III:8.

Review of McGovern's early successes in her career, including playing Evelyn Nesbit in Ragtime.

416   Benson, Sheila. "'Ragtime'--An Optimistic Novel Lost In Transla-
      tion." Los Angeles Times 15 November 1981:"Calendar,"29.

The film is intricate and rich, but lacks the optimism, most of the interesting historical characters, and important social interrelation-ships contained in the novel. The film focuses on the negative quali-ties of obsession and injustice. But the casting, performances, and music are excellent. Mostly reprinted in "Ragtime," Film Review Annual (book 1982).

417   Buckley, Tom. "The Forman Formula." The New York Times Magazine
      1 March 1981:28,31,42-44,50-53.

Comments on the adaptation and casting of Ragtime lead to a re-counting of Forman's life and career. Particularly valuable are Forman's remarks about his mental breakdown after the commercial failure of Taking Off, receiving the offer from Michael Douglas to make Cuckoo's Nest, his devotion to a strong story and practical techniques, and his love of America.

418   Canby, Vincent. "Film: 'Ragtime' Evokes Real and Fictional
      Pasts." New York Times 20 November 1981:III:10.

Provocative, but alternately disappointing because the narrative becomes too confused, though the performances are excellent. Brief analysis of the novel included.

419   ------------. "Why 'Reds' Succeeds and 'Ragtime' Doesn't." New
      York Times 6 December 1981:21-22.

Warren Beatty's Reds informs people about an era and makes them want to go back to the original sources. Ragtime does not. It is not boring, but confused, the novel probably being unfilmable.

420   Chase, Chris. "At The Movies." New York Times 20 November
      1981:III:10.

Discusses life and career of Kenneth McMillan, racist fire chief Willie Conklin in Ragtime. McMillan compares working in theatre and films and expresses love of James Cagney, Milos Forman, and London (filming site).

421   ------------.   "Cagney, 82, Is Embarrassed Anew at Being a 'Star.'"
New York Times   17 November 1981:III:11.

Brief review of Cagney's career, his disdain for being called an
artist (he always thought of acting as "a job"), and his health problems. He decided to return in Ragtime after a twenty-one-year absence
from the screen because of the encouragement of his doctor and friends.

422   Harmetz, Aljean. "When Emma Goldman Hit Cutting-Room Floor." New
York Times 12 December 1981:21.

Description of the Emma Goldman scene cut from Ragtime when Forman
was outvoted by producer DeLaurentiis and author Doctorow. Forman
admits the scene was not necessary. Also, summary of Mariclare
Costello's career. She played Goldman.

423   Kernan, Michael. "High-Voltage Vamp." Washington Post 25 June
1981:F8.

Re-tells the life of Evelyn Nesbit, her affair with Stanford White,
and his murder by her husband Henry K. Thaw. Falsely claims that Brooke
Shields will paly Nesbit in Ragtime.

424   Levy, Francis. "Hollywood Embraces the Difficult Novel." New York
Times 22 March 1981:II:13.

Cites Ragtime as one of several complex literary works being filmed
as a result of Cuckoo's Nest's success. Filmmakers choose difficult
novels because of their originality, ability to entertain on several
levels, and appeal to top talent, and the availability of new cinematic
techniques and increased audience sophistication.

425   Martin, Judith. "Eight Holiday Films." Washington Post (Weekend)
18 December 1981:17.

Unfortunately, much of the novel was cut for Ragtime, but even more
should have been. Audiences will not understand what is happening with
the New Rochelle family or Thaw, Nesbit, and White. The performances
are good, and those of Howard Rollins, Jr., James Cagney, and Kenneth
McMillan make seeing the film worthwhile.

426   Pond, Steve. "Dateline Hollywood." Washington Post 26 November
1981:C7.

Brief mention of the large amount of final cuts required for Ragtime and the problems they caused for composer Randy Newman.

427   Quindlen, Anna. "Will He Go From 'Ragtime' To Riches?" New York
Times 15 November 1981:1,23.

Howard E. Rollins, Jr.'s background, how he got the part, his
commendations and future prospects, experiences during the filming, and
incidents of racism that helped him understand Coalhouse Walker, Jr.

428   Raynor, Vivien.   "Ragtime: The Book, the Film, the Show."   New
      York Times   27 December 1981:XXII:16.

      Account of New Rochelle's museum exhibition of Ragtime era arti-
facts, related to the film as a fund-raising effort.

429   Taylor, Clarke.   "Rollins: The Rage of 'Ragtime.'"   Los Angeles
      Times Calendar   29 November 1981:53.

      Brief review of Howard E. Rollins, Jr.'s life and career.
Awareness of the realities of racism in America allowed Rollins to
identify with the rage of Coalhouse Walker, Jr., whom he sees as a very
principled character.

430   Williams, Christian.   "The Model Role."   Washington Post   18
      December 1981:C1,C3.

      Howard E. Rollins provides a good description of how Forman audi-
tions and works with his actors.   He also discusses working with Kenneth
McMillan (who plays the racist fire chief Willie Conklin) and James
Cagney.

Periodicals

431   Berger, Thomas.   "I Am Not a Movie Person."   American Film December
      1981:34-36.

      Novelist Berger describes his attempt to write a filmscript of his
book Vital Parts with Forman in the winter of 1971-72.   Berger claims he
contributed very little and Forman wanted more disagreement than what he
gave.

432   Buck, Joan Juliet.   "'Ragtime' Dreaming America."   Vogue   November
      1981:440-43,492-93.

      Describes E. L. Doctorow's novel as being about the connection
between public and private events and the classes in American society.
Also describes filming the assassination of Stanford White, how Norman
Mailer played the scene, the actors' background knowledge about their
characters and the work, and Forman's preparation for the filming.

433   Corliss, Richard.   "One More Sad Song."   Time   23 November 1981:97.

      Ragtime is impressive, but lopsided.   Forman understands the book,
includes many good effects, and gets many fine performances.   But his
attention to nuance loses E. L. Doctorow's sweep.   Mostly reprinted in
"Ragtime," Film Review Annual (book, 1982).

434   Crist, Judith.   "Dazzling 'Ragtime.'"   Saturday Review   December
      1981:68-69.

      Forman and screenwriter Michael Weller maintain the rhythm, themes,
and purity of concept of E. L. Doctorow's novel.   They present early
20th-century America as a place full of possibilities and repressions.

Forman blends unknown actors with veteran stars such as James Cagney
very well, evokes great performances, and shows beautiful scenery.
Mostly reprinted in "Ragtime," Film Review Annual (book 1982).

435 Denby, David. "Slow Motion." New York 30 November 1981:63-65.

Ragtime demonstrates complete miscalculations in every aspect of
its production. Forman has taken all the fun out of the novel and made
an oversimplistic social drama. James Olson as Father, Mary Steenburgen
as Mother, and Brad Dourif as Younger Brother are irritatingly slow in
delivering their lines. Making Coalhouse Walker, Jr. immaculately
polite and condescending and placing his story at the film's center
gives it unwarranted significance in relation to American culture.
Moreover, Walker's story takes too long to reach an obvious conclusion.
James Cagney's scenes are also very awkward. Mostly reprinted in
"Ragtime," Film Review Annual (book 1982).

436 "Dialogue on Film: Mary Steenburgen." American Film October
     1981:12-22.

Steenburgen describes working with Forman as weird because he does
not let the actors see the daily footage. But, despite the insecurity
of not knowing how she was doing, she respected his talent. She wanted
to play Mother in Ragtime because the character is intelligent.

437 "For James Cagney's Return, New York Throws An Old-Time 'Ragtime'
     Premiere." People 7 December 1981:52-53.

Description of Ragtime's gala New York premiere, with a large
amount of respect paid to Cagney.

438 Hatch, Robert. "Ragtime." The Nation 12 December 1981:650-51.

Hatch takes time to describe several of the performances and finds
irony in James Cagney being billed over Howard E. Rollins. Forman
stuck to the center of the novel by concentrating on Coalhouse Walker's
story. The scenes of Stanford White's murder and Walker's car being
desecrated are particularly powerful.

439 Holloway, Robert. "Columbia U.'s Film School Now Attracts Europe's
     Helmers." Variety 14 January 1981:24.

Lecturing at Columbia has become a valued stop for European filmmakers since Forman took the job as co-chair of the film department
along with Frank Daniels. Forman's former teacher at Prague's film
school agreed to come to New York when he realized Forman was serious
about teaching and considered the depth of instruction Columbia offers
in several related fields.

440 Jacobs, Diane. "Making Books." Horizon December 1981:70-71.

Forman starts well, but Ragtime loses its energy when it focuses on
Coalhouse Walker's story. Except for a few moments, the characters are
mainly stereotypes.

441 Kael, Pauline. "The Swamp." New Yorker 23 November 1981:180-85.

Forman has no knowledge of American cultural history to enable him
to make a film like Ragtime. Producer Dino DeLaurentiis should have
kept Robert Altman as director. Forman tries to simplify things too
much, but even what is left does not make sense. Though the movie
centers on an angry black man, it has no social conscience. The actors
do well, but Forman handles them crudely, fully exploiting Elizabeth
McGovern's body.

442 Kauffmann, Stanley. "Turning the Century." The New Republic 2
     December 1981:24-26.

The book of Ragtime was great, built on cinematic conceptions and
ragtime rhythms that reflect America at its most optimistic point. What
the film keeps from the book is never explained. Forman himself has
always been overrated, and even his best work, Cuckoo's Nest, was
probably more of Jack Nicholson's product. The casting was all wrong
except for James Olson as Father and Robert Joy as Harry K. Thaw.

443 Kennedy, Harlan. "Ragtime: Milos Forman Searches for the Right
     Key." American Film December 1981:38-43.

Describing Ragtime as a thinking man's disaster film of sociological rather than physical change, Kennedy follows Forman's attempts
to cope with the myriad of scenes, characters, and plots. Forman and
writer Michael Weller talk about giving the story a strong narrative
spine based on its New England family. Forman discusses the relationship of individuals to institutions and how he and cinematographer
Miroslav Ondricek obtained the look they wanted for the film.

444 Kroll, Jack. "Ragtime in Waltz Time." Newsweek 23 November
     1981:124.

Believes Forman was too calculating in his creation. The energy,
wit, and memorable events of the novel are all missing. Even the
passion of Coalhouse Walker's rebellion is gone. The performances are
good, but the overall tone uncertain. Mostly reprinted in "Ragtime,"
Film Review Annual (book 1982).

445 McCourt, James. "Cynicon: Movies for Cynics." Film Comment
     November/December 1981:59-60.

Blasts Taking Off as a dated film with only one good scene: the
parents getting high.

446 Moss, Robert F. "The Americanization of Milos Forman." Saturday
     Review December 1981:14-18.

Discussion of Forman's work on the set of Ragtime, the development
of that project and Cuckoo's Nest, his success since Taking Off at
learning how to construct a tight narrative structure, and Forman's
biography.

447   O'Toole, Lawrence. "Broadway to Hollywood." Film Comment
      November/December 1981:22-25.

      Michael Weller, one of several playwrights who have also written
for the screen, comments that he was able to write the dialogue for
Ragtime after watching a silent film of a woman at the beginning of the
century.

448   "Ragtime." Variety 18 November 1981:14.

      Forman captures the novel almost perfectly. He maintains a con-
sistent emotional pitch while juggling characters and evoking the times
perfectly. The performances, production values, and score are remarkable as well, but the mass appeal of the film is still hard to predict.

449   Reed, Susan K. "'I Always Wanted to Be a Farmer.'" Saturday
      Review December 1981:17.

      James Cagney discusses his life in retirement on the farm and his
decision to work on Ragtime for health reasons. Forman and screenwriter
Michael Weller praise him as an actor and a person.

450   Rothenbuecker, Bea. "Ragtime." The Christian Century 16 December
      1981:1322.

      High praise for the cast, but the story lines fail to link up.
Robert Altman should have directed.

451   Sarris, Andrew. "Ragtime: Irony Plays Hide and Seek With
      Ideology." Village Voice 18-24 November 1981:57,60.

      Whatever the individual judgment, Ragtime is an intelligent
achievement that must be seen. Forman waves liberal causes and a
radical view of American history in the Reagenites' faces. James
Olson's and Mary Steenburgen's performances as Father and Mother, showing all of America's good intentions gone awry, allow the film to
surpass the novel. Mostly reprinted in "Ragtime," Film Review Annual
(book 1982).

452   Schickel, Richard. "'Some Kind of Genius.'" Time 16 November
      1981:120.

      Forman, Schickel, and fellow actor Pat O'Brien comment on James
Cagney's natural ability and grim determination in this review of his
career and plans for the future. Schickel finds him as sharp and witty
as ever in Ragtime.

453   Wolf, William. "When a Book Becomes a Movie." New York 30
      November 1981:66-67.

      Director Robert Altman explains that he and Ragtime author E. L.
Doctorow had wanted to recreate the novel on screen in the form of a
ten-hour tapestry that the viewer would form into a whole at the end.
Forman counters with his beliefs in a strong storyline and the need for
the director to have the same creative freedom with the materials that

the author had. Screenwriter Michael Weller agrees with Forman but
suggests the film would have gained excitement through the addition of
scenes vetoed by producer Dino DeLaurentiis. Wolf concludes that finding the cinematic means for expressing a great novel's spirit is the
only justification for filming it. Producers will always choose a
skillful, but predictable, director like Forman over an idiosyncratic
one like Altman, though the latter is more capable of genius.

454 Yakia, Dan. "Howard Rollins: Playing a Rebel, Not a Terrorist."
     American Film December 1981:42.

Brief biography of Rollins, how he came to understand the character
Coalhouse Walker, and his hopes for the future.

1982

Books

455 Kagan, Norman. Greenhorns: Foreign Filmmakers Interpret America.
     Ann Arbor, MI: Pieran Press, 1982.

Repeats the story about Forman's troubles getting financing for
Taking Off. Forman comments that creative freedom depends upon trust
from producers and help from cast and crew and tells about how much Buck
Henry helped him on his first American film. Following a lengthy synopsis of Taking Off, Forman comments about the lack of political content
in his films and the lack of runaways in Czechoslovakia. Kagan quotes a
few other critics and then offers his opinion that Taking Off accurately
reveals youth and adults acting within their own worlds, without placing
any false labels on either generation.

456 Simon, John. Reverse Angle: A Decade of American Films. New
     York: Charleson W. Potter, Inc., 1982.

Contains a reprint of Simon's "Forman Against Man" (periodical,
1971).

457 Willis, John. Screen World 1982. New York: Crown Publishers,
     Inc., 1982.

Contains stills and full production credits of Ragtime.

Newspapers

458 Brown, Geoff. "Uncluttered but Ominous Line." London Times 19
     February 1982:13.

Ragtime shares some themes with Forman's earlier work, but not the
same attention to human nuances. Forman strips down the narrative and
uses Hollywood veterans as a substitute for the book's use of historical
figures. The cast is excellent.

459 Caulfield, Deborah. "Forman: He Can Go Home Again." Los Angeles Times 3 November 1982:VI:1,6.

Forman discusses the origins of his interest in making Amadeus, why he has not worked with producer Saul Zaentz since Cuckoo's Nest, and his anticipation of working in Czechoslovakia again and seeing his twin sons. He has no idea who the leads will be.

460 Combs, Richard. "One man's sense of humor." Times Literary Supplement 26 February 1982:215.

E. L. Doctorow's Ragtime lacked a well-defined point, but it provided a fascinating picture of an era. Milos Forman's Ragtime makes only a tame social point made in 1950's "racial problem" films and does not tell enough about the era. Forman lingers too long on scenes which Doctorow skimmed through, picking out the most telling facts.

461 Kristal, Marc. "Making a Case for 'Ragtime.'" (letter) New York Times 7 February 1982:2:12.

Arguing with Times critic Vincent Canby, Kristal states that Ragtime is better than Reds because Forman gives it character and tone and comments positively about dissent and change throughout American history. Forman's film also artistically surpasses the novel.

Periodicals

462 Asahina, Robert. "Sorting Out the Film Glut." New Leader 25 January 1982:20-21.

In Ragtime, Forman is out of touch with his material. He spends too much time on the wrong episodes. Coalhouse Walker becomes foolish looking. The film is pretentious where the novel was humorous and inventive. Mostly reprinted in "Ragtime" Film Review Annual (book, 1982).

463 Buckley, Michael. "Ragtime." Films in Review January 1982:48-49.

Mainly a brief evaluation of each actor with special appreciation mentioned for James Cagney. Buckley calls the film interesting but flawed and ultimately depressing. Mostly reprinted in "Ragtime," Film Review Annual (book, 1982).

464 Coleman, John. "Exteriors." New Statesman 19 February 1982:29-30.

Mainly a plot description and high praise for the novel. Coleman finds both novel and film as highly entertaining and sometimes more. Mostly reprinted in "Ragtime," Film Review Annual (book, 1982).

465 Dickstein, Morris. "Time Bandits." American Film October 1982:39-43.

In Ragtime, decor triumphs over substance. The film looks good but gets dragged down in the Coalhouse Walker plot. It is neither good

history nor good drama. Forman is mainly concerned with the human elements that resist history. But he lets himself get trapped in the
strict plots and nostalgic liberalism of others.

466 Greenspan, Roger. "Rhythm and Blues." Penthouse February
     1982:50.

     Ragtime is broadly ambitious, sometimes inspired, but empty of
ideas. Forman redeems some of his effort in his handling of the actors.
But the film loses too much in what it cuts out of the book.

467 Harris, William. "'Do it my way.'" Forbes 6 December 1982:46,50.

     Summary of career and working methods of producer Dino
DeLaurentiis. Notes Ragtime is one of his few films to ever lose
money--about $6 million. Foreign distributors thought it too
intellectual.

468 Hey, Kenneth. "Films: Ragtime." USA Today March 1982:65.

     Another believer that Robert Altman was the man for this job. The
photography and production design yield some enchanting tableaux, but
Forman focuses too much on American shortcomings rather than the change
from values to institutions as a basis for society.

469 Jefferson, Margo. "Ragtime." Ms. February 1982:25,28.

     The performers valiantly attempt to overcome simplistic direction
and script. The film lacks psychological and historical texture and
even the rich visual details of the novel.

470 Miller, Edwin. "Movie of the Month." Seventeen January 1982:71.

     High praise for Ragtime. Miller summarizes the era and the plot.
Characters are introduced like themes in a symphony and woven together
until the whole is revealed.

471 Norment, Lynn. "'Ragtime' Star Is Rich in Talent." Ebony
     February 1982:115-122.

     An account of Howard E. Rollins, Jr.'s youth in Baltimore and rise
to stardom through Ragtime. Includes various critics' comments on
Rollins' performance.

472 Pulleine, Tom. "Fact and Fiction." Sight and Sound Spring
     1982:134.

     The performances and sets in Ragtime are fine, but the film is too
anecdotal. Forman fails to evoke the spirit of the times that Doctorow
managed. James Cagney's performance reveals more about legend and
popular memory than the entire remainder of the film.

473   Quart, Leonard and Barbara Quart. "Ragtime Without a Melody."
      Literature/Film Quarterly X.II (Spring 1982):71-74.

      Forman achieves some cinematic effects, especially in focusing on
individual characters, that the novel cannot match. But the film lacks
Doctorow's subtle irony regarding the futility of political and artistic
aspirations. Forman suffers from an over-reliance on traditional narrative and a lack of familiarity with American culture. The film needed a
director like Robert Altman who could turn American history into rol-
licking, but intelligent, entertainment.

474   Schlesinger, Arthur, Jr. "Ragtime and Reds." American Heritage
      April/May 1982:42.

      Forman captures E. L. Doctorow's sense of violent tendencies burst-
ing through an optimistic period, but not the historical complexity of
the novel. The performances are unusually good.

475   Seitz, Michael H. "Hits and Misses: Ragtime." The Progressive
      January 1982:47.

      Forman does his best, and the film starts brilliantly. But the
script reduces a complex historical work to a simple social problem
film.

476   Simon, John. "Wrong-Note Rag." National Review 5 February
      1982:122-23.

      The book was unfilmmable because the movies cannot capture a
kaleidoscopic structure originally created in print, and producer Dino
DeLaurentiis limited Forman even further to a conventional moral tale.
Some scenes and performances are good. The production values handsome.
But it does not work.

477   Smith, Ronn. "Organizing Ragtime." Theatre Crafts January
      1982:16-17,43-47.

      Art director Patrizia von Brandenstein describes the planning of
work and consideration for budgets and lenses needed in creating the
sets for a period film such as Ragtime.

478   ------------. "Ragtime on East 11th Street." Theatre Crafts
      January 1982:21,48-52.

      Set designer Patrizia von Brandenstein discusses choosing New
York's East 11th Street as the ideal place to recreate a 1906 immigrant
ghetto, remodeling the buildings and filling the street with sand to
achieve the proper look, and working with the community to benefit them
and the film.

479   Sragow, Michael. "Ragtime." Rolling Stone 18 February 1982:28.

      E. L. Doctorow created a novel full of the complex comedy and
tragedy of social possibilities in America. His ghetto dwellers could

rise out of poverty; his middle-class could fuel economic growth; and he examined the whole problem of celebrity in America. Forman and co-writer Michael Weller reduce the story to an Old Left critique of society.

480   "The Five Films Nominated For 'Best Cinematography' of 1981:
      'Ragtime.'" American Cinematographer 63.5 (May 1982):450,472-73,
      480,482-83.

Cinematographer Miroslav Ondricek talks about working in different countries, his research, filming, and crew on Ragtime, the influence of his career in documentary films on his work, and his desire not to let the photography interfere with the story.

481   Thomson, David. "Redtime." Film Comment January-February
      1982:11-16.

The key to Ragtime is in the contrast of two murders: that of Stanford White by Harry K. Thaw and that of racist, but defenseless, firemen by Coalhouse Walker and his men. The audience is left to question the nature of sanity, the American justice system and values, and the subtle effects of racism. The film is about looking, often from the viewpoint of a child. And that viewpoint produces the staring at and questioning of images prevalent in the film. Forman often focuses on faces, a key contrast being evident in the humble righteousness of Mary Steenburgen as Mother versus the carefree practicality of Elizabeth McGovern as Evelyn Nesbit. The film falters towards the end, but, together with Reds, it has helped return dignity to the big budget film. American critics need to re-assess their opinions.

482   Westerbeck, Colin L., Jr. "Rags to Revolution." Commonweal 12
      February 1982:87-89.

Entertaining. No character is around long enough to become dis-enchanting. Forman has modest, but sure-fire, talent.

483   Williamson, Bruce. "Movies." Playboy February 1982:28.

Ragtime is like an ode to the joy of cinema. Forman captures Doctorow's spirit perfectly and seems to have affected everyone involved with the film. The actors are outstanding.

                                    1983

Books

484   Bodeen, DeWitt. "One Flew Over the Cuckoo's Nest." Magill's
      American Film Guide Vol. 4. Englewood Cliffs, NJ: Salem Press,
      1983:2462-64.

Reprint of essay originally published in Magill's Survey of Cinema (book, 1980).

485   "Forman, Milos." The Illustrated Guide to Film Directors. Ed.
      David Quinlan. Totawa, NJ: Barnes and Noble Books, 1983:99-100.

Forman's best films were made in Czechoslovakia, The Firemen's Ball
being the most inventive. His Hollywood films are flamboyant, dealing
with innocents suffering within society. Cuckoo's Nest shows a dis-
tasteful manipulation of mentally ill people, but Ragtime captures the
spirit of a novel that many had thought unfilmable.

486   Paul, David W., Ed. Politics, Art, and Commitment in Eastern
      European Cinema. New York: St. Martin's Press, 1983.

Drawn from the proceedings of a conference held in Seattle,
Washington in October 1980, this essential work covers the experiences
of Eastern European nations in general and some of the leading artists
in particular. Much of the discussion focuses on the relationships
between the artist and his nation and what happens when these artists
move to the West. Many ideas and even more new areas for study are
suggested, particularly in the ambiguous area of style. The book includes the following essays that relate most directly to Forman.

487   Biro, Yvette. "Pathos and Irony in East European Film":28-48.

For Eastern European cinema as a whole, there was a movement from
pathos in the late 50s and early 60s to irony in the films of 1963 to
1970. Pathos is most clearly evident in Polish and Hungarian films from
the 50s. They reveal a concern with broad issues, an identification of
universal guilt, and a hope for the return of goodness. Sixties' irony
resulted from a shift in focus towards diversity and the particular.
Forman was part of a movement in Czech film back towards banality.
Insecure characters move through a world in which the rules are not
clear, but they somehow survive. Other forms of irony were more severe.
The films of both periods were conditioned by their eras and brought out
universal truths.

488   Daniel, Frantisek. "The Czech Difference":49-56.

In Czechoslovakia, irony always dominated pathos. Czech film had a
greater continuity with its own past and greater integration with the
national theatre and literature than did Hungarian or Polish film. All
Czech art forms saw the value of irony and satire as a weapon. Also,
Czechs lost illusions about communism slowly in the fifties, but the
sixties directors had few following reprisals in 1959. These perspec-
tives steered film away from pathos.

489   Liehm, Antonin J. "Milos Forman: The Style and the Man":211-24.

Forman's early artistic growth was based on a reaction against the
broad, empty symbols of Stalinism. Beginning with Competition (1963),
he began viewing people microscopically as humans in a way that was both
gentle and cruel. The Firemen's Ball (1967) represents his most merci-
less attack on human folly, mixed with sympathy for human helplessness.
Taking Off (1971) proved that Forman's style had become substance and
could adapt to any material. The Decathlon (1972) exemplifies his

vision in microcosm. With Cuckoo's Nest (1975), his style remained
constant, but a new optimistic tone crept into the conclusion. Hair
(1979) revealed a definite desire to please and reassure the audience.
The final question is whether or not Forman will be able to cope with
being part of the system.

490   Paul, David W. "Discussion":57-65.

All Eastern European films share a view of history as a living
reality. Stalinism attempted to impart a common heritage and enforced
optimism. Its downfall produced differing responses in various countries. Czech culture is plebian in origin. It tends to be concerned
with the lowly and find beauty and ideals tarnished by baseness. Polish
and Hungarian culture both reflect aristocratic influences. All Eastern
European films tell something about their makers' experiences but are
still universal.

491   ------------. "Discussion":252-76.

Considering the emigration of several Eastern European directors to
the West, what seems clear is that America needs some form of public
subsidizing of filmmakers in order to preserve film as an art. Milos
Forman and Roman Polanski have both succeeded in the West because their
styles were malleable, but Forman seems to have emphasized certain
aspects of his style in order to satisfy his audience's desires for
conformity. In both Hair (1979) and Ragtime (1981), Forman was not
familiar enough with his subject. Ragtime lacks the kaliedoscopic
vision of its source novel and continues the optimism of Cuckoo's Nest
and Hair.

492   "Ragtime." Film Review Annual 1982. Englewood Cliffs, NJ: Film
      Review Publications, 1983:951-69.

Includes full production credits and large excerpts from reviews in
the Los Angeles Times (newspaper 1981), the Monthly Film Bulletin, New
York, Newsweek, the Saturday Review, Time, the Village Voice,
(periodicals 1981), Films in Review, the New Leader, Sight and Sound
(periodicals 1982), Cineaste, the New Statesman, the New York Post,
Newsday, and Women's Wear Daily.

Newspapers

493   Borsten, Joan. "'Amadeus' Takes Forman Back Home." Los Angeles
      Times 29 May 1983:"Calendar,"17,19-20.

Forman is able to celebrate Prague's spectacular eighteenth-century
beauty in Amadeus. Much of the city remains the same as it was two
centuries ago. Besides architecture, Czechoslovakia also provided set
builders, costumes for the hundreds of extras, and processing. The
article also describes changes in the work from stage to screen, the
filming of Mozart's funeral scene, and bureaucratic difficulties
encountered with the Czechs.

494   "Czechoslovakia Bans Entry of New York Times Reporter."   New York
      Times   10 May 1983:I:6.

      Times reporter Henry Kamm was denied entry to the country to report
on the filming of Amadeus when he refused to allow Czech officials to
look through his address book.

495   Kamm, Henry.   "Milos Forman Takes His Cameras and 'Amadeus' to
      Prague."   New York Times   29 May 1983:2:1,15.

      Mainly an account of Forman's expressing his desire to film Amadeus
upon seeing the first public preview of the play in London. Forman and
Shaffer discuss their efforts to totally rewrite the work. Forman talks
about the reasons for filming in Prague, what it was like to be there,
and what winning an Oscar for Cuckoo's Nest meant to his career.

496   Sandler, Ken.   "Writers' Reel Tales: From Book Into Film."
      Washington Post   9 November 1983:D4.

      E. L. Doctorow, author of Ragtime, charges that films are "cultural
regression," and he will have nothing to do with them. Doctorow claims
he spent two years arguing with Forman and got some of what he wanted in
the film.

Periodicals

497   Ansen, David and Edward Beha.   "The Return of the Native."
      Newsweek   11 July 1983:41.

      Article discusses dealing with the Czech bureaucracy, changes from
stage to screen, and the casting of Mozart. Most Czechs had not heard
of Amadeus or Forman, even though he had great success there just twenty
years earlier.

498   Palumbo, Donald.   "Kesey's and Forman's One Flew Over the Cuckoo's
      Nest: The Metamorphosis of Metamorphosis as Novel Becomes Film."
      CEA Critic   45.2 (1983):25–32.

      Palumbo provides an excellent explanation of McMurphy's degenera-
tion in the novel from man to vegetable and reciprocal metamorphosis of
the Chief and the other patients. He also analyzes Kesey's questioning
of Christianity and the method of art. Palumbo then looks for these
same ideas in the film and, when he does not find them, accuses Forman
of producing a meaningless work.

499   Sasanow, Richard. "Scoring With Mozart."   American Film   September
      1983:13.

      Conductor Neville Marriner comments about Forman and Shaffer's
desire to work with complete recordings of Mozart's music as he wrote it
and not mere arrangements that could be fit in various places. Marriner
found the method of recording the music first and then filming around it
to be very unusual.

500   Whitmen, Peter O.   "Ken Kesey's Search for the American Frontier."
      Saturday Review   May-June 1983:23-27.

      Kesey expresses his ideas about the future, his anger about his
lack of income from the movie of Cuckoo's Nest, his belief that the
filmmakers missed the point by making Nurse Ratched the villain (though
he has never seen the movie), and his disgust with Jack Nicholson having
played the lead. He would have preferred Gene Hackman.

                                    1984

Books

501   Cagin, Seth and Philip Dray.   Hollywood Films of the Seventies:
      Sex, Drugs, Violence, Rock 'n' Roll, and Politics.   New York:
      Harper and Row, 1984.

      Cagin and Dray basically provide a plot summary of Cuckoo's Nest,
but actually say nothing about how the film relates to its time. They
comment that it equates manliness with sanity and shows competitiveness
as a positive quality.

502   "Josef Skvorecky."   Contemporary Authors Autobiography Series,
      Volume 1   Detroit: Gale Research Publishing Co., 1984.

      Includes Skvorecky's account of his collaboration with Forman on a
screenplay of "Eine Kliene Jazzmusick" in 1959 originally published in
All the Bright Young Men and Women (book, 1971).

503   Lieberman, Susan and Frances Cable, comps. Memorable Film
      Characters: An Index to Roles and Performers, 1915-1983.
      Westport, CN: Greenwood Press, 1984.

      Contains brief characterizations of Billy Bibbit, Chief Bromden,
R. P. McMurphy, and Nurse Ratched from Cuckoo's Nest and Willie Conklin,
Evelyn Nesbit, and Coalhouse Walker, Jr. from Ragtime.

504   Skvorecky, Josef.   "Forman, Milos."   The International Dictionary
      of Films and Filmmakers: Volume II Directors/Filmmakers.   Ed.
      Christopher Lyon.   Chicago: St. James Press, 1984:194-95.

      Influenced more by Czech novelists than Western cinema, Forman's
early films used nonprofessional actors, lively dialogue, and music to
take a detailed look at Czech society that differed with the tenets of
socialist realism. Forman's support by liberals within the Communist
Party and capture of awards at festivals made him a star of the 60s'
Czech New Wave. Except for Taking Off and Cuckoo's Nest, Forman's
American films have lacked the touch of his Czech works. His decision
to create only adaptations of popular works has made him a less innovative force. But his portrayal of people attempting to cope with forces
over which they have no control answers critics who accuse him of
cruelty. Chronology, filmography, and selected bibliography included.

505   Urgosiikova, B.   "Lasky Jedne Plavovlasky."   The International
      Dictionary of Films and Filmmakers: Volume I Films.   Ed.
      Christopher Lyon.   Chicago: St. James Press, Inc., 1984:251-52.

      Forman's early films, such as Loves of a Blonde, derive from their
concentration on average young people who dream of romance and greatness
but will never achieve either.   His staring camera could be cruel, but
he softens the effect by noticing the humor in every situation.   His use
of documentary style disrupts the traditional narrative form, creating
instead a mosaic that the viewer must piece together.   This style was
something totally new in Czechoslovakia.   Complete credits and selected
bibliography included.

Newspapers

506   Anthony, Michael.   "Trying To Get The Most Out Of Mozart."   Los
      Angeles Times   7 October 1984:"Calendar,"26-27.

      Conductor Neville Marriner, of the Academy-of-St. Martin-in-the-
Fields Orchestra, selected by Forman and producer Saul Zaentz to record
the music for Amadeus, applauds the filmmakers' attention to detail.
Marriner agreed to the work only if the music could be recorded intact.
He explains the reasons for using his British orchestra, why they did
not use period instruments, and Forman's devotion to using the music
during the filming of particular scenes.

507   Benson, Sheila.   "The Music of Mozart, The Magic of the Film
      Maker--That's 'Amadeus.'"   Los Angeles Times   19 September
      1984:"Calendar,"1,6.

      The music, acting, directing, screenwriting, cinematography, and
sets all create an enthralling film experience.

508   Canby, Vincent.   "Film: 'Amadeus' Arrives on Screen."   New York
      Times   19 September 1984:22.

      Canby may not like the film as much as the play, but he praises
Forman for preserving its heart.   He also praises the settings, the
music, and most of the performances, taking particular exception to
Elizabeth Berridge.   Canby particularly admires Amadeus' celebration of
genius.

509   ------------.   "Stage and Screen Go Their Separate Ways."   New York
      Times   30 September 1984:2:1,19.

      The stage provides restrictions within which modern playwrights
have learned to work to allow the audience to share their imagination.
But this style has increased the difficulty of adapting their work for
the screen.   Amadeus preserves the heart of Peter Shaffer's play, but it
also loses the emotional qualities present in the stage work.   Though
well-made, the film often wanders aimlessly while the play continually
holds the imagination.

510   Farber, Stephen.   "Casting the Coveted 'Amadeus' Roles."   New York
      Times   20 September 1984:III:18.

      Forman mentions the qualities he looked for in casting the roles of
      Antonio Salieri and Wolfgang Amadeus Mozart. F. Murray Abraham and Tom
      Hulce, who got the parts, discuss their relationship on the set and how
      they immersed themselves in their characters and the culture in which
      they lived.'

511   Gendel, Morgan.   "A European Fortissimo For Forman's 'Amadeus.'"
      Los Angeles Times   23 December 1984:"Calendar,"40.

      Forman reports on the phenomenal success of Amadeus throughout
      Europe, the success of the soundtrack album on American popular music
      charts, and his hope that the film will be seen in Czechoslovakia.

512   Gosney, Cynthia.   "Chewing a Cream Puff, and Other Sounds."
      Washington Post   3 July 1984:D2.

      A discussion of "Foleying" (creating sounds) for films, specifi-
      cally Amadeus. The cream puff sound was created by chewing rotten
      cantaloupe, and carriage sounds by jumping on a wooden baby seat.

513   Haithman, Diane.   "The Animal Plays Amadeus."   Tulsa World   30
      September 1984:H2.

      Brief summary of Tom Hulce's career. Mostly famous for his role in
      Animal House, Hulce was attracted to the role of Mozart because the
      character is just an average man who happens to be a genius.

514   Henahan, Donal.   "Never Mind Salieri, Sussmayer Did It."   New York
      Times   23 September 1984:2:1,21.

      Recounts the role Mozart's pupil Franz Xavier Sussmayer actually
      played in Mozart's final years that Amadeus attributes to Salieri.
      Credits the film for highlighting the music, Tom Hulce's convincing
      pianist imitations, and the revealing musical composing and dictation
      techniques in the final scene. Showing the composers conducting from
      the podium instead of the keyboard, however, was totally inaccurate.

515   Kakutani, Michiko.   "How 'Amadeus' Was Translated From Play to
      Film."   New York Times   16 September 1984:2:1,20.

      Peter Shaffer works on the stage--a verbal medium. Milos Forman
      works in film--a visual medium. Their collaboration on the filmscript
      of Shaffer's play Amadeus, therefore, involved several arguments as
      Shaffer attempted to hold onto his original work and Forman tried to
      create something entirely new, using the same characters and ideas.
      Shaffer basically agreed with Forman because earlier films of his plays
      had attempted to re-create the original works and had all failed. In
      the end, they cut a lot of dialogue and added several new characters and
      scenes. Most importantly, a great deal of Mozart's music was added.
      This article gives good insights into how Shaffer and Forman did it and
      Forman's basic screenwriting methods.

516 Kempley, Rita. "Some Power, Much Glory in 'Amadeus.'" Washington
     Post (Weekend) 21 September 1984:23.

A positive review, focusing on Mozart's suppression by bureaucratic
forces. Kempley likes every aspect of the film except for the performances of Tom Hulce and Elizabeth Berridge.

517 Klein, Alvin. "Larchmont Actress to Open in Play." New York Times
     9 December 1984:XXII:14-15.

Life, career, and plans of Elizabeth Berridge, Constanze Mozart in
Amadeus. Berridge responds to critics of her performance and talks
about working with Forman. She received the part a week before shooting
began when Meg Tilly broke an ankle.

518 Mann, Roderick. "'Amadeus' Stars Take Shine To Challenge." Los
     Angeles Times 26 September 1984:"Calendar,"1,7.

Actually, a pair of articles about F. Murray Abraham and Tom Hulce.
Abraham's career is reviewed. Forman found him for the role during a
casting call. Hulce discusses learning to play the piano, his Broadway
debut in Peter Shaffer's Equus, and the audition process for the role of
Mozart in Amadeus.

519 Maslin, Janet. "At the Movies: A Standing Tribute." New York
     Times 5 October 1984:III:8.

Jeffrey Jones remarks that the role of Emperor Joseph II in Amadeus
appealed to him because everybody would stand when he walked into a
room.

520 Matthews, Jack. "'Amadeus' is as brilliant as Mozart." USA Today
     19 September 1984:D1.

Matthews calls the film as close to perfect as possible and praises
Forman's use of music as dialogue in particular.

521 McLellan, Joseph. "'Amadeus': Music, Mystery and the Grandeur of
     Genius." Washington Post 19 September 1984:B1,B12.

A detailed plot description that praises Amadeus for its beauty,
humor, use of music, and presentation of genius. The historical fal-
lacies are unimportant, but the question about the nature of God is not.

522 ------------. "Who Killed Mozart?" Washington Post 30 September
     1984:H1,H4-H5.

Factual article about Mozart's life, relationship with Salieri, and
best recordings of his music. Designed to help those in conversations
sparked by Amadeus.

523   Miller, Bryan. "At New Pastry School, A Special Cake." New York
      Times 12 September 1984:III:3.

Describes the creation of an eight-foot cake for the Amadeus
premiere party.

524   Shaffer, Peter. "Paying Homage to Mozart." The New York Times
      Magazine 2 September 1984:22,25,35,38.

Shaffer talks of using specific pieces of Mozart's music as evidence of divinity in the world. Yet, Mozart's music demonstrates
restraint, a mixture of shadows and joy. The last section of the film
Amadeus attempts to show these two attitudes conflicting in him. The
film also uses masks to celebrate Mozart as dramatist. Article partially reprinted in the Lonton Times, 16 January 1985.

525   Swan, Christopher. "'Amadeus' plays with musical genius, and
      strikes wrong chord." Christian Science Monitor 2 October
      1984:26.

The film does violence to history by presenting a Mozart who has no
knowledge of the human spirit and puts no effort into his achievements.
It also labels everyone else as mediocrites instead of being exalting.

526   Wadler, Joyce. "A Little Mozart." Washington Post 28 October
      1984:H1,H5.

In this brief interview, Forman discusses his personal life from
childhood through his two marriages and his move to America. He also
tells how he became interested in Amadeus.

527   Yardley, Jonathan. "'Amadeus': Minimally Mozart." Washington
      Post 3 December 1984:C2.

Amadeus is a beautiful but shallow movie because it blatantly lies
about Mozart's life and reduces his genius to being a mere instrument of
God. While Lawrence of Arabia and Ghandi sought to illuminate history,
Amadeus is a cynical work that misconstrues history for the sake of
melodrama.

Periodicals

528   Aloff, Mindy. "Degas: The Dancers." "Amadeus." Nation 22
      December 1984:692-93.

Amadeus creates a direct correlation between dance and exuberant
life through the character of Mozart. Twyla Tharp's choreography is not
authentic, but it does work well with the music and settings to create
splendid effects. Forman's Mozart is like Berger in Hair, crashing
elite social functions through his liveliness.

529   "Amadeus."   Variety   5 September 1984:12.

Still a potent drama, but now too heavily dependent on a one-dimensional characterization of Mozart as opposed to the play, where the focus was on Antonio Salieri. F. Murray Abraham and Jeffrey Jones are excellent as Salieri and the Emperor. But Forman seems to have miscast Tom Hulce and Elizabeth Berridge as Mozart and his wife. The amount of opera in the film will probably hurt it at the box office outside of major cities.

530   Ansen, David. "A Genius Despite Himself."   Newsweek   24 September 1984:85.

Amadeus is sumptuous for both eye and ear. It is strongest when it stays close to musical matters, but Salieri's revenge plot does not make sense. Forman's biggest mistake is in the monumental nature of his directing. He seems to have lost the personal touch of his Czech years and makes his points much too forcefully.

531   Blake, Richard A. "God's Grandeur."   America   13 October 1984:210.

Amadeus powerfully presents the mystery of God's greatness. The plot structure resembles Salieri's attempts to place a human order on creation and shows man's hopelessness in such an effort.

532   Boyum, Joy Gould. "Movies."   Glamour   October 1984:238.

Amadeus is a blackly comic exploration of genius, fame, and jealousy. The sets and performances are beautiful.

533   Conniff, Richard. "Milos Forman."   GEO   April 1984:10-22.

Forman discusses in detail the last times he saw his parents and the effect that the Nazi occupation had on his life. The conversation also reveals some of his ideas about parent-child relationships. Other topics are the differences between European and American films, going back to Prague to film Amadeus, working with Jimmy Cagney and Norman Mailer on Ragtime, and film critics.

534   Corliss, Richard. "Mozart's Greatest Hits."   Time   10 September 1984:74-75.

The play seemed unfilmmable, but Forman found a way by returning to a conservative narrative structure after the failures of Hair and Ragtime. Forman and Shaffer highlight the music and challenge the audience about the nature of genius. Tom Hulce and F. Murray Abraham, as Mozart and Antonio Salieri, give brilliant performances. The setting, style, and budget of the film make it questionable at the box-office, but audiences will respond to a film that says they too can be Mozart.

535   Czarnecki, Mark.   "A Duet of Jealousy and Genius."   <u>Macleans</u>   1
October 1984:83.

<u>Amadeus</u> boasts beautiful sets that fail to obscure a fine cast and
subtle script.   It cannot completely succeed in capturing the essence of
Mozart's music, but its achievements are awesome.

536   Delloff, Linda-Marie.   "Current Cinema."   <u>The Christian Century</u>   24
October 1984:995-96.

Forman exploits all of film's ability to present grandeur in
<u>Amadeus</u> while spanning the emotional spectrum of life itself.   The film
questions the value of art and focuses on Antonio Salieri's changing
relationship to God.

537   Denby, David.   "Mozartomania."   <u>New York</u>   24 September 1984:93-95.

Denby has both high praise and heavy criticism for <u>Amadeus</u>.   He
likes most of the acting except for that by Tom Hulce and Elizabeth
Berridge.   He likes what the film does for classical music and opera,
probably more than any film ever.   He does not like Shaffer's
implication that Mozart was divinely inspired, an idea that reduces the
scope of his genius, the carrying of the Salieri legend to extremes, and
the idea that contemporary society would have appreciated Mozart.
Actually, though Mozart's society persecuted him, it was also the only
one that could have produced him.

538   Edelstein, David.   "Wolfiegate."   <u>Village Voice</u>   25 September
1984:63.

<u>Amadeus</u> is opulent and well-paced, but not much more than a kinky
biopic.   The horror is that it defines talent as a random gift of God,
not the result of hard work and character.   F. Murray Abraham and
Jeffrey Jones (as Emperor Joseph II) give excellent performances.
Shaffer powerfully states that being praised for poor work is worse than
being damned for good.   But the new conclusion makes the film a rich
buddy-buddy story.   Finally, <u>Amadeus</u> uses the music to produce all of
its emotion.   The film has none of its own.

539   Fayard, Judy and Nancy Griffin.   "Madcap Mozart."   <u>Life</u>   September
1984:66-68.

Tom Hulce and F. Murray Abraham talk about their satisfaction at
landing the roles of Mozart and Salieri and their preparations.

540   Flatley, Guy.   "The Wolfgang's All Here?"   <u>Cosmopolitan</u> November
1984:28.

Presenting Mozart as a buffoonish American college student took
nerve, but it works.   His antics can be irritating, but the music is
sublime.

541   Gelatt, Roland.   "Mostly Amadeus."   <u>Horizon</u>   September 1984:49-52.

Biography of Peter Shaffer and a few details about life with the
<u>Amadeus</u> company in Prague.   Shaffer discusses the themes and inspira-

tions of his plays, adapting Amadeus for the screen, and highlighting Mozart's music in the film.

542 Greenspan, Roger. "Class Acts." Penthouse December 1984:60.

Except for Mozart's music and Jeffrey Jones' performance as Emperor Joseph II, not much in Amadeus is of any value. Forman's direction is ponderous and the character analysis is at a kindergarten level.

543 Hodenfield, Chris. "The Czech Bounces Back." Rolling Stone 27 September 1984:19-23.

Discussion of Forman's ability to overcome all the upheaval in his life including the loss of his parents in concentration camps, his inability to go home to Czechoslovakia for several years, and his nervous breakdown following the failure of Taking Off. Forman also talks about choosing Tom Hulce to play Mozart in Amadeus and working with Peter Shaffer and Twyla Tharp.

544 Hoffman, Eva. "Mozart on the Couch." Vogue October 1984:636,696-97.

Amadeus succeeds in accurately linking Mozart's music with his environment and his era, but fails in its attempt to reveal the source of his genius. The play distanced viewers from Mozart by showing him solely through Salieri's eyes, but the film presents him more unsatisfactorily by moving closer to him. Forman and Shaffer equate Mozart's genius with his lack of sexual inhibitions, a questionble notion, and Tom Hulce's performance takes the character far out of his time. The conclusion, the music, the beauty, and the drama are all great elements, but the film does not allow an adequate suspension of disbelief.

545 "It's a Glittering Guest List, Not Mostly Mozart, That Makes Amadeus A Hollywood Hit." People 24 September 1984:45-46.

Description of the party following Amadeus's Los Angeles premiere. Some of the stars in attendance see the film as a tale of Hollywood greed.

546 Jacobson, Harlan. "As Many Notes as Required." Film Comment 20.5 (1984):50,53-55.

A rare type of article, focusing on the relationship between director and producer: Forman and Saul Zaentz. Jacobson cites examples of creative conflicts in the two films on which they have worked together, Cuckoo's Nest and Amadeus, to show that Zaentz is a successful producer because he is not primarily concerned with money. Jacobson also suggests that Cuckoo's Nest presents an oppressive society while Amadeus reveals problems within individuals, thus showing the difference between 1975 and 1984.

547   Kael, Pauline.   "Mozart and Bizet."   The New Yorker   29 October
      1984:122-23.

      Amadeus is little more than a stale costume drama to which the
music and Twyla Tharp's choreography bring an occasional reprieve.
Forman and Shaffer insult Mozart by claiming that his genius was a gift
from God.   F. Murray Abraham never gets to bring his performance
together and Tom Hulce is disgusting.   See also Kael's The State of the
Art   (1985).

548   Kauffmann, Stanley.   "Divertimento."   The New Republic   22 October
      1984:30-32.

      Amadeus is Forman's best directorial effort.   He balances a his-
torical view with present day satire very nicely.   The script is still
weak—Salieri is more angry about Mozart's manners than jealous of his
genius.   But having Salieri confess to a priest instead of the audience
and making the ending ironical are improvements over the stage version.
Of the three lead actors, only F. Murray Abraham does well.

549   Krupp, Carla.   "Twyla Tharp Takes On Amadeus."   Glamour   October
      1984:238.

      Tharp researched eighteenth-century dance for six months and
attempted to make it accessible to modern audiences.

550   "A Movie That's Music to Our Ears."   Mademoiselle   October
      1984:80.

      Comments most significantly on Tom Hulce's learning to play the
piano for his role as Mozart in Amadeus and Forman's reasons for selecting Elizabeth Berridge to replace Meg Tilly as Constanze Mozart.

551   O'Brien, Tom.   "Mozart and Murder."   Commonweal   19 October
      1984:557-58.

      In Amadeus, Peter Shaffer stretches the historical credibility of
the Mozart character too far in order to create a conflict of a
primitive genius and a modern sophisticate.   But the music is moving,
revealing spiritual truth and characterization.

552   Seitz, Michael H.   "School Daze."   The Progressive   December
      1984:38.

      Some aspects of Amadeus are grating, but it has a fast pace,
beautiful sets, and glorious music.

553   Shaffer, Peter.   "Making the Screen Speak."   Film Comment October
      1984:50-51,56-57.

      Shaffer discusses how Forman convinced him to help adapt Amadeus
for the screen, their method of collaboration, the degree of historical
accuracy in the film, the dramatic necessity of the climactic scene, and
the role of producer Saul Zaentz during the filming.

554   Simon, John. "Bizet's Carmen, Shaffer's Amadeus." National Review
       19 October 1984:55-57.

       The whole idea, and especially the conclusion, is tremendously
       appalling. Characters have no depth, the acting is terrible, and Forman
       makes the most heavy-handed and obvious use of symbolism and music to
       support points.

555   Stark, John. "Going Home to Prague to Film Amadeus Evokes Bitter-
       sweet Memories for Milos Forman." People 8 October 1984:113-117.

       Discusses Forman's two marriages, his agreements with Czech author-
       ities to allow him to work in Prague again, the casting of Tom Hulce as
       Mozart, and critics' complaints with historical inaccuracies in Amadeus.

556   Travers, Peter. "Picks and Pans: Screen." People 1 October
       1984:14.

       The music in Amadeus, as the voice of God, is a new central
       character added from the play. The expertly chosen cast adds to it
       marvelously. Only the flashback technique hinders the pace.

557   Walsh, Michael. "'Amadeus,' Shamadeus." Film Comment 20.5
       (1984):51-52.

       Walsh accuses Amadeus of mangling history. Salieri was not a
       mediocrity. Mozart was not unpopular in his own time, and his family
       was never broke. The music could have been played on 18th-century
       instruments but was not. Walsh also mentions funeral customs under
       Joseph II and Mozart's relationships with aristocrats.

558   Williamson, Bruce. "Movies." Playboy November 1984:18.

       The grandest epic ever made about a composer's life. F. Murray
       Abraham does not quite carry the role of Salieri, but the rest of the
       cast is fine. Amadeus is a beautiful, daring film that celebrates great
       music passionately.

                                    1985

Books

559   Boyum, Joy Gould. Double Exposure: Fiction Into Film. New York:
       Universe Books, 1985.

       Ragtime was a failure because the filmmakers did not realize that
       the novel's substance was in its style, for which they made no attempt
       to find a cinematic equivalent. The film opts for a traditional narra-
       tive flow, reducing the novel's historical scope and completely losing
       its vision. The film is also too slow, has no equivalents for the
       novel's many shocking images, and completely loses the ambiguous rela-

tionships between fiction and reality that the book contains. Finally, the music is entirely conventional, which leaves ragtime out of the film altogether.

560   De Nitto, Dennis. Film: Form and Feeling. New York: Harper and Row, 1985.

In some brief comments, De Nitto cites Forman's Czech films as all sharing a semidocumentary tone and revealing the way a nation's mores and conventions affect its people. He also calls Hair the most sensitive and intelligent rock musical ever made.

561   Finler, Joel W. The Movie Director's Story. New York: Crescent Books, 1985.

Brief summary of Forman's career. Forman is at his best in small scale projects, and he will hopefully return to them in the future. Loves of a Blonde has significant insights, but Amadeus is only a middle-brow view of high culture.

562   Hames, Peter. The Czechoslovak New Wave. Berkeley: University of California Press, 1985.

Approaching his subject from an autuerist perspective, Hames discusses the films of each director in relation to social, cultural, and artistic trends both within Cezchoslovakia and internationally. With Forman, for example, Hames explains his use of cinema-verité, Italian neo-realism, and French nouvelle-vague techniques all within the context of his distinct brand of realism that both reveals and questions life in Czechoslovakia and the assumptions that all of us make. Forman, in his Czech films, uses a basically episodic approach to scriptwriting. But he does not attack narrative conventions. Hames concentrates mainly on Black Peter, Loves of a Blonde, and The Firemen's Ball, but also mentions how Forman continues focusing on his favorite themes in Taking Off and Cuckoo's Nest. Forman rarely acknowledges the political dimension to his work because he does not wish to have his films reduced to that context.

563   Kael, Pauline. State of the Art. New York: E. P. Dutton, 1985.

Contains a reprint of her review of Amadeus (periodical, 1984).

564   Lorenz, Janet E. "Amadeus." Magill's Cinema Annual 1985. Ed. Frank N. Magill. Englewood Cliffs, NJ: Salem Press, 1985:63-68.

Acting, cinematography, costuming, scenery, and music all worked together splendidly to bringing Amadeus eight well-deserved Oscars. The film states that man cannot make bargains with God, but must watch helplessly as life continues amid the ruins of his plans. Long plot summary included.

565 Oumano, Ellen. Film Forum: Thirty-five Top Filmmakers Discuss Their Craft. New York: St. Martin's Press, 1985.

Forman cites patience and the inability to turn back as keys to his American success. He also discusses how he likes characters to talk rather than discuss. In Hair, characters never had to discuss issues because the song lyrics did. Forman mentions tricks he uses to get natural performances from actors and his involvement in the whole film-making process from writing through shooting to editing.

566 Rusinko, Susan. "Loves of a Blonde." Magill's Survey of Cinema Foreign Language Films, Vol. IV. Ed. Frank N. Magill. Englewood Cliffs, NJ: Salem Press, 1985:1848-52.

Similar to Chekov, Karel Capek, and other Eastern European artists, Forman captures universal truths in trivial objects or brief moments. These moments carry Loves beyond its banal truths. Forman draws no conclusions and causes no great changes in his characters' lives. Clinging to dreams in the face of reality is the basis of his art. In contrast to conventional comedies, the humor does not undercut tragedy, but vice-versa.

567 Willis, John. Screen World 1985. New York: Crown Publishers, Inc., 1985.

Contains stills and full production credits of Amadeus.

568 Wilson, John. "The Firemen's Ball." Magill's Survey of Cinema Foreign Language Films, Vol III. Ed. Frank N. Magill. Englewood Cliffs, NJ: Salem Press, 1985:1086-90.

Despite Forman's disclaimer at the start of the American version, The Firemen's Ball contains specific political messages. On the whole, it has a well-paced feeling of artlessness that reveals human cruelty without condemning. But the self-conscious images of the house burning down are difficult to interpret. Forman's American films have not reached this level, meaning the quality here probably stems from his collaboration with Ivan Passer and Jaroslav Papousek and the creative climate of the times.

Dissertation

569 Slater, Thomas J. "Milos Forman: The Evolution of a Filmmaker." Ph.D. Dissertation: Oklahoma State University, 1985.

A chronological examination of Forman's life and work incorporating all of his films. Emphasizes the combination of Forman's thematic con-sistency along with his continual relevance. Also examines Forman's writing, filming, and editing techniques and use of such elements as music and color in relation to each film.

Newspapers

570   "'Amadeus' Tops Golden Globes." Washington Post   28 January
      1985:132.

      Brief mention of Forman winning for Best Director, the film for
Best Film, and Peter Shaffer and F. Murray Abraham for Best Screenplay
and Best Actor.

571   "Angry town to erect statue." London Times   25 March 1985:5.

      Salieri's birthplace, Legrano, Italy, decides to honor him in
response to Amadeus's insinuation that he murdered Mozart.

572   Attanasio, Paul. "The Decline and Fall of Oscar." Washington Post
      17 February 1985:F1,F5.

      While lambasting the Ocars, Attanasio draws some parallels between
them and Amadeus. The film can be seen as a parable of Hollywood, where
professional jealousy abounds. Out-of-work film people want to believe
that talent will simply descend on them. Amadeus will win because
Hollywood wants to prove it has taste.

573   Brown, Geoff. "Darkly Comic Tale of Human Glory and Infamy."
      London Times 18 January 1985:13.

      The opulence of Amadeus does not detract from its substance.
Forman shows a strong sense of narrative possibilities. The editing
makes crucial points, and the cast is excellent.

574   ------------. "Delicacy in the Quest for Mozart." London Times
      12 January 1985:18.

      Story of organizing Amadeus. Original play was entirely rewritten,
actors were chosen for believability, Prague was chosen as location
with Forman forced to make agreements with the Czech government.

575   Champlin, Charles. "Jeffrey Jones Rising On Musical Note." Los
      Angeles Times 10 January 1985:V:1,6.

      A review of Jones' career and his research for the role of Emporer
Joseph II in Amadeus. Forman found him doing a play, Cloud 9, in New
York.

576   Cummings, Judith. "Joy, Astonishment, and Pain Are Part of Oscar's
      Aftermath." New York Times 26 March 1985:III:13.

      F. Murray Abraham comments that half of his best actor award should
belong to Tom Hulce. Forman reveals that Amadeus may become his first
American film to be shown in Czechoslovakia.

577   Davis, Ivor.   "Hollywood's Symphony of Oscars for Amadeus."
      London Times   27 March 1985:36.

      List of the awards. Forman comments on the international involve-
ment in the film and its appeal to both young and old. Teenagers loved
Mozart's rebelliousness while adults enjoyed the music and philoso-
phizing.

578   "Directors' Guild of America Announces Award Nominees." New York
      Times   2 February 1985:13.

      Announcement that Forman has been nominated for the Guild's award
for Amadeus, the winner of which almost always wins the Academy Award as
well.

579   Dunlap, David W. and Sally Rimer.   "An Oscar For the Professor."
      New York Times   27 March 1985:II:3.

      Comments on Columbia University students' reactions to Forman's
winning an Oscar for Amadeus. They were happy though some did not like
the film. Forman teaches courses on directing at Columbia.

580   "Golden Globes for 'Amadeus.'" London Times   28 January 1985:6.

      Notes winning of four Golden Globe awards: Best Picture, Director,
Screenplay, and Actor.

581   Hall, Carla.   "Twice Around With Oscar." Washington Post   1 April
      1985:B1,B4.

      Account of Forman's celebrations after winning the Oscar for
Amadeus, his early struggles to succeed in America, and what winning
means to him. Forman comments on the appeal of the Salieri character
and praises the performance of Jeffrey Jones as Emporer Franz Joseph II.

582   Harmetz, Aljean.   "'Amadeus' in Sweep of Oscars, Wins Best Film and
      Seven Other Awards." New York Times   26 March 1985:III:13.

      Notice of awards given to Amadeus.

583   ------------.   "Milos Forman Wins Directors' Guild Award." New
      York Times   11 March 1985:III:13.

      Forman announced as winner for Amadeus. Only two Guild winners
ever failed to get Oscars.

584   ------------.   "Two Films Top Oscar Nominations." New York Times
      7 February 1985:III:19.

      Announcement of Forman's nomination for Best Director and other
nominations for Amadeus.

585   London, Michael. "'Amadeus': Box-Office Strategy." Los Angeles
      Times 27 March 1985:VI:1,7.

Orion Pictures plans heavy booking of Amadeus following the Oscars.
Initial bookings were light, with the company counting on some Oscars to
boost the box-office returns. However, success at the Academy Awards
does not bring in the audiences that it used to.

586   ------------. "DGA Nod To Forman For 'Amadeus.'" Los Angeles
      Times 11 March 1985:VI:1,5.

Announcement of Forman as winner of the Directors' Guild of America
Award for Best Director. He did not attend the ceremonies.

587   Preston, John. "Going Home to First Principles." London Times   9
      January 1985:13.

Forman talks about missing his native land, about choosing to work
with adaptations in America as a means of losing his foreigner status,
and about choosing Tom Hulce to play Mozart in Amadeus because audiences
would believe he is the composer.

588   Shaffer, Peter. "Mozartian Magic Behind the Masks." London Times
      16 January 1985:9.

Partial reprint of article originally appearing in the New York
Times 2 September 1984.

589   Shales, Tom. "Mozart's Night!" Washington Post   26 March
      1985:C1,C8.

Review of the Academy Awards ceremony at which Forman won for Best
Director and Amadeus for Best Picture. Amadeus also won for Best Actor,
Best Sound, Makeup, Costume Design, Screenplay Adaptation, and Art
Direction.

590   Sofer, Anne. "A Fitting Homage to Genius." London Times   25
      February 1985:14.

Amadeus at first seems to have too much of a Hollywood facade, but
eventually the audience becomes entranced by the music, which lifts it
onto a higher plane than what most modern entertainment offers.

Periodicals

591   Adair, Gilbert. "What's Opera, Doc?" Sight and Sound Spring
      1985:142-43.

Forman's version of Peter Shaffer's Amadeus is a genuine
adaptation, enlivening and clarifying the plot by presenting a cartoon
version of the eighteenth century. Salieri and Mozart are reminiscent
of many combatting characters from American film, but mostly of the
Roadrunner and Wily Coyote.

592   "'Amadeus' Score Adaptors Honored by Picture Academy."   _Variety_ 27
      March 1985:5,28.

      Orchestra conductor Neville Marriner and music supervisor John
Strauss received special commendation from the Academy of Motion Picture
Arts and Sciences for their work on _Amadeus_. The two were unable to
receive Oscars because there was no category in which they could
compete.

593   Clarke, Gerald. "Eight Cheers for the Music Man."   _Time_ 8 April
      1985:74.

      An account of _Amadeus_' winning of eight Academy Awards, including
statements by Forman and fellow director Ivan Passer about the reasons
for its success. Clarke also mentions the marketing strategy for the
film.

594   Coleman, John. "Musical Shares."   _New Statesman_ 18 January
      1985:34.

      In _Amadeus_, Milos Forman provides comedy, lush music, and wonderful
opera stagings and successfully does away with the old convention that
only British actors can play cultured Europeans.

595   Corliss, Richard. "Larger Than Life."   _Time_ 8 July 1985:94.

      Forman expresses his gratefulness to America and his admiration for
its diversity. He believes that his large vision of the country is
accurate. Corliss notes how Forman's American films have maintained the
themes of the individual versus the system from his Czech projects, but
they also have the grandness of Hollywood style.

596   Craft, Robert. "B-flat Movie."   _New York Review of Books_ 11 April
      1985:11-12.

      Perhaps, to portray Mozart on the screen at all is simply impos-
sible, and the makers of _Amadeus_ simply chose the best solution in not
attempting to be accurate. The film's worst mistakes are in attempting
to show Mozart conducting and in insensitively editing the music.
Finally, the audience can never understand Salieri's self-pity or
motivation to murder something he loves. But, after all, the music
itself holds the audience. The film does give them that.

597   "Dialogue on Film: Saul Zaentz."   _American Film_ January-February
      1985:14,68-69.

      The co-producer of _Cuckoo's Nest_ and producer of _Amadeus_ talks
about working, and arguing, with Milos Forman, but still liking him.
Included are comments about hiring Nicholson for _Cuckoo's Nest_, the
script Ken Kesey wrote for it, production problems on _Amadeus_, hiring
Tom Hulce to play Mozart, Mozart's laugh, and writing the script for
Amadeus.

598 Elley, Derek. "Amadeus." Films and Filming June 1985:33.

The film features many excellent performances, if one can tolerate the American accents. The music is effective, and the imagery is full of spectacle. But Forman's directing is always portentious. The work has lost all of its lightness and humor.

599 Frost, Polly. "The Salieri Variations." New Yorker 22 April 1985:40-41.

Satirical proposal to Milos Forman for a sequel to Amadeus in which Salieri confesses to the murder of every other composer he knew. Parallels the liberties with history taken by Amadeus.

600 Gendel, Morgan. "'Amadeus' Heard Around the Globes." Los Angeles Times 28 January 1985:VI:1,4.

Notice of Amadeus winning for best dramatic film, best director, (Forman), best actor (F. Murray Abraham), and best screenplay (Peter Shaffer).

601 Gianakaris, C. J. "Drama Into Film: The Shaffer Situation." Modern Drama March 1985:83-98.

Detailed accounts of how Shaffer was disappointed by earlier films of his plays, how Forman convinced him to collaborate on the screenplay for Amadeus, and how Shaffer achieved the transition from stage to screen by basing the film on huge amounts of Mozart's music. The film helps Shaffer pursue his ideas about music and art and their possible relationship to divinity, but it also contains a too-simplistic plot line, an episodic structure that makes it too long, and an annoying characterization of Mozart.

602 Harwood, Jim. "'Amadeus' Provides Oscar Crescendo." Variety 27 March 1985:5,105.

Account of Academy Awards competition and ceremonies at which Amadeus garnered eight Oscars.

603 Lee, Nora. "Miroslav Ondricek and Amadeus." American Cinematographer 66.4 (April 1985):94-101.

Details Ondricek's use of candlelight to give Amadeus a realistic eighteenth-century pastel look. Contrasts his work in actual settings with his lighting on constructed sets. Also provides a brief history of his cinematography.

604 Plantinga, Cornelius, Jr. "How Odd of God." Christianity Today 19 April 1985:32.

Amadeus demonstrates that man cannot understand God's ways and that to partake of God's glory, we must give up our own.

605 Schipper, Henry. "'Amadeus' Vid Compares Mozart With Van Halen,
     Twisted Sister." Variety 20 March 1985:131,34.

     Description of a two-and-a-half-minute video of scenes from Amadeus
intercut with scenes from several rock music videos set to a piece of
Mozart's music. Purpose is to describe Mozart as having the same
attitudes and impact in his time as rock musicians do today and thereby
lure rock fans into the movie theaters. Forman saw a rough cut and
approved the video's completion.

606 Slater, Thomas J. "Milos Forman: An Interview, Part I." Post
     Script: Essays in Film and the Humanities 4.3 (Spring/Summer
     1985):2-15.

     Forman talks a great deal about the difference between working in
Czechoslovakia and America. In America, he chooses to work from already
completed materials because of cultural differences. He has experienced
failure and rejection in both places, but winning the Oscar for Cuckoo's
Nest has smoothed out all the rough spots in his career. He discusses
inspiration, his long desire to film Hair, and his belief that American
movies offer a good amount of quality. Also, his belief that art is a
neverending process.

607 ------------. "Milos Forman: An Interview, Part II." Post
     Script: Essays in Film and the Humanities 5.1 (Fall 1985):2-16.

     A discussion of working with other writers on Hair and Amadeus.
The origin, in whole and in part, of The Firemen's Ball. Forman's
belief that in adopting a novel or play, he has the right to develop his
own film vision. The struggle of developing his own artistic values and
emerging from the oppression of the 50s in Czechoslovakia into the hopes
of the 60s. His goals for the future.

608 Thomson, David. "Salieri, Psycho." Film Comment January-February
     1985:70-75.

     In digging down to the substance of Amadeus, Thomson creates an
elaborate comparison with what the movie Psycho could have been. Like
Norman Bates, Salieri is the evil spirit dominating the film and
replacing substance with glamourous facades. Salieri is a genius of the
superficial.

609 Young, Vernon. "Of Mozart, Proust and Cambodia." Hudson Review
     (Spring 1985):110-14.

     Amadeus is simply tasteless and pointless excess. The acting is
unconvincing and Shaffer's script only weakens his originally thin idea.
People probably like it because it makes Mozart look no better than
themselves.

1986

Periodicals

610   Bloom, Michael.   "Going Through Stages."   <u>Saturday Review</u>   June
      1986:24-29.

      Focuses on Elizabeth Berridge as exemplary of a number of new,
young character actresses. Berridge comments that Forman was cruel in
his casting methods for the role of Constanze Mozart and dictated her
performance completely.

611   "Cutting controversy."   <u>Broadcasting</u>   27 January 1986:63-64.

      Report of a panel discussion about the editing of films for
television. Involved were Forman, fellow directors Mark Rydell and
Warren Beatty, and some television executives. Forman complained about
a version of <u>Hair</u> appearing on non-network television that was virtually
incomprehensible. All agreed they would like to see networks make
regular announcements about when a film has been edited without the
director's approval.

612   Kearney, Jill.   "What's Wrong With Today's Films?"   <u>American Film</u>
      May 1986:53-56.

      Forman, as one of several respondents to the question, states his
belief that there is a lot of variety and quality in American films. He
believes that good stories will always attract people to theatres
despite the video market.

1987

Books

613   Slater, Thomas J.   "<u>One Flew Over the Cuckoo's Nest</u>: A Tale of Two
      Decades."   <u>Proceedings of the Nineteenth Annual Texas Tech Compara-
      tive Literature Symposium: Literature and the Movies: A Compara-
      tive Approach to Adaptation</u>.   Lubbock: Texas Tech University
      Press, 1987.

      Forman transformed Ken Kesey's novel into film by substituting his
camera as narrator for the author's use of the schizophrenic Indian,
Chief Bromden. Through the camera's eyes, the story becomes one of a
contest for power between patients R. P. McMurphy and Dale Harding and
ward supervisor Nurse Ratched. Forman captures the spirit of Kesey's
work and makes the story significantly relevant to the immediate post-
Watergate era.

Index

About the Author

THOMAS J. SLATER is an Instructor in the Department of English at Missouri Western State College and the University of Missouri—Kansas City. He has published interviews with and articles about Milos Forman. He has contributed to various collections of literary and dramatic biographies and has written and produced a video documentary about shelters for battered women.